Prevention and Coping in Child and Family Care

Mothers in adversity coping with child care

Michael Sheppard

with Mirka Gröhn

Jessica Kingsley Publishers
London and New York

First published in the United Kingdom in 2004
by Jessica Kingsley Publishers Ltd
116 Pentonville Road
London N1 9JB, England
and
29 West 35th Street, 10th fl.
New York, NY 10001-2299, USA

www.jkp.com

Copyright © 2004 Michael Sheppard

This work was funded by a grant from the Economic and Social Research Council, United Kingdom.

Library of Congress Cataloging in Publication Data
A CIP catalog record for this book is available from the Library of Congress

British Library Cataloguing in Publication Data
A CIP catalogue record for this book is available from the British Library

ISBN 1 84310 193 9

Printed and Bound in Great Britain
by Athenaeum Press, Gateshead, Tyne and Wear

Prevention and Coping in Child and Family Care

of related interest

The Child's World
Assessing Children in Need
Edited by Jan Horwath
1 85302 957 2

Good Practice in Risk Assessment and Management 1
Edited by Jacki Pritchard and Hazel Kemshall
1 85302 338 8

Divorcing Children
Children's Experience of their Parents' Divorce
Ian Butler, Lesley Scanlan, Margaret Robinson, Gillian Douglas and Mervyn Murch
1 84310 103 3

Making an Impact – Children and Domestic Violence
A Reader
Marianne Hester, Chris Pearson and Nicola Harwin
1 85302 844 4

Parental Substance Misuse and Child Welfare
Brynna Kroll and Andy Taylor
Foreword by Jane Aldgate
1 85302 791 X

Imprisoned Fathers and their Children
Gwyneth Boswell and Peter Wedge
1 85302 972 6

Engaging with Fathers
Practice Issues for Health and Social Care
Brigid Daniel and Julie Taylor
1 85302 794 4

Contents

Part IV: Using Social Support

Part V: Epilogue

Acknowledgements

This book was based on research carried out with the support of a grant from the Economic and Social Research Council, for whose support I am grateful.

I am also grateful for those in social services who provided crucial help in gaining access to the women involved in this study. These are Tony Marchese and Fiona Hadden.

The study would not have been written, of course, without the co-operation and time of the women themselves. These were women, as the title suggests, largely in circumstances of considerable disadvantage. They had suffered, and often were suffering, great stress and distress in their lives. They were, however, prepared to talk about matters which referred to that pain. Some women became distressed in the interview, and yet were determined to tell their story. One sometimes wonders at the circumstances of people where it takes researchers to provide the opportunity for such stories to be told. I am most grateful of all to these women. I hope that this book, and any effects it may have, will do them justice. All names have been deleted, including those of the children.

Finally, Mirka Gröhn worked with considerable energy and commitment, as well as personal strength, on this project. Some stories, and examples of these are in Chapter 11, can be very sad, and test the fortitude of the listener herself. I am grateful to Mirka for all her efforts.

Mirka carried out all the interviews on which this study is based. The design and direction of this study was carried out by myself, Michael Sheppard, who also wrote all the drafts, including the final one, which appears as this book. I, therefore, am responsible for any errors or deficiencies that may appear.

Michael Sheppard, University of Plymouth, July 2003

Introduction

This study arose from previous work carried out in relation to social work practice with depressed mothers in child and family care. The focus of that research, as the title of the programme indicates, was primarily on sustained social services intervention. However, in the various stages through which that research programme passed, parts involved a focus on intervention by community child care professionals. A focus on the work of health visitors showed how they dealt with a socio-demographically diverse client group, but also that there was a continuum from those who managed the challenges of childcare well, to those who had considerable problems.

This was a group with problems which became ever more entrenched and severe until they reached the same kinds of severity as – indeed began to merge with – families on social work child and family care caseloads. The continuum showed that this growth of severity occurred alongside a range of factors: a growth in social and economic deprivation, greater reliance on state benefits, poorer housing more likely to be rented, lower educational achievement, a steady growth in rates of depression. As child and parenting problems became more apparent, so each of these indices rose in frequency.

That much is, perhaps, not surprising. Health visitors deal with a general population group of mothers, and, as such, their work spans the range of families which might be expected in a general population group. A minority will have major child and parenting problems. What was of considerable interest, however, was that many families with quite significant problems were not referred for social services intervention. This, furthermore, involved deliberate decisions by the health visitors, the most significant of which was their belief that even these families would not have sufficient levels of need to be given a service. The threshold which families had to meet, in other words, was so high that even families with significant problems were not being referred, because, it was thought, such referral was pointless.

This is consistent with what we know about child and family social work from other research. There has been a strong emphasis on child protection, and social services are confronted by a constant stream of referrals for children who, such referrals suggest, are in some sense 'at risk' (of significant harm). For all these referrals, only a small fraction actually end up on child protection registers, but assessment nevertheless takes up considerable time and resources. The degree of emphasis on child protection, indeed, generated concern in influential quarters, and a 'refocusing' debate emerged in which a greater emphasis on families in need and family support was promoted. In some respects this was a mindset, in that children at risk were also children in need. Certainly, limited resources means that child care social work time is inevitably going to continue to be spent overwhelmingly on child protection.

Thus we have families with considerable child, parenting and associated problems, who do not get social work support. The question, then, emerges (one that appears deceptively simple): how do these families cope? Indeed, in view of women overwhelmingly being primary caregivers, this can be stated more precisely: how do these *mothers* cope? Of course, there are alternatives. Family centres, youth advisory services, child and adolescent psychiatry and counselling services also exist (although access to these can be restricted and often gatekeeping processes are involved). What was not clear was the extent to which such families took up these services. The health visitor research suggested that the health visitors themselves viewed these as alternatives only to a small extent, and that, in the absence of social work support, they did what they could themselves. For most families there was little evidence of involvement in alternative services beyond the primary health care team.

Once we take this focus, a number of highly significant empirical and conceptual questions emerged. One involves the centrality of the women themselves. Much of research on child welfare revolves around issues of need and support. At heart these are issues, in practical terms, of what can be provided: what does someone need? What support may be provided? Of course such issues have been researched, while including something about the client or service users' perspective. These perspectives, however, are solicited primarily in terms of individuals being *receivers or users of services* (hence the term 'service user') rather than *initiators of action*. What about looking at the women themselves as the dynamic force initiating and carrying out strategies designed to manage problems? What about placing women at the heart of the whole process? This, after all, is the reality of any child care and parenting, as any parent can say. It is they who deal with the day-to-day challenges emerging in the processes of childcare, and it is they who have primary responsibilities for managing problems as they escalate and become more severe.

That leads us to a conceptual 'space' which has not been the focus of attention in much of the welfare literature on child and family care. Terms like (social or family) support, need and, in particular, prevention, have been used as frames into which a range of empirical research and practical developments have been placed. Far less of a focus has been the notion of coping, particularly in relation to the extensive conceptual and theoretical edifices which have emerged in relation to this concept. Coping has been much more of a focus for psychology, and it became obvious, fairly quickly, that the notion of coping would be of central importance in extending understanding of this area. At the heart of coping theory is the notion of the subject's *appraisal* of the threat posed by particular problems. This meant, as far as these women were concerned, that we needed to focus on the *meanings of actions, events and behaviours, as the mothers saw them*. In this respect, the women, and their perspectives, must be at the heart of our understanding.

This, however, leads to the important theoretical question of the connection between these two major conceptual areas: prevention and coping. Prevention has for some time been a central focus for welfare provision in child and family care. It combines, as a concept, two elements: that there are distinctive 'stages' of intervention, which may be distinguished by their degree of 'intrusiveness', and that the aim, at each stage of intervention, is the prevention, or avoidance, of children and families receiving more intrusive forms of intervention, or mitigation of the worst effects of that intervention. These levels span, at one end, primary prevention – largely universalist services designed to prevent acquisition of client status – and, at the other end, quaternary (4th level) prevention. This involves action beyond the point of a child's admission to care and seeks to minimise the damage arising from the breakdown of the integrity of the family and admission of children to care. The underlying theme is that preventive services are *provided* for families. Coping, on the other hand, is something *undertaken* by them (and the mother in particular).

Coping enables us, in principle, to reconsider prevention in a significant way. For example, is the provision of universalist services really the primary, or first, stage of intervention? What about the practices of the families themselves? It is surely patronising in the extreme to consider prevention as something only provided for families, rather than something which they undertake themselves. Indeed, we can take this further: what about the practices of the families themselves (and, of course, the mother in particular) at the various stages of intervention? What about their work as initiators of action (rather than receivers or users of services) at each stage? Coping, therefore, enables us both to widen and deepen our understanding of prevention, while, furthermore, bringing the mother far more to 'centre stage' as part of the prevention process.

This book focuses on mothers in adversity coping with child and parenting problems. It concentrates on families referring themselves, or referred by others, for social service intervention, who are subject to assessment, but who, despite the identification of child or parenting problems, do not get taken on to social work caseloads, and receive sustained intervention or support. This is exactly the group for whom we earlier asked the question: how do they (mothers) cope?

The book seeks to provide the answer to the question, as follows. Part I seeks to place the research in context. This involves focusing on a number of important themes. The first deals with the policy and practice developments in child care, particularly the different ways in which notions of prevention, need and family support have emerged in recent decades. It charts, for example, the growth in perception of the importance of the birth families (even those whose parenting at times falls below general expectations), and of the need to provide support for families in difficulty. Of course, where great emphasis is placed on the birth family and the capabilities of parents, then their coping strategies become a matter of first-rate importance. The next theme is that of coping. Here the key theoretical issues are critically examined, in particular the concepts of threat, challenge and control, and the appraisal of those carrying out the coping strategies. The third theme is that of parenting. Key elements of parenting, from the behaviours of the parents to the temperament of the child, the significance of attachments, and the different challenges at different stages in the child and young person's development are all the focus for our attention. We can, after all, only understand coping in this context. The final chapter of Part I focuses on the area of study and methods used. Particular attention is placed on critical appraisal of meaning and the manner in which this was examined within an overall framework of our concern for coping and prevention.

With Part II we move to the first group of findings. The key initial concerns are the 'threat meanings' attached to the problems confronted by these women. Thus we are able to focus on the way in which child behavioural, child emotional and parenting problems, which are the main domains of concern to the women, are considered respectively in terms of the egocentricity of the child, the sensitivity of the child, and the self-blame attached to the mother. However, meaning did not simply involve definition of problems, but also the ascription of responsibility or blame; this is the subject for Chapter 6. This was complex, involving identification of levels of responsibility, distinguishing causal from influencing factors. Women blamed themselves (inducing poor self-worth), the father and the environment. Where blame was perceived to rest with the child, it was attributed to personality. Chapter 7 places these problems in psychosocial context. The women were very aware of contextual factors which impacted on their child care coping capabilities. Poverty and deprivation were at the heart of interrelated problems, including housing, social relationship and psychological wellbeing, all of which affected their coping.

Part III examines direct coping with parenting and child problems. Chapter 8 looks at direct actions by the mother with the child. Women largely regarded these as the most significant element of their coping strategy. There were two broad types: child-controlling and child-responsive. The latter centred on enabling the children to feel more secure, stable and understood. The former rested on crude behaviourist principles, and could be positive or negative. However, the latter, which involved negative responses to negative actions, was more widely used, and often self-defeating, aggravating conflict. Chapter 9 is about child-responsive coping. A number of dimensions of this coping were identified and defined. These included areas such as instrumental-oriented coping, protective commitment, normalising, cognitive-affective coping, proximising, caring-affective nurturing, encouragement through firmness, and parent-oriented coping. These situations presented women with considerable personal strain, and their response to this is the subject of Chapter 10. They had to cope not just with the problem, but also with their feelings about the problem (emotion-focused coping). There were two main strategies: avoidance, which included denial and disengagement, and adjustment, which included acceptance of the situation, positive reinterpretation and growth. Snapping was a more immediate response reflecting the loss of women's self-control. Chapter 11 focuses on four case studies which enable us to examine in detail the processes of coping and their relationship to the problems and stressors with which women sought to deal.

Part IV moves on to the use of social supports. Here, consistent with our overall theme of women as active agents, we see much of the use of social support as originating in the actions of the women soliciting such support, rather than its mere provision. Chapter 12 examines informal support. Some women were unable to identify such support, while conflict could provide further problems. An important issue for a woman in terms of actively soliciting support was the extent to which supporters agreed on her fundamental perceptions of the situation. Key factors examined included: integration in her social network, routine support, acceptance and encouragement, and the degree of reciprocity involved. Chapter 13 focuses on the search for formal support from social services. This involved links between voluntary referral and the search for control on the part of the women. Social services were most frequently approached to enable their problem-focused strategies. Where emotion-focused strategies were their concern, this included a need for validation, seeking security and support, and stress relief. With unsolicited (often child protection) referrals, women were predominantly motivated to gain control of the definition of the situation. Chapter 14 examines discourses through which women made judgements about social services. A range of discourses emerge. They had a right to service discourse, based on notions of desert and need. There was a response of service discourse arising from perceptions of social services' role and function. Important elements were contextualised judgements and abstracted judgements. There were, additionally, discourses on problem control and convergence–divergence. Chapter 15 focuses on women referred on to other agencies. Where women had not wanted referral in the first place, their main drive was to get away at the first opportunity. Hence referral on, where it took them away from social services, was often welcome. When they were not referred on, they were generally happy if they had got what they wanted from social services, or if they felt referral on was unnecessary. They were unhappy when they felt undervalued and unimportant. When they were referred on, the key elements determining their attitude were the timeliness, helpfulness and appropriateness of the referral.

Part V is the Epilogue. Chapter 16 examines women's appraisal of their coping. Coping theory would suggest that this would be based on the extent to which control had been achieved, but the meaning of controllability in these circumstances required elucidation. There was a range of ways in which coping was appraised, including outcome-oriented judgements, coping as an ongoing process, the 'character issue', capacity to use supports, and personal growth. Chapter 17 is the conclusion and develops theoretical ideas on prevention through a fusion with the concepts from coping, and the empirical and conceptual data emerging from this study. We are able to develop and extend the prevention process, and establish a multidimensional model through which these data may be considered, and which is applicable to other areas of prevention.

That, then, is the broad thrust of the book. It behoves us now to move to the first part, and set the context for the work.

PART I

Context

CHAPTER 1

Policy, Prevention and Practice

The capacity of parents to cope with the challenges of bringing up their children is of central importance in child care. Indeed, this point may be immediately refined. In the overwhelming majority of instances women are the primary caregivers, and this means that, in general, the central issue is the capacity of *mothers* to parent. The importance of the birth parents and family of origin has been strongly recognised in the 1989 Children Act, so this issue is not simply one of profound ethical and humanitarian import, but also a key element of child care policy. This book focuses on the capacity of mothers to cope with child care in adversity, adversity which is related to social disadvantage and child care problems. It focuses on families where referral is made to child care social services for support but where, because of pressure on resources and the high 'threshold' of problems and needs, they are not taken on to caseload for medium- or long-term support. The families who are the subject of this study were all, as a result, only the subject of fairly brief contact with the childcare social work service.

This chapter will outline the major dimensions of child care policy, by identifying facets which are important in our understanding of the position of parents, and hence, in view of the *de facto* dominance of women as primary caregivers, that of mothers in particular. Key elements of parental responsibility, partnership and family support which provide birth parents with unrivalled significance in child care policy, will be examined, and placed within debates through which these emerged, such as issues of permanence, substitute care, cycle of abuse and social disadvantage in policy development.

Parenting and parental responsibility

In the pursuit of the best interests of the child, policy has veered, at different points in the recent past, between approaches which, on the one hand, seek to retain, as far as possible, the integrity of the birth family, to those which, on the other, seek to find a permanent solution for problematic child care in substitute families (a rescuing approach). Current child care policy tends very much towards the former. A central feature underlying the Children Act, 1989, indeed, its overriding purpose, is to promote and safeguard the welfare of the child. To that end, the courts are required to treat the welfare of the child as the paramount consideration. When operating to this welfare principle, this means that the court's decision will be that which most promotes the welfare of the child.

It is the means by which this is to be achieved that places birth parents to the fore. In one of its volumes on the Act, the Department of Health (1989, p.1) comments that 'the Act rests on the belief that children are generally best looked after within the family, with both parents playing a full part and without resort to legal proceedings'. Indeed, where such proceedings occur, the court is prohibited from making any order unless it is satisfied that the order will *positively contribute* to the child's welfare.

This is made overt through the concept of *parental responsibility*. This is a collection of rights, powers, duties and responsibilities which accrue to parents from the Act in relation to the upbringing of children. Its effect is 'to empower parents to take most decisions in the child's life' (Department of Health 1989, p.10). It emphasises the duty of parents to care for the child and to raise him or her in a way which encourages moral, physical and emotional health. Where married, both parents have parental responsibility. Where unmarried, the father does not, without recourse to the courts (s 4). Even where a child is subject to a Care Order, the Act provides for parents to retain parental responsibility and for them to have reasonable contact with the child unless the court directs otherwise. This serves to emphasise the significance, from a legal standpoint, of the tie with the birth parents.

These central features of the Children Act do not prevent children being separated from their parents, through, for example, a Care Order, but they do require that such action should have positive benefits, and that it is undertaken with an eye to the significant harm which could be done to a child if it were not taken. However, there is also a recognition that separation from birth parents could also involve damage to the child, who should be protected from 'the harm which can be caused by unwarranted intervention in their family life' (Department of Health 1989, p.4).

The idea of prevention

Prevention has been considered in a variety of ways. In part, it can be considered in terms of what it is that we are trying to prevent. Holman (1988) distinguished prevention in terms of its proactivity and aim. A positive or proactive approach has a universalist and societal focus. It involves, he thinks, policies and practices focusing on quality of life, including promoting adequate standards of living, appropriate levels of health, suitable environments for bringing up children, and a quality of community life which maintains and promotes good-quality child development. A reactive approach is more concerned with avoidance of harm at an individual, group and societal level. This form of prevention seeks, for example, to avoid separation from parents, and where it is not necessary, to avert, as far as possible, placement in care. Where such placement occurs, we should seek to avoid placing the child at a distance which would reduce, with other factors, the possibility of contact; and seek to have the child remain in care for as short a time as possible before being returned to the birth family.

Holman (1988) also considered that prevention could have diverse aims, apparently related to three domains. The first related to the quality of parenting, and here he identified the prevention of neglect and abuse, and the effects of poor parenting. The second related to what may be broadly termed the socio-economic environment. Prevention here related to the effects of disadvantage, such as low income, poor environment and social and cultural experiences. The third, perhaps more conventionally, related to the processes of intervention and institutional care, and included preventing the reception of children into care, preventing their having to remain in care, the search for rehabilitation, and preventing their isolation (particularly from their families) while in care.

There is clearly some overlap in these two conceptualisations of prevention. Hardiker, Exton and Barker (1991), like Holman, sought to widen the ways in which we understood prevention, but they did so through a two dimensional approach which emphasised, on the one hand, models of welfare (residual, institutional, developmental and radical) and on the other, the actual levels of prevention. These levels, Hardiker *et al.* (1991) think, can be conceptualised in terms of client 'career', which relates to the journey the client takes through ever more intrusive levels of intervention. Their notion of prevention is therefore firmly linked to that of intervention, rather than focused, as, for example, in Parker (1980) on the nature, extent and response to problems.

Hardiker *et al.* (1991) identified a number of levels of intervention, the purpose of which, at each stage, was the avoidance, as far as possible, of further, more intrusive intervention, or the unnecessary continuation of intervention which might be potentially damaging. Prevention should be considered an objective at all stages of intervention. Using their notion of client career, the first level was defined as aimed at the prevention of the acquisition of client status. This will apply where there are difficulties in personal or social functioning – problems which are relatively common, but where failure to act or deterioration may lead to client status. Prevention services are very diverse, and can range from universal services, and policies designed to ameliorate the effects of social and economic disadvantage, to particular services in the community, such as support for one-parent families or parent training programmes (which may also be used as an aspect of more intrusive intervention).

Secondary prevention arises at the point when an applicant to a social agency becomes accepted as a client. This can involve early intervention in a situation in which, while the family have problems, they have not yet reached crisis point. Intervention may be undertaken to prevent a potentially worsening situation arising, or in response to some crisis where short-term help can help restore the family to its normal, adequately functioning state (see Department of Health 1991). Secondary prevention ideally involves a rapid response at an early stage. In traditional, case based models of intervention, the client/family becomes the main focus, although with more systemic approaches there is a concern about the interaction between the individual and the environment.

Tertiary prevention is the third level, and involves action to prevent the child being taken into care. This involves working with families with more severe difficulties, often with long established multi-problem families. Action at this level often seeks to avoid the worst effects of chronic family difficulties. There tends to be a greater emphasis on the more authority based, often child protection, elements of the agency statutory responsibilities. The case based model predominates at this level, difficulties tend to be seen in terms of family or individual dysfunction, and targets for intervention tend to be the family unit or individual within it.

Quaternary intervention is the fourth level identified, and is often considered to indicate a level involving the failure of preventive practice. This is where children are admitted to care. However, care may here be considered a constructive option, where it is a response to short-term family crises. As with the notion of accommodation in the Children Act, it can be seen as a means of supporting families through particularly difficult times in raising their children. It can also refer to attempts to rehabilitate the child with their family, or to limit the potential damage which may occur to all family members from the breakdown of its integrity. This can be achieved through, for example, encouraging contact between the child and family, and seeking to reduce the possible loss of self-esteem, threats to identity, and so on.

The ideas of Hardiker and colleagues, and to some extent Holman, are consistent with the assumption underwriting the 1989 Children Act, that the best place for the child is generally with his or her birth family. While there has been a wide recognition for some time that there are different levels of prevention, particularly evident in mental health (Goldberg and Huxley 1992), in social work the notion of prevention has historically, and particularly among the social work force, been identified with one particular level – the secondary level. Social workers frequently bemoan that the emphasis on child protection, and shortage of resources, means that they are unable to undertake early intervention, before families' problems have become severe. Work is all 'heavy end', and some families could avoid being placed (or placing themselves) in that position – had earlier and appropriate support been given, the child protection circumstances would not have developed.

Packman (1981) recounts how, from the inception of children's departments, this notion of prevention began to emerge. The central task of the child care service at its beginning was the provision of good substitute care for deprived children. From this, however, in the 1950s and 60s there was a gradual emergence of field social work in which there was a growing concern with preventing children coming into care. Of course, there was a concern that some families were not capable of caring adequately for their children, and that they could be downright dangerous, a concern underlined by child death scandals during the 1970s. There was, though, a two-pronged concept of prevention: prevention of admission into care, and prevention of neglect and cruelty within the family. Both tend to emphasise secondary prevention, and early intervention before familial problems reach crisis proportions.

Rescuing children and permanence

This secondary notion of prevention has been consistent over the last 40 years of British child care policy. However, prior to the 1989 Children Act there was, relatively speaking, less emphasis on tertiary and quaternary prevention (though, it must be emphasised, these were far from excluded). It may be that it is the consistent aspects of prevention which have led many social workers to interpret prevention, as a whole, as being about its secondary, and to some extent primary, levels. (The latter tends to be less of a concern to social workers, in view of their non-universalist service.) Anything which goes beyond secondary level has tended to be seen in terms of, for example, contact and rehabilitation. Thus, while the aims may be the same, the terminology used can differ.

This has a profound significance, since the emphasis in child care policy in relation to the birth family, before and after the 1989 Act, was significantly different, reflecting major differences in values, and in perceptions of the relationship between birth family and child, where major problems arose. These differing values are reflected in the degree of emphasis which can be placed on the different levels of prevention in child care policy.

Much of pre-1989 child care policy arose from a twin concern about (a) the dangers of leaving children with their birth families in abusive situations and (b) the problem of children who, having been admitted to the care system, were left in residential establishments, without any clear long-term and stable provision being made for them. Of particular significance was the death of Maria Colwell, which received wide publicity, and evoked widespread disgust and horror (DHSS 1974). The circumstances of her death, preceded as it was by what amounted to sustained torture, produced widespread revulsion, and a concern that the birth family was given too great an importance in the child's life by social workers involved with such families. Indeed, while Maria's was perhaps the most high profile death, it was not the only one (Department of Health and Social Security 1982). These inquiries have had the effect of introducing a more proceduralised form of practice in an attempt to enable greater control and direction of social work actions and practices (Howe 1984).

However, the developments after the Colwell tragedy also had the effect of altering significantly perceptions of the appropriate balance between the birth family and substitute care in cases where there was concern over children. The influential study by Rowe and Lambert (1973) *Children Who Wait* reinforced this. Their study can be viewed within an overall concern about 'welfare drift' in which children brought into care, after a relatively short period of time, were unlikely to be returned to their birth family. Indeed, unless adopted, they could experience a series of foster placements, the effects of which could easily be destabilising (Fuller and Stevenson 1985). Rowe and Lambert (1973) found that social workers sought first to rehabilitate children with birth families, resulting in delays in decisions about placements. However, rehabilitation could often be an optimistic scenario, workers expecting that only a minority of children were likely to be rehabilitated.

A third element took a positive view of the possibility of successful substitute care. This was linked with the 'cycle of abuse' thesis propounded by Sir Keith Joseph and others (Buchanan 1996). This thesis, for which there is some empirical support, indicated that there was a greater tendency for parents who themselves had been abused as children, to abuse their own children. This, it should be emphasised, is a tendency, and parents who were abused as children do not necessarily abuse their children, while some parents who were not themselves abused as children do abuse their own children. However, the notion of a cycle of abuse suggested there was a need to break the cycle, and substitute care seemed a good way to achieve this. Pringle (1974) as well as Goldstein, Freud and Solnit (1979; 1980) were critical of an over-valuation placed on birth family, and a misplaced faith in the blood tie. There was some concern that parents were seen to have some kind of 'property rights' over their children. While attachment theory had initially emphasised the significance of the mother for healthy child development (Bowlby 1951), there was growing evidence that substitute care, appropriately given, could provide for children's developmental needs (Rutter 1977). Hence there was a stress on the importance of psychological parenthood rather than biological ties.

The danger presented, in some cases, by the birth family, together with concerns about insufficient direction and planning for children who came into care, led to an emphasis on permanence and the greater use of substitute care. These concerns were underlying features of the 1975 Children Act. In broad terms, the powers of local authorities over children in care were extended, and measures were introduced which made adoption easier. The most symbolic (and certainly subsequently contentious) element, perhaps, was that which widened the powers of local authorities to assume parental rights. There was, as a result, a 'shift towards concentrating on the removal of children rather than on the social disadvantages which put them at risk' (Colton, Drury and Williams 1995). They were, in a sense, being 'rescued' from unsatisfactory and dangerous familial situations. In the late 1970s there were increases in the numbers of children in care, and of (emergency) place of safety orders, and the use of voluntary care diminished (Hallett and Stevenson 1980; Parton 1985; Packman 1993).

The emerging emphasis on the birth family

These key elements of child care policy were heavily criticised in some quarters, and the cause of considerable disquiet in others. Two reports were of central importance in developments leading to the 1989 Act. These were the Short Report (House of Commons 1984) and the *Review of Child Care Law* (DHSS 1985). A key theme of the Short Report was a concern with the way permanence operated, and the need to improve preventive services for children and families. The committee argued that the stress on permanence, and on adoption in particular, had as a consequence the neglect of policies which enabled parents to retain contact with children in care, and to care permanently for their own children. The practical consequence of the legislation was too often to drive a wedge between the child and their family of origin.

The committee blamed managers for this state of affairs, commenting on a lack of a concerted strategy to prevent children entering care. They considered there was neither the impetus nor the commitment in relation to prevention that there was in relation to adoption and fostering. Social workers, likewise, were viewed as giving prevention an insufficiently high priority. In these respects, however, they were only mirroring the central themes of recent legislation, and the influential groups who had advocated permanence and the potential dangers of too great an emphasis on birth families. They also criticised policies which financed expensive facilities for rescuing victims, while failing to invest in supporting families in social circumstances which could lead to family breakdown.

Their criticisms resonated with the work of some influential writers. Foremost among these was Holman (1980, 1988). He strongly argued that there was more to healthy child development than psychological ties of the sort to be found in attachment theory. We can, he felt, only understand the nature of the ties which children develop with their parents if we understand the social construction of the family, in particular the birth family. The 'normal' family is one in which the child lives with his or her birth parents, or at least one of them. It is a biologically related unit, not one that is simply defined by its psychological ties. There is, as a result, a stigma attached to children who do not live with their family of origin, and their circumstances are not defined as normal.

There is, furthermore, a psychological dimension to this biological relationship. There is a strong sense that an individual's identity, their sense of self, is tied up with their birth family. The result of this is that where the birth family is not known to an individual, they may seek to identify and contact them. This is evident in the cases of adults who, as children, were adopted without knowing who their birth parents were, who also subsequently had no contact with them. It is frequently the case that such individuals make considerable efforts to locate and get in touch with their parents (Melville 1983).

A third dimension was the systematic disadvantage which accrued to some birth families as a result of their poverty. Poverty has impacted widely on families, and particularly among those likely to be subject to social services intervention, such as families with single mothers. Between 1979 and 1987 the proportion of children living in families with an income below 50 per cent of average went up from 12 per cent to more than a quarter (Bradshaw 1990). A roughly equivalent increase occurred in children in families relying on supplementary benefit, or income support. Immediately prior to the inception of the 1989 Act, there was clear evidence that 90 per cent of new referrals to social workers came from social security claimants, and over half these were dependent on income support (Becker and Selburn 1990). As many as three-fifths of social service clients sought help from the Social Fund (Stewart *et al.* 1989).

Holman (1980) and Parton (1985), noted the significance of this link between deprivation and case status. They argued that families which suffered state-facilitated separation from their children were overwhelmingly those living in poverty and disadvantage. In marked contrast, those who adopted children (and adoption was one of the preferred alternatives in order to secure permanence) were generally middle-class and considerably more affluent, with fewer social and economic pressures. Some poor families, it appeared, were losing their children to more affluent families, and much of this could be ascribed to their poverty and disadvantage.

The social pressures associated with disadvantage are well documented (see Chapter 3 for an extended discussion) and affect many poor families, whether or not they become involved with social services, or their children are received into care. Holman suggested that social disadvantage affected the parents themselves, from the everyday stresses they experienced, thus affecting child care, and from a lack of material resources with which to carry out their parenting tasks. It was not surprising that a disproportionate number of children from socially deprived families populated the care system.

In a highly influential article, Bebbington and Miles (1989) demonstrated this link between care status and social disadvantage, based on a survey of 13 social services departments in 1987. They commented that entry into care was more closely associated with social deprivation than had been the case in 1962. Living in single-parent households was the greatest single risk factor: children from such families were almost eight times as likely to enter local authority care. Children living in overcrowded accommodation were over three times as likely as children from other families to enter care (the second highest risk factor). This was followed by families being in receipt of benefits, having a mother whose age was under 21, coming from a family of four children or more, and residing in a deprived neighbourhood. The clear association here was between social and economic deprivation, as evident in terms of factors such as poor neighbourhood, receipt of benefits, overcrowded living accommodation, and the personal circumstances of the parent, such as their young age and single parent status. The significance of single parenthood was perhaps not surprising, since such families are often among the poorer and more disadvantaged, and they are likely to feel the pressure of childcare without the support of a partner.

Milham *et al.* (1986) found that children frequently came into care in crisis, and many of the placements were made in emergencies (Packman 1986). Furthermore, evidence emerged that placement changes (breakdown) occurred in over half the children coming into care within the first six months, and many long-term placements were made in a hurry following previous breakdown (Berridge and Cleaver 1987). Finding an adequate match between child and substitute family was not straightforward. Furthermore, the longer the period in care grew, the less likely were the family to remain in contact with the child. Milham *et al.* (1986) found that barriers experienced by children and parents were key factors in limiting or eliminating contact between them. These included factors such as changes in the parents' situation and limited social work support, or even ambivalence about contact.

Supporting (birth) families: the importance of parents

These four factors – the positive importance of the social construction of links with birth parents/family, the importance of identity and the place of the birth family in this, the significance of social disadvantage to parenting and the likelihood of entering care, and the inadequacies of the care system, particularly in its aspirations towards permanence – were instrumental in the swing towards a greater emphasis on the importance of the family of origin, and natural parents in particular, evident in the 1989 Children Act. From this emerged the importance, for childcare policy, of the parent (and hence the mother), and parental responsibility.

These very much link with a strategy for prevention which is consistent with the four-level framework developed by Hardiker *et al.* (1991). Among the features signalling a reduction in the intrusiveness of state intervention were the abandonment of local authorities' power to make parental rights resolutions, and a reduction in the time allowed for emergency admission to care (Place of Safety to Emergency Protection Orders). While the 1975 Act focused on rescuing children, the Review of Child Care Law (DHSS 1985), which underlay the 1989 Act, concentrated on enabling parents to keep, or to receive back, their children. The 1989 Act sought to create a balance between the need to protect children at risk, while supporting families finding it difficult to cope.

There are a number of key concepts which underlie the approach to families, and in particular the role of parents in relation to child care, encapsulated in the 1989 Act. One of the most significant is the emergence of family support as a key aspect of child care policy and practice, through which parents are to be enabled to parent more effectively, or through periods of crisis. Family support was a key element of the emphasis on keeping children, where possible, with their family of origin. Support was to be provided for families with children in need (of which more later), with the view that the best place for the child to be brought up is usually his/her own family. They 'can be helped most effectively if the local authority, working in partnership with the parents, provides a range and level of service appropriate to the child's needs' (Department of Health 1991, p.1).

Family support comprised two forms of resources: those which could be provided for families who remained intact – community resources, so to speak – and the use of accommodation where the problems faced by the family were such that it was not possible for it to remain intact, but nevertheless, the aim was to support these families. Local authorities have a general duty to provide a range and level of services appropriate to children in their area who are in need, to promote their upbringing by their families, in so far as this is consistent with their welfare. In pursuit of this, while they were not expected to meet every individual need, they were expected to identify the extent of need, set priorities for service provision in their area, and provide a range of services to meet the nature and extent of need in their area. Among those aspects for which provision should be made were included advice, guidance, counselling, assistance and home help services. They were also empowered to provide social, cultural or leisure activities or assistance with holidays (Department of Health 1991, schedule 2).

Accommodation provided by the local authority (the nearest thing to voluntary care under the previous legislation) endorsed the idea that even such intrusive involvement could be undertaken in order to support families, and, in the medium term, ensure they remained intact. This form of support would be appropriate if families reached a stage where they were not able to resolve their problems, and were therefore providing inadequate care for their children. Accommodation was designed to replace reception into care 'with its unhelpful association with parental shortcomings' (Department of Health 1991, p.8). Accommodation was intended to be a service provided under a voluntary arrangement, as part of a wider framework of prevention, and the child was not to be considered to be in care, unless subject to a care order.

The issue of partnership linked together parental responsibility and family support. Partnership with parents was to be undertaken on the basis of 'careful joint planning and agreement' (Department of Health 1991, p.5). There was a recognition that parenting could be affected by experiences of illness or disability, social, relationship or unemployment problems, and bereavement. Partnership involved building on the strengths of the family and minimising any weaknesses. While partnership is at times a confused and complex concept in official guidance, and is particularly problematic where child protection is concerned (see Sheppard 2001 for an extended discussion of the concept of partnership), there can be little doubt that it affirmed the importance of the birth parents to the child, even where families were in difficulty and parenting became problematic.

Need and thresholds for intervention

The central importance of parents and parenting emerges clearly in the 1989 Act and the support it sets up for them through the provision of resources by local authorities. However, child protection inevitably remained a major consideration, and the level of needs experienced by different families varies greatly. In a climate which sought to provide family support, there nevertheless remained a resource and rationing issue, because of the importance which was placed on child protection. This raised the question of the extent to which, in practical terms, local authorities could devote attention to the provision of support for families which were not involved in child protection, or in the assessment of the need for it. Was the threshold for the provision of services, in practical terms, so high that it precluded concentrating on cases other than child protection?

At the heart of the 1989 Act is the concept of need. Need, it has been clearly established in philosophical analysis, involves the issue of harm. An individual is 'in need' when, without some action to alleviate that need, they would suffer harm (Sheppard and Woodcock 1999). Once this is understood, it is clear how the child protection function becomes an aspect – admittedly a very serious one – of work with children in need. For Section 31, which deals with this matter, the legislation is concerned with children 'who are suffering, or likely to suffer *significant* harm'. It is the *severity* of the harm which, in common parlance, distinguishes those who are simply 'in need' from those who, while in need, are 'at risk'.

The definition in the Act is essentially a practical one, although deliberately wide. The principal responsibility of local authorities, in relation to children, is 'to safeguard and promote the welfare of children within their area who are in need' (s 17.1). Indeed, concern is for those *likely to suffer difficulties* as well as those who already have them. Section 17 defines children in need as those who:

- are unlikely to achieve or maintain (or to have the opportunity to achieve or maintain) a reasonable standard of health or development

- without such services their health and development, would be likely to be significantly impaired (or further impaired)
- have a disability.

The practical consequence of this wide definition is that there are wide divergences in the way that need is interpreted by different local authorities. Aldgate and Tunstill (1995) commented that, in their policy documents, local authorities frequently went little further than the definitions provided in the 1989 Act and official guidelines in their attempts to identify and respond to need. Colton *et al.* (1995), however, noted that the Act and official guidelines gave little guidance as to how terms like 'reasonable standards', or 'significant' or 'further impairment' should be understood. Furthermore, departments gave very little guidance to social workers on how to interpret the concepts in practice.

Another practical consequence, one which helps explain the divergences in local policy and practice, is that need has tended to be far too great for local authorities to respond to all cases. There has inevitably been a rationing of resources. In these circumstances, notwithstanding the emphasis of the 1989 Act on family support, as well as child protection, the emphasis of local authorities has been on the child protection function. These, practitioners define as 'statutory work' (Aldgate and Tunstill 1995), bemoaning the fact that they are no longer able to engage in preventive work, which, as we have seen, tends to be defined as work at the secondary level of prevention with families who have not yet reached a crisis, and where intervention is designed to prevent such a crisis occurring.

This situation, Williams (1997) felt, was analogous to the 1970s. Problems arose when social workers attempted to implement preventive policies in child care where large numbers of families were materially deprived and where that material deprivation affected their capacity to parent. Packman (1981, p.181) observed that social workers in the newly created social services departments were at times confused and distressed at being faced with clients in desperate need, all of whom they felt were in need of help. Faced with budget restriction, at the same time as overwhelming need, they were forced to ration services, at times in ad hoc ways, with the consequence that they were at times seen as withholders of resources, rather than providers of services.

In the light of large scale need, and rationing, there was an increasing emphasis on child protection work. This was despite the emphasis in the 1989

Act on parental responsibility and on supporting families. In an effort again to 'kick start' the preventive, family support/need response elements of the 1989 Act, the Refocusing Debate began.

The refocusing debate was concerned with changing culture in social services departments, so perceptions and practice moved away from a narrow child protection focus to one that was concerned more widely with a response to need. Instrumental in this was the Audit Commission Report (1994) *Seen But Not Heard*. The Audit Commission argued that the central expectations of the 1989 Act were not being achieved in practice, particularly in relation to a concern with children in need rather than a narrow concern with child protection. However, rather than view this as an issue of the rationing of limited resources, the Commission saw this as a matter of efficient use of resources. They suggested that child care resources were poorly managed and planned, resulting in considerable wastage of expenditure on families who did not need support. They argued for a greater emphasis on prevention and less on responsive inter-ventions and expensive residential resources. The solution was in better planning, co-ordination and management. In pursuit of this they recommended that, together with Health Authorities, social services departments should produce Plans for Children's Services, lending a more strategic approach to the provision of resources. The focus should be on identifying, assessing and responding to need, and on the development of services enabling this to happen.

The concern with widening the focus of concern to family support for children in need was a central theme of the influential official publication *Child Protection: Messages From Research* (Department of Health 1995). Like the Audit Commission, *Messages From Research* suggested that there was a wastage of resources, arising from child protection investigation where only a small minority were considered severe enough to warrant intervention. Commenting on Gibbons, Conroy and Bell's (1995) examination of the operation of the child protection system, they drew attention to how through a series of filters, only one in seven child protection investigations ended up on the child protection register. Indeed, three-quarters of investigations never reached the case conference stage. In nearly half the cases the investigation led to no action at all. The system itself, furthermore, is experienced as extremely alienating by those subject to it. Many children and their parents felt alienated and angry. There was emphasis on investigation, but little on support or a more positive approach to problem resolution, when child protection assessments occurred. There was little attempt, on a community-wide basis, or in individual cases, to develop a co-ordinated preventive strategy.

Rose (1994) drew these strands together, arguing that Section 17 (family support) was no less statutory than investigations carried out under Section 47 (contrary to the use of the term 'statutory' by social workers). There was a need to develop an integrated child care system, which brought together family support. There was also a need for a lighter touch in the conduct of practice, and the term 'enquiry' rather than 'investigation' has subsequently been increasingly used in pursuit of this.

While there has been a response to this, it is arguable that, at heart, social workers and other child care professionals remain unconvinced about the capacity of the system to respond more widely in support of families, because this could reduce the resources available for the assessment of child protection, where the danger to the child is greater (Sheppard 1998). Parton (1997) has argued that a central problem of this analysis is the failure to place child protection concern within the context of widespread poverty and disadvantage, suggesting that it is no coincidence that child protection investigations or enquiries are frequently carried out among the poorest and most disadvantaged families. Furthermore, it fails to address the embattled culture which has emerged in social services, and among social workers in particular, as a result of the severe criticisms following child deaths occurring during social work supervision. The philosophy of permanence and rescue may have been eclipsed by family support-prevention, but the effects of these child deaths and the public response which underlay the pre-1989 approach to child care policy continues to exert an influence on social work actions.

We can, as a result, understand many of the actions of social workers in relation to child protection as an approach which is 'risk aversive', that is, governed by an approach which seeks to reduce to the minimum the possibility of a child being harmed. This is exactly reflected in results by Gibbons *et al.* (1995), which demonstrate that social workers are prepared to risk the possibility of investigating a large number of cases where it transpires that child protection concerns do not exist, so as to ensure that they uncover the maximum number of cases where child protection concerns legitimately do exist.

Bringing matters together: prevention and thresholds, coping and need

Emerging from the Refocusing Debate, and in pursuit of these broad objectives of supporting families, and particularly parents, in need, there have been a number of initiatives. On a wide level the Home Office document *Supporting Families* (Home Office 1999) sought to enhance service provision at the primary and secondary levels of intervention. This was a broad-brush programme looking at a range of factors which bear on the issue of children in need. These include financial support for families, helping families balance work and home, strengthening marriage, and the provision of better support for serious family problems. Among the initiatives of greatest significance were a new national parenting helpline, an enhanced role for health visitors, embracing the whole wellbeing of parents and children as well as their physical health, and the Sure Start initiative to help children in their early years.

More specifically in relation to social service provision, and relationships with health authorities, the development of the Framework for Assessment of Children in Need and their families (Department of Health 2000) is designed to ensure that the overall framework for assessment is based on the concept of need, and that assessment and response should reflect the level of need in families. To this end, and deliberately derived from the research literature, the framework seeks to identify the range of needs and the domains within which they reside, in order to enable assessments to be made in a needs based way. There is no division between child protection and non-child protection/family support cases, and need is broadly divided into three areas: child's development needs, parenting capacity, and family and environmental factors.

The Quality Protects Programme (Department of Health 2001), designed to encourage the improvement of service provision in key areas, monitored by central government, includes within it a concern with thresholds, and response to need. Objective 7 seeks 'to ensure that referral processes discriminate effectively between different types and level of need, and produce a timely response' (Department of Health 2001, p.63). In pursuit of these objectives, responses have been mixed, and at times marked by an absence, in local authority returns, of data which could shed light on progress.

Family support services are not, of course, limited only to those provided by mainstream qualified social workers, and the Guidance (Department of Health 1991) identifies a number of these, already noted. The example of family centres certainly suggests they can and do operate in a supportive manner with families in need. Although family centres are very diverse, they frequently are used by families suffering social disadvantage (Batchelor, Gould and Wright 1999; Gibbons 1990). Among the more frequent characteristics of those who use open access services are problems with health, unemployment and lone parenthood (Smith 1996). Family centre uses include: a drop-in for social purposes, parental support, and play and therapeutic activities with children (Pithouse and Holland 1999; Smith 1996).

Within mainstream, district based services, the rationing of resources and high threshold for service provision remains a significant restraint on providing a response to those cases not labelled 'child protection'. There is little doubt that community child care professionals are aware of this, and, as a result, the actions of both social workers and other community child care professionals create a high threshold of need or risk before a family is likely to obtain social work support. Sheppard's (1996, 1998) research demonstrated how the referring actions of health visitors were actually predicated on the anticipation of a high threshold of need in social services. The result was a rationing of families which they sought to refer to social services, since referral, they reasoned, was pointless. Thus, while the health visitors had significant concerns about child behavioural problems in over 10 per cent of their cases, only a minority of these received social work support. Indeed, only one third of the 6 per cent of the families where health visitors had concerns about possible abuse were in receipt of social work intervention. In other cases, the traditional role of monitoring was being carried out by the health visitor herself. Many families about which health visitors had considerable concerns, and whom they felt could benefit from social work intervention, were nevertheless not referred, because the threshold expected was too high. This is consistent with the very high level of problems and needs consistently found in studies of child care social work practice.

Two key realms come together in this. One is a practical one about the ways in which women respond in circumstances of adversity, and where the service sought is not available to them. How do mothers cope when they seek help, or are referred by others, and they are unable to obtain sustained intervention through being placed 'on caseload'? This will remain significant in terms of policy and practice, because it is difficult to imagine the circumstances in which resources are not rationed, and hence some families fall below the needs threshold to receive a service.

The other is a conceptual one. The concept of need is one which is focused on providing resources for those with problems. That much is clear from the theoretical analysis of Sheppard and Woodcock (1999). The key issue with need is, what is it that is needed to deal with the particular problem which is confronted? However, this, in essence, concerns what others will do or provide in order to help families or parents. These are the family support services, as well as other services. The concept of need, as a result, tends not to conceptualise the individual as an active agent. Even the attempt to elicit support involves decision making on the part of parents, acting as active agents seeking to direct their own lives. However, we can go further than this. From the point of view of the parent, the key issue when faced with problems or challenges in child care is one of coping: how will *they* cope with the challenges with which child care presents them, particularly if they are in some ways disadvantaged? So while the concept of need, to put things a little simplistically, tends to represent the parent, child or family in a passive way as recipient of services, the concept of coping treats them as active agents seeking to manage and control the challenges, difficulties and disadvantage with which they are confronted.

Likewise, the issue of coping comes into the realm of prevention. All levels of prevention, like need, are concerned with the provision of help or resources. Coping, on the other hand, is about the manner in which parents themselves seek to negotiate the challenges and difficulties with which they are confronted, and this can involve their eliciting services for whichever level of prevention required, or involving themselves in decisions made. Coping can be linked with the operation of partnership, and a focus on different coping strategies can throw light on the different ways in which partnership works.

Coping, then, has significant policy, practice and conceptual relevance for families in adversity. This is the basis on which this study was conducted. Where we know that families can be in adversity, defined both in terms of the child care challenges with which they are presented, and the social disadvantage they suffer, then the issue of coping is important. We also know that this adversity can be extreme, and yet, because of resource rationing and high thresholds, parents are still unable to have access to social work services. This raises the deceptively simple question (in view of the complex answer): how do they cope?

This study focuses on families who:

- refer themselves, or are referred, to social services

- have child care problems acknowledged by both the assessing social worker and the mother herself, but

- do not get taken on to caseload (and hence have only fleeting social work involvement).

The key questions addressed under these circumstances are:

- How does the mother cope? What is the range of coping strategies adopted to deal with child care problems?

- What is the nature and severity of her problems and needs, and how do these impact on her coping strategies?

- How, if at all, are other services accessed, and how do women use these as part of their coping strategies?

- What is women's judgement of the efficacy of their coping strategies?

Clearly, this emphasis on coping requires further elucidation, and it is to this that we shall now turn.

CHAPTER 2

Dimensions of Coping

Coping theory generally approaches humans as active agents, that is conscious beings who bestow meaning on situations, and act in a motivated and self-directed way. The coping process is generally about two key concepts. The first is that of *threat*, which derives primarily from the stressor which is confronted, but may also arise because of the response that is made by the individual; the stressor presents the individual with some threat, with which they seek to cope. The second is that of *control*. Faced with the threat of the stressor, the individual seeks, through coping processes, to gain some measure of control over the situation, or themselves, including their feelings.

Lazarus (1993 p.237) has stated that 'coping consists of cognitive and behavioural efforts to manage psychological stress'. Lazarus and Folkman (1984 p.141) regard coping as the 'constantly changing cognitive and behavioural efforts to manage specific external and/or internal demands that are appraised as taxing or exceeding the resources of the person'. Cohen comments (1987 p.301) that it is 'efforts, both action oriented and intra-psychic, to manage (that is to master, tolerate, reduce, minimise) environmental and personal demands and conflicts...which tax or exceed a person's resources'. Sarafino (1998) describes it as 'the process by which people try to manage the perceived discrepancy between the demands and resources they appraise in a stressful situation'.

Stress and the primary appraisal of threat

The start point for understanding coping is, therefore, stress. Stress can be seen as a *response* to particular, difficult circumstances confronted by individuals. It is a state of tension – anxiety, frustration, etc. – which resides within the individual – primarily psychic – which occurs in response to some unwanted external situation (Coyne and Holroyd 1982). Stress is also seen as a process (as, indeed, is coping). Where the stress itself is seen as a process, it is contextualised within the relationship between the person and their environment (of which more later). This involves a continual process of interactions and adjustments between the person and their environment, which are frequently termed 'trans-actions' (Hobfell 1989).

Coping occurs in the face of some stressor. According to Sarafino (1998 p.70) this 'is the condition that results when person–environment transactions lead the individual to perceive a discrepancy – whether real or not – between the demands of a situation and the resources of the person's biological, psychologi-cal or social systems'. A stressor is generally considered to be circumstances, or particular facets of a circumstance, which are threatening or harmful (or perceived to be such) to the individual. Examples of this include catastrophic events, such as tornadoes, major life events (for example, the break up of a significant relationship), or chronic circumstances, such as living with severe pain from arthritis (Baum 1990). Although there are some variations in approaches to stress (Elliot and Eisdorfer 1982; Vingerhoets and Marcelissen 1988) if an event typically leads to psychological distress, behavioural disruption, or deterioration in performance, then it is characterised as a stressor.

Meaning and appraisal

A stressor is not a simple objective thing, but achieves its definition of threat through a process of appraisal by the individual concerned, which is dependent on the meaning of that event for that individual in terms of their wishes, feelings, concerns or interests.

Coping theorists generally distinguish between the *primary appraisal* of threat and the *secondary appraisal* of controllability. Primary appraisal relates to the appraisal the individual makes of the stressor: it is the process of perceiving a threat to oneself (Carver, Weintraub and Schieir 1989). Events which are threatening involve harm and/or loss and challenge. Harm/loss relates to the appraisal of the amount of damage that has already occurred, as when someone is incapacitated and in pain following a serious injury. Challenge relates to future harm/loss, and involves the opportunity to achieve growth or mastery by using more than routine resources to meet a demand.

At a personal level – and this is the level which interests us when we interview the women, in the first instance – meaning is subjective, and yet affected by the norms and expectations of the social group, and the history and experiences of individuals. The ways in which, for example, a mother makes sense of an argument with her teenage son depends on her perceptions of his motivation, on her interpretation of the content of what he says and his motivation for saying it. If she sees, for example, his argumentative behaviour as a response to some stress which has occurred in his life (for example, that he has been bullied at school, and the stress of the situation is getting to him), she will interpret, or appraise, this behaviour very differently from an argument based, in her view, on an unwarranted and stubborn attempt to get his own way. New and different information can also change the way a situation is appraised. Suppose, for example, this woman does not know about the bullying at school. She may then see him as argumentative and stubborn. She may subsequently learn of the bullying, and change her view not just of his behaviour, but also of herself (at least in relation to that incident). She may feel guilty, and even criticise herself for failing to realise that his behaviour was a response to external pressure.

The same event can have quite different meanings for different people and in different contexts. Take, for example, the case of a woman who finds she is pregnant. We can quite easily understand the uninhibited joy of this woman when we realise that she has been trying (and failing) to have a child for a number of years. Another woman, however, may feel desperate in finding that she is pregnant. She may be a woman who is very career-minded, and the prospect of having children will represent a major disruption, or even barrier – or a threat – to her life plans.

Factors in an individual's personal history may affect the meaning they attach to the particular event. Apparently straightforward tasks can be imbued with negative meanings and become stressful in the face of a problematic past. Many of the women whose children are subject to social work intervention have themselves been abused in their childhood. Women subjected to sexual abuse in childhood have described their own inhibitions when having to deal with the physical care of their own children, such as bathing, which they trace directly to their own childhood experiences (Sheppard 2001b).

The importance of meaning is discussed by Brown, Bifulco and Harris (1987). Their view is that an event or difficulty becomes more important – more stressful – when it has particular significance for the individual. It then has considerable, and negative, meaning for them, and, according to Brown *et al.* has an aeteological relationship to the onset of depression. They identified three ways in which negative events would develop particular significance for women. Each of these involved a 'match' between the negative event and certain characteristics of the woman and her life context at the time.

The first concerned marked difficulties which were already being experienced. If, for example, women were already worried because of financial difficulties, an additional burden of unexpected debt was likely to be perceived as far more problematic than if long-term financial difficulties were not already being experienced.

A second area where stress was likely to gain particular significance or meaning concerned areas of life which had particular value because of the extent of commitment which the woman experienced. This generally concerned a role or activity. Brown *et al.* identified five areas of women's lives: children, marriage/partner, housework, employment, and other activities outside the home. For example, a woman might describe herself as highly committed to her marriage, or close relationship. An event presenting a threat to her marriage would have particular significance.

The third area was role conflict. Role conflict related to roles where good performance in one area was inconsistent with good performance in another. This particularly related to conflicts between diverging occupations, for example, between the domestic and external spheres of a person's life. Where, for example, work and domestic responsibilities collide in trying to get children to school on time, an additional factor, such as an illness or injury, which makes the smooth performance of these tasks even more difficult, is likely to be experienced as stressful. Add to this an insistence by the boss that the woman must arrive at work on time, or else they will have to review her employment, and this is a recipe for considerable stress.

Coping: emotion-focused and problem-focused

While threat underlies appraisal of stressors, control, or the need to gain it, underlies coping responses. The way an individual seeks to gain control may be classified in terms of the functions of coping, involving a basic division between problem-focused coping on the one hand and emotion-focused coping on the other. Lazaraus and Folkman (1984 cf Carver *et al.* 1989; Lazarus 1993) define problem-focused coping as coping directed at altering the problem causing the distress. It involves efforts to change the troubled person–environment relationship. Emotion-focused coping they define as coping that is directed at regulating the emotional response to the problem. Emotion-focused coping is aimed at reducing or managing the distress that is associated with, or caused by, the situation.

Within these two broad domains, there is a wide range of more detailed coping actions which comprise these coping functions. There are two major groupings of problem-focused activities. Those directed at the environment include strategies for altering environmental pressure, barriers, resources, procedures, and so on. Inward-directed coping, focusing on the person him- or herself, includes strategies that are directed at motivational or cognitive changes, such as shifting the level of aspiration, reducing personal involvement, finding alternative channels of gratification, developing new standards of behaviour or learning new skills and procedures.

Lazarus and Folkman (1984) suggest that, while we can identify generic emotion-focused coping actions identifiable in a wide range of situations, there seems to be greater specificity in problem-focused coping, limiting opportunities for generic classification. Others do not agree, and Carver *et al.* (1989) identify a number of dimensions of problem-focused coping. These include, first, *active coping*, which is the process of taking active steps to remove or circumvent the stressor, or to ameliorate its effects. This includes initiating direct action, increasing one's efforts, and trying to execute a coping attempt one step at a time. *Planning*, which can occur alongside active coping, is thinking about how to cope with a stressor. Planning involves coming up with action strategies, thinking about what steps to take, and how best to handle the problem. This involves weighing up the resources available to deal with the problem, and considerating alternative approaches.

Some forms of problem-focused coping can involve limiting or delaying action, rather than taking it, where this is believed to facilitate problem amelioration or resolution. *Suppression of competing activities* means putting aside other projects, trying to avoid becoming distracted by other events, even letting other things 'slide', if necessary, in order to concentrate more fully on the threat. Another form of problem-focused coping is the exercise of restraint. *Restraint coping* is waiting until an appropriate opportunity to act presents itself, holding oneself back and not acting prematurely.

Lazarus and Folkman (1984) suggest that emotion-focused coping strategies are more likely to occur when there has been an appraisal that nothing can be done to modify harmful, threatening or challenging environmental conditions. However, there is no reason why emotion-focused strategies cannot occur alongside problem-focused strategies, for example, a mother seeks to express her distress when she feels she has not responded well enough to her young child's needs, and also seeks to deal with this as a problem.

Emotion-focused coping can be grouped into various domains. One domain involves attempts at *lessening emotional distress*, and includes strategies such as avoidance, minimising (importance), seeking to find positive value in negative events, distancing oneself from the problem, and so on. Some people even try to increase their emotional levels, as when athletes 'psych themselves up' for a competition.

Another domain involves *reframing encounters*. This is where the individual seeks to change the way an encounter is construed, without changing the objective situation. This might be the case if, for example, a family suddenly finds itself with debts, but then considers itself lucky still to be together ('and that is the most important thing'). The event can thereby change from a catastrophic event to a challenge (with the supportive imagery of the family around them). Another strategy involves *selective attention*, rather than seeking to change the meaning of an event. The change in meaning occurs because there is a change in what is being attended to, and what is being avoided. However, the meaning of an encounter can remain the same, even if some of its aspects are being screened out, or thoughts about it are being put 'to one side' temporarily.

Self-deception can also occur. Emotion-focused coping can be used to maintain hope and optimism, to deny both the fact of an event and its implications. By this the individual refuses to acknowledge the worst and acts as if what has happened does not matter. Of course, the individual may not know this is happening: one cannot simultaneously deceive oneself and be aware of what one is doing. Successful self-deception, therefore, generally occurs unawares (Suls 1983).

The person–environment interface

Coping occurs in a context. The manner in which coping takes place and the opportunities for taking particular coping actions are, it is generally accepted, considerably influenced by the 'internal' psychological state and 'external' environmental opportunities and constraints. Besides these internal feelings and cognitions, Moos and Schaeffer (1993) have suggested that the environment acts in two ways in the coping process: in the demands placed on the person, and in the action and resources available to meet those demands. Together, they consider this to be the *person–environment interface*, which provides the context for the coping responses of individuals.

This is the context for considering *secondary appraisal*, the process of bringing to mind a potential response to a threat: our assessment of the resources we have available for our coping. Two key aspects of appraisal seem to influence the perception of our capacity to cope. The first relate to the person – these include intellectual, motivational and personality characteristics (e.g. people with high self-esteem may believe they have the resources to meet the demands – if they perceive an event as stressful, they may perceive it as manageable rather than a threat (Cohen and Lazarus 1983). The second relate to the situation – the stressful context, including barriers which make management of the problem difficult, and the degree of support available to deal with the problem (Paterson and Neufield 1987).

Stress and constraints

The instigator for coping actions, as we have seen, is the existence of a stressor. However, the particular stressor which is the subject of coping actions may itself occur within a context of stress and constraints experienced by the individual (Williams 1999). Constraints can often be cultural, whereby group norms generate expectations which create a context unpropitious for the woman to cope when confronted with a problem. Constraints can operate as mechanisms linking external and internal states, and this can make productive coping more difficult, by, for example, affecting the individual's self-esteem. Feminist literature has emphasised how women who are mothers in traditional roles are often engaged in work which is routine, repetitive, unrewarding and not highly valued (Williams 1999). Such work includes housework, and even child care, particularly if a mother bears sole responsibility, and finds herself socially isolated.

Linked to this can be reinforcing negative responses from those in the social network if the woman tries to transcend the limitations of her role (Sheppard 1993). Strongly expressed disapproval may (deliberately or otherwise) leave a woman with a sense of 'wrongness' about her actions, and consequent guilt feelings. Powerful sanctions, such as accusations of neglecting her children, may be supported behaviourally by, for example, refusal to provide child care support where the woman's child care and employment responsibilities clash.

A particular problem, secondly, can be experienced within a wider context of stresses or disadvantage which makes resolution of that problem more difficult. A range of stressors have been associated with the women who are the subject of this study. These again can link the external context with the internal psychological state, including mental health. One significant area is that of domestic violence (Mirlees Black 1995), which has been associated with poorer physical and mental health outcomes for women, and even as an important cause of suicide and attempted suicide (Peterson *et al.* 1997; Ratner 1998; Stark and Flitcraft 1995).

Poverty is another stressful context. The association between poverty and mental health state is an unsurprising and well established research finding (Belle 1990). Poverty among women, evidence suggests, is associated with being a single parent, divorced, or a member of an ethnic minority group (Payne 1991). Family life itself can be stressful, with a well established association between psychological distress and motherhood (Pound and Abel 1996). Indeed, women may find their normally exhibited behaviours defined as indicators of mental health problems, as feminine attributes have been found to be considered inconsistent with those of mental health (Becwith 1993; Broverman *et al.* 1970).

Social support

One of the key dimensions of the person–environment interface is the presence (or absence) of social support. Social support has been the subject of various definitions (Henderson 1984), but it generally refers to help or aid provided by one or more persons for another. Pierce, Sarason and Sarason (1990) usefully define it as social transactions which facilitate coping in everyday life and are perceived as such by the recipients. As such, in general, its relevance for coping is fairly obvious. The presence of social support provides a potential avenue for coping whereby the individual facing a stressor mobilises the help of others to deal with the problem (problem-focused coping), or the emotional consequences of the problem (emotion-focused coping).

When seen as part of a coping process, the individual becomes much less of a passive recipient than s/he appears through social support theory alone. In the latter case, social support is something which is given or provided by others. In coping theory, while this of course can be the case, social support may be *actively solicited by the individual*. This is very much part of the conceptualisation of the individual as active agent (and, indeed, there is some correlation in this study between the women's perception of themselves as active copers, and the soliciting of social support as part of that active coping).

While some have presented social support as a kind of single, undifferentiated 'commodity', in general it has been accepted that it has a variety of conceptually distinct facets (Antonucci 1985; Thoits 1982). Of course, the first issue for coping is whether or not social support is available. The absence of social support, therefore, closes off a potential avenue for help in coping.

The issue of appraisal is relevant here. In this case, social support is a key element of *secondary appraisal* – appraisal of resources with which to cope with a problem. It may, for example, be the case that an individual does have support available (for example, her mother may be prepared to help), but she is either not aware of this, or does not see it that way. Alternatively, she may perceive herself as having support, but when put to the test, it 'evaporates' with potentially catastrophic psychological consequences (Brown *et al.* 1986). Thus the perception or secondary appraisal of support is crucial in the coping process.

A differentiated concept of support is widely accepted as necessary for the understanding of the link between social support and coping processes (Thoits 1982, 1986). Where support is available, its functional properties are most significant (Henderson 1984; Thoits 1986). These functional properties relate to that which is on offer, or provided, through social support. Here, there is an important distinction between availability and adequacy. Henderson, Byrne and Duncan Jones (1981) found that the availability of social support (that is, potential avenues for support) was much less significant for mental health outcomes than its adequacy (i.e. the potency of the support when provided). It is not enough, in other words, for support to be available, it must be enacted (and presumably, from the point of view of the person seeking to cope, solicited – cf Brown *et al.* 1986). Vieil (1985) distinguishes various dimensions of social support, based on type (psychological/affective or instrumental), relational context (formal and informal), and crisis versus everyday support. The difference between crisis and everyday support is the difference between support directed at a particular stressor that is creating a time of particular or discrete difficulty, and routine support derived from everyday interactions with friends, relatives and acquaintances. The latter is generally seen as helping provide a general psychological robustness, helping endow an individual with self-esteem, as well as a sense of 'belonging'.

Thoits (1986) gives a variety of ways in which social support may be engaged as part of the coping process. One obvious way is by *direct intervention*. For example, an individual may be helped by a loan, or being taken on vacation, or, indeed, by provision of child care when a mother's energy or patience runs out. Others can, alternatively, provide *advice or information*, like students who recommend study strategies, and books containing useful overviews, to each other. Others can help the individual to *reinterpret situations* so they seem less threatening, and reinforce less threatening perceptions by repetition and selective attention to cues. Friends can reassure parents, for example, that their teenager's difficult behaviour is 'quite normal' rather than the manifestation of some problematic behaviour. Others can also *manipulate the individual's expressive performance*, for example, by allowing them to ventilate their emotions outside the threatening situation, or enabling them to 'keep up a front' by helping direct and reinforce the individual's positive expressive gestures (such as giving off a sense of confidence).

Locus of control

An obvious alternative to soliciting help from others is to try and deal with the problem yourself. In this respect the issue of locus of control has some significance. Locus of control relates to an internal state that explains why some people actively, willingly and resiliently try to deal with difficult circumstances, while others succumb to a range of negative emotions (Lefcourt 1991). The term 'locus of control' refers to a construct originating from Rotter's (1966, 1975, 1990) social learning theory, and relates to the sense in which an individual feels they can influence, or determine, events, particularly when these are difficult, threatening or perceived to present them with a challenge. It develops as a general sense as a result of accumulated experiences in which individuals perceive a trend of relationships between their actions and the outcomes of their actions. Perceived controllability affects appraisal of threat. People tend to appraise an uncontrollable event as being more stressful than a controllable one, even if they do not do anything to affect it (Sarafino 1998).

A distinction is made between internal locus of control and external locus of control. Those with an internal locus of control believe that events are a consequence of their own actions and thereby under their personal control. Those with an external locus of control believe that events are unrelated to their actions, and are thereby determined by factors beyond their personal control. In principle, an internal or external locus of control may be a generalised attribute (i.e. applying to most or all circumstances encountered by an individual), or more specific (i.e. related only to particular areas of their lives).

These basic differences can have profound implications for the conduct of individuals. For example, 'internals' are likely to be prepared to expend more effort in an attempt to solve a problem, because they believe that such effort is likely to lead to a good outcome. Furthermore, they are more likely to attempt to resolve the problems themselves. Indeed, this can lead to the perception of a direct relationship between effort expended and good outcome (the more effort I put into something, the more likely that I am to succeed). Furthermore, the more difficult the problem confronted, the more likely is the individual to redouble their efforts. Conversely, 'externals' are likely to see raised effort in relation to a difficult problem as pointless.

This gives a clear indication of likely task persistence. Internals are likely to show greater task persistence than externals, and the more difficult the problem faced by the individual, the more marked this difference is likely to be. To the extent that task persistence is likely to lead to a successful outcome, internals are likely to develop a greater general sense of task competence: i.e. that they can deal with what life throws at them. This, in effect, is likely to create a sense of confidence in themselves as individuals, and to contribute to a higher level of self-esteem. The opposite is likely to be the case with externals.

While locus of control relates to an internal psychological state, the environment itself may be such that this reflects the real circumstances of their lives. For example, where individuals live in less responsive environments, they may, rightly, fail to see connections between their efforts and outcomes. Here again the issue of systematic disadvantage can have an impact on perceptions of locus of control. Individuals in disadvantaged, discriminated-against groups would, by definition, feel they have a more limited capacity, by their own efforts, to achieve successful outcomes. Young black males in deprived areas are likely to be fully aware of the higher rates of unemployment compared with similar white populations, and of the link between this and discrimination.

Research and conceptual development in relation to locus of control has been most marked in relation to health. Researchers are concerned with the extent to which individuals are likely to engage in 'healthy behaviours' i.e. behaviours liable to contribute to the development and sustainment of good health (Norman and Bennett 1999). The initial position was that those with an internal locus of control would be most likely to engage in healthy behaviours, because they would see themselves liable to determine health outcome through their own efforts. Those with an external locus of control, it was supposed, would be less likely to engage in healthy behaviours, regarding health outcome as more liable to be the result of 'fate'. Thus, in theory, there should be a strong association between health internal locus of control and health-promoting behaviours.

However, matters are not that straight forward (Norman 1995; Steptoe *et al.* 1994; Waller and Bates 1992; Weiss and Larson 1990). It has been suggested that insufficient attention is paid to the value placed by individuals on their health (the 'value placed on particular outcomes'). An individual might be expected to devote energy and effort to achieving a particular outcome if they place value on the achievement of that outcome, but not to do so if it is not highly valued (Abella and Helsin 1984; Weiss and Larson 1990). So an internal locus of control involves a sense that the individual is able to bring a difficult situation under control by their own actions, and is liable to be associated with direct action by the person themselves, and with task persistence and competence, provided it is in an area considered valuable by the individual.

Those with an external locus of control might be expected not to seek actively to cope themselves with a problem, or not to be persistent in doing so, or to seek help from others who might be considered more effective at bringing the problem under control. The belief in powerful others can be a strong factor in engendering a sense that a problem can be brought under control, though not by the individual him- or herself. This is not an internal locus of control construct, but is rather linked to the use and effectiveness of social support. This would be the case, for example, with professionals who are seen as being able to create change in a positive direction. Such is the case with medical professionals in relation to illness states (Wallston 1989).

Thoits (1986) has suggested a further factor in the effective use of social support for coping, which may be used by externals. She believes that socio-cultural and situational similarity between the individual and their supporter are key factors in the acceptability and likely success of the support. Both, she thinks, are likely to enhance a sense of empathic understanding, a condition under which she thinks coping assistance is likely to be most effective. Socio-cultural similarity increases the probability that a significant other will suggest coping techniques, or attempt to influence circumstances in ways that individuals view as acceptable. Individuals, furthermore, are more likely to compare themselves with, and affiliate with, others who have faced similar stressful circumstances. Distressed individuals tend to feel that others who have experienced similar situations are most likely to understand their position (Gottlieb 1985).

Trait and process, stability and change

Coping has been presented in terms of a particular trait or style characteristic of individuals. The assumption underlying this approach is that coping styles are more or less stable, with individuals learning to cope in particular ways. People do not approach each coping context anew, but rather employ a preferred set of coping strategies that remains relatively fixed across time and circumstances (Carver *et al.* 1989). More recently, there has been a growing emphasis on process. According to these writers, an individual's coping is not a stable trait, but may change over time, and in accordance with situational contexts (Lazarus and Folkman 1984).Coping is not static, but is a function of continuous appraisals and reappraisals of the shifting person–environment relationship. Any shift in the person–environment relationship may lead to a reappraisal of what is happening, its significance and what is to be done.

This approach assumes that we should be concerned with what a person actually thinks or does, in contrast with what the person 'usually does', and that the former and latter frequently diverge. The coping actions, like the circumstances in which the coping takes place, are considered to have a high degree of specificity, always directed towards particular conditions. It follows that coping is a shifting process in which a person may rely on different coping strategies at different times.

One example of changes in the coping process may be found in loss and bereavement, and in the frequently long duration of grief work, beginning with the moment of loss. Initially there may be frantic activity, tearfulness or brave struggles to carry on socially or at work. Later stages often involve temporary disengagement and depression, followed ultimately by acceptance of the loss, re-engagement and even attachment to other persons (Littlewood 1992). This process can last some time, even years, and be characterised by many emotional difficulties and ways of coping. To an observer (according to those who consider coping to be a process) these may well appear quite different at different times.

There is, indeed, evidence that different modes of coping are used in dealing with different aspects of a stressful situation, and at different stages in a stressful encounter (Cohen *et al.* 1986; Folkman and Lazarus 1985). However, there may be dispositions evident where coping strategies are consistent over time, or across different types of stress (Carver *et al.* 1989). Where a consistent pattern of this sort is shown, this would indicate coping patterns characteristic of the individual.

Nevertheless, the degree of variance over time, as observed in the process approach, can depend on the time period over which observations are made. What may be identifiable as a process over a lengthy period may appear to be stable when focusing on a shorter period of time; even a process such as adjusting to loss may involve shorter periods of stability. Denial, for example, may occur over some time. However, one can take this further. There may be relatively stable elements in the key individual and situational factors relating to particular stressors which lead to stability in coping response. Particular behaviours may elicit particular responses. For example, aggressive behaviour by a teenager may elicit argumentative responses in the parent.

There is a case to be made, therefore, that while process is a very important aspect of coping, elements of continuity should not be lost in pursuit of elements of change. Where we are concerned with practical implications and responses, elements of continuity, and the time period concerned, may assume greater significance than change. For example, where a particular coping response leads to danger to children, it may matter little whether the parent would have adjusted their coping behaviour one year down the line. By that time a child might be injured or even dead. A crucial variable in the focus on elements of continuity and change, therefore, is the *relevant time period* concerned. Under some circumstances it is the issue of stability of coping behaviour which assumes greatest importance.

Conclusion and summary

It is evident that there is a need for clarity about a wide range of factors which serve to situate the coping process. Obviously, the stressor itself has to be identified, but so, too, do background stresses. The coping functions used in response to the stressor are central to our understanding of the individual's response, as is their appraisal both of the stressor and the resources available to cope with it. The context, both in terms of internal psychological factors and the external environment, provides the setting through which coping strategies can develop, including the persistence and perceived competence of the individual to respond. Broadly, we can summarise the key factors as follows:

1. Coping theory generally approaches humans as active agents, that is, conscious beings who bestow meaning on situations, and act in a motivated and self-directed way. This allows them to initiate actions and respond to problems with which they are confronted.

2. Coping is a response to some stressor. There are two key dimensions to coping, which underlie the perspectives taken by the individual and their need to respond. These are: the threat posed by the stressor, and the need for (some) control, which is the main purpose of the coping attempts.

3. Appraisal is key to understanding both stressor and coping strategy, defining and bestowing meaning upon both. Neither stress, nor coping, therefore, is straightforwardly and unproblematically defined.

4. Stress is defined in terms of the primary appraisal of threat, which is defined in terms of harm/loss or challenge to the individual. Events and difficulties are likely to be more stressful when endowed with particular value or significance by the individual.

5. The way individuals seek to gain control of a stressful situation is through their coping strategy. Coping is generally divided into two basic functions: problem-focused and emotion-focused. Problem-focused is coping directed at altering the problem causing the distress. Emotion-focused is coping directed at regulating the emotional response to the problem, reducing or managing the distress associated with or caused by the problem.

6. Coping occurs in a context, considerably influenced by the 'internal' psychological state of the individual and the 'external' environmental opportunities, background stresses and constraints.

7. Secondary appraisal is bringing to mind appraisal of resources – personal and environmental – to help deal with a stressful situation and bring it under control. This is considered the person–environment interface.

8. Individuals may possess a sense of an internal locus of control – where they believe they have considerable capacity to bring events under control – or external locus of control, where they do not.

9. Those with internal locus of control are likely to have a greater capacity for task persistence and sense of task competence, and will be likely to make more effort to resolve a problem, the more difficult it is.

10. For those with an external locus of control the opposite is the case.

11. Social support is a key aspect of coping, and refers to help or aid provided by one or more persons for another. It is differentiated by type (affective and instrumental) and source (formal and informal).

12. Coping is largely a process, i.e. it is not static, and changes with changes in the environment. While it is responsive and changes with changed circumstances, there is also some degree of continuity and persistence in coping approaches.

CHAPTER 3

Parenting

The care of children is a task which calls upon the coping capacities of parents, so the dimensions of coping outlined in the previous chapter are relevant to the consideration of parenting. However, there is a wide literature on parenting which itself has a variety of dimensions. While parenting is clearly a task, it is also an interaction with the child. Of central importance here are ideas derived from attachment theory in the encouragement of healthy child development. However, these need to be considered, following Belsky (1984), in the wider contexts of the characteristics of the parent (particularly the mother, who is generally the primary caregiver), the child and the environment. It is to these issues that we now turn.

Attachment and child development

As attachment theory has gained influence, so has a widespread view that the prime task of parenting is the facilitation of child development. Belsky (1984) argues that caregiver warmth and sensitivity is the most influential dimension of parenting in infancy. It not only fosters healthy psychological functioning but also lays the foundation on which future experiences will build. There is remarkable consistency of research in this respect: warm and sensitive parents who often talk to their infants and try to stimulate their curiosity contribute positively to the establishment of secure emotional attachments, and facets of child behaviour which is associated with such security: the child's interest in their environment and willingness to explore.

The early experiences of children, although not exclusively contributing to their positive development, are nevertheless of considerable significance. The primary developmental task during the child's early years is to promote an environment which engenders feelings of security and trust (Fahlberg 1991). This has been, to a considerable degree, associated with what Ainsworth (1973), assuming the mother as primary caregiver, has called *maternal sensitivity*. This is the mother's ability and willingness to interpret her infant's behaviour from the infant's point of view. Responsive mothers will be able to recognise their baby's social signals, and regulate their behaviour in a way that co-ordinates with that of the child.

The conceptualisation of this relationship between parenting and child development is made through the notion of *inner working models*. These are the models children develop of themselves, their environment and their interactions with it. The quality of the child's relationship with their primary caregiver becomes internalised and influences the development of *self*. An accepting, responsive parent will tend to engender in the child positive feelings about him- or herself. A rejecting parent will have a tendency to generate feelings in the child of being unimportant and unlovable. Insensitivity can also generate feelings that the environment is hostile and unresponsive.

The Attachment Classification System developed by Ainsworth and colleagues (1978), and extended more recently (Main 1991) illustrates how different parental behaviours have identifiably different outcomes. These vary from the most well-adjusted parent–child relationships, which engender secure attachments, to less desirable outcomes of different types of insecure attachments (insecure avoidant attachments, insecure and ambivalent attachments, insecure and disorganised attachments), to the non-attached, for whom no attachment is developed (Fahlberg 1991). Mothers of securely attached infants tend to hold and cuddle their children on a regular basis in their caregiving. They have a sensitive and warm quality in their verbal interactions, and they respond to infant vocalisations more frequently than insensitive mothers. By contrast, for example, mothers of ambivalent children are inconsistent in their responses to the child, being available and helpful on some occasions, but not on others. Indeed, they may later use threats of abandonment as a means of securing the child's compliance. Such a mother is both inconsistent and insensitive in her response to the child, generating confusion rather than co-operation in her relationships with the child (Bowlby 1991).

Although later parent–child interactions have an impact on child development, the Ainsworth Strange Situations classification has proved helpful in focusing on the relationship between early life experiences and later personality development. This provides some testimony to the persistent impact of early life experiences, and hence parenting of young children, on their long-term development (Howe 1995).

Two major dimensions of parenting

This warmth and receptiveness has been considered one dimension of parenting: that of acceptance and responsiveness, a feature relevant to child development beyond infancy (Maccoby and Martin 1983). The general feature of warmth towards the child as positive parenting is contrasted with criticism. Accepting-responsive parents often smile, praise and encourage their children, expressing a great deal of warmth, although they can become quite critical when the child misbehaves. By contrast, less accepting and relatively unresponsive parents are often quick to criticise, belittle, punish or ignore the child. They rarely communicate to the child that they are valued or loved.

'High warmth, low criticism' in parenting, encouraging stable, positive child developments, has been generally identified in contradistinction to 'low warmth, high criticism' parenting, which is frequently associated with children with emotional or behavioural difficulties (Department of Health 1995). A major contribution to poor relations, clinical depression and other psychosocial problems later in life is a family setting in which one or both parents have treated the child as if he or she was unworthy of their affection and attention (Ge, Conger and Elder 1996; MacKinnon-Lewis *et al.* 1997; Bifulco and Moran 1999). Not only do children not thrive when ignored or rejected, they are unlikely to become happy, well adjusted adults (MacDonald 1992).

The other dimension of parenting relates to child regulation. In this respect, and at extreme ends of a spectrum, demanding parents place restrictions on their children's freedom of expression by imposing many demands and actively surveying them to ensure compliance with rules and regulations, while undemanding parents are less restrictive, allowing children considerable freedom to pursue their interests and make decisions about their own activities, regardless of consequences.

Baumrind (1967, 1971) has carried out considerable research around these two dimensions of parenting. Taking into account Maccoby and Martin (1983), four types, or styles, of parenting have been identified. The first, *authoritarian parenting* has a very restrictive pattern, in which parents impose many rules, expect strict adherence to them, and rarely, if ever, explain why it is necessary to comply with those regulations. They also often rely on punitive, forceful tactics (power assertion and love withdrawal) to gain compliance.

The second (at the opposite extreme) is *permissive parenting*. This is an accepting but lax pattern of parenting, in which adults make relatively few demands, permit their children freely to express their feelings, do not closely monitor their children's activities and rarely exert control over their behaviour.

In recent years, it has become clear that the least successful parenting is *uninvolved parenting*: an extremely lax and undemanding approach displayed by parents who have either rejected their children, or are so overwhelmed by their own stresses that they have little time or energy to devote to child rearing (Maccoby and Martin 1983).

The final pattern of parenting is *authoritative parenting*. This is a controlling but flexible style in which parents make reasonable demands on children. They are careful to provide rationales for complying with the boundaries they set, and ensure that the children follow these guidelines. They are much more responsive to the child's point of view than authoritarian parents, and often seek their children's participation in family decision making. These parents seek a more rational, democratic style, compared with the more domineering approach of authoritarian parents.

Baumrind was able to link these styles of parenting with characteristics, in the first instance, of pre-school children. Children of authoritative parents had the best prognosis: they were cheerful, socially responsible, self-reliant (for their age) and co-operative with adults and peers. When further studied at age eight to nine years, these children tended to be higher in cognitive competencies (i.e. showed originality in thinking, had high achievement motivation). They tended, compared with other children, to have greater accomplishment in social skills, that is, they were sociable and outgoing, participated actively and showed leadership in group activities (Baumrind 1977; 1991).

Pre-school children of authoritarian parents tended to be moody, apparently unhappy for much of the time, easily annoyed and unfriendly. At age eight to nine, these children were generally average or below average in both cognitive competencies and social skills. Pre-school children of permissive parents were often impulsive and aggressive, and this was particularly the case with boys. They were more self-oriented, and lacking in self-control. At age eight to nine, like children of authoritarian parents, these children were also relatively poor in relation to cognitive competencies and social skills.

The least successful parenting is uninvolved or neglectful parenting. Already, by the age of three, children are high on levels of aggression, and externalising behaviours, such as temper tantrums (Miller *et al.* 1993). They tend to perform poorly in the classroom in later childhood (Eckenrode, Laird and Doris 1993), and are more likely to display hostility and be rebellious as adolescents. They are more likely to be lacking clear goals or direction, and to be more persistent users of alcohol or drugs, to be frequent school non-attenders, and to be offenders (Kurdeck and Fine 1994; Lamborn *et al.* 1991; Patterson, Raid and Dishion 1994; Weiss and Schwartz 1996).

In teenagers the greater efficacy of authoritative parenting remained apparent. Compared with other children, children of authoritative parents were relatively confident, achievement-oriented and socially skilled. They were also more likely to stay clear of drug use and other behavioural problems (Baumrind 1991).

The adolescent period presents, as most parents of teenagers are aware, particular challenges. A key developmental task during the teenage years is the development of autonomy, and this requires a delicate balance between the regulatory function of parenting and the granting of an ever greater degree of independence to the teenager. There is evidence from a variety of cultures and countries that conflict occurs between parents and children during the adolescent years (Steinberg 1996).

This conflict occurs, to a considerable degree, because of the different perspectives adopted by parents and adolescents, derived from the tension between the search for autonomy and parental regulation. Parental concerns are often moral, but may also relate to matters such as safety and age appropriateness of behaviours, all essentially related to regulatory functions. Young people frequently see matters from the perspective of personal rights (to do or be what they want), both related to their search for greater autonomy, and as a result view their parents' regulatory actions as nagging, restrictive and even offensive. Behind this is also an issue of greater equality: as the young people are able to assert themselves more, and parents are gradually able to relinquish their regulatory functions, so a greater degree of interpersonal equality occurs between parent and child, as the latter moves closer to adulthood, by which time, ideally, self-regulation largely replaces parental regulation.

The quality of psychosocial adjustment in teenagers is related to a combination of the relationship with parents and the response of the young person. Teenagers who consider their relationships with their parents to be conflictual and non-supportive appear to be better adjusted when they distance themselves from their families and become emotionally autonomous (Fuhrman and Holmbeck 1995). However, those who are gradually able to achieve greater behavioural autonomy, at the same time as maintaining close attachments to family members, display the best overall pattern of psychosocial adjustment (Lamborn and Steinberg 1993; Steinberg 1996).

A key issue, therefore, for parenting of teenagers lies in the capacity of parents to respond appropriately to young people's demand for autonomy. The period of adolescence, ideally, sees the transfer of responsibility for behavioural regulation from the parents to the child him- or herself. It would appear that parents of well-adjusted teenagers are able gradually to relinquish control of these young people, as they display a readiness to accept a greater degree of responsibility. They nevertheless continue to monitor the conduct of their adolescent children, and at the same time demand more self-regulation (Younniss and Smollar 1985). Furthermore, where parents continue to insist on exerting some regulation, there is a good outcome when they try to explain it and continue to be warm and supportive even in the face of conflicts that arise (Steinberg 1996).

There is, then, a degree of flexibility manifested by such parents at the same time as paying the courtesy of reasoning with the young person – seeking to explain and give reasons for their actions. This interaction is most successful where there is some degree of reciprocity also, that is, a recognition on the part of the young person that parents may relinquish the bounds of their regulatory function gradually, and where the young person recognises some degree of parental right of regulation.

Characteristics of the child

Parenting, it is now appreciated, is not carried out in a vacuum, nor a process in which the child is the recipient, and the parent the donor or initiator, of all developments. Current theoretical thinking, especially that influenced by Belsky (1984), views parenting as determined by multiple factors grouped broadly into three main areas: the characteristics of the parent, the characteristics of the child, and sources of stress and support in the wider environment.

The focus here is on the child's temperament, and the extent to which this influences both the child's development and the processes of parenting. What, in other words, is the interaction between child temperament and parenting? And how does this interaction affect child development?

Temperament refers to the child's characteristic mode of responding emotionally and behaviourally to environmental events, or tendency to act in predictable ways. Attributes of temperament include areas such as activity level, irritability, fearfulness and sociability. To the extent that temperament remains stable over time, from early infancy through to adulthood, this would suggest that child characteristics, rather than parenting, are the key factor determining child development and psychosocial adjustment (Caspi and Silva 1995). Some longitudinal research does indeed suggest some degree of temperamental stability from infancy, through childhood, to the early adult years. A team in New Zealand found that a number of components of temperament at age three predicted problems in psychosocial adjustment at age 18 to 21, including individual differences in subjects' antisocial tendencies, and the quality of personal and family relationships (Caspi and Silva 1995; Henry *et al.* 1996; Newman *et al.* 1997).

One dimension which has been examined in this respect is behavioural inhibition – a tendency not to participate, or to withdraw from social activities and interaction. One research programme examined children aged 4 months, 21 months, and 4, $5\frac{1}{2}$ and $7\frac{1}{2}$ years (Kagan 1992; Kagan and Snidman 1991; Snidman *et al.* 1995). The heightened physiological arousal (such as high rates of heartbeat) with which inhibited infants responded to novel situations or objects, was reflected in a greater degree of shyness at a later age when encountering unfamiliar people, toys or settings. Less inhibited children showed far less arousal at the younger age, and reacted quite adaptively to the novel events. By the age of $7\frac{1}{2}$, inhibited children remained less sociable with strange adults and children, and more cautious than uninhibited children. However, it would appear that only children at the extremes of the inhibited/uninhibited continuum displayed long-term stability. Others showed considerable fluctuations in levels of inhibition over time (Kerr, Lambert and Benn 1994).

Such an extreme would be apparent in children with Attention Deficit Hyperactivity Disorder (ADHD). This can involve unpredictable behaviours, or predictably aggressive and hyperactive behaviours, with problems in attending and maintaining attendance to important environmental stimuli and controls.

Parental regulation of behaviour becomes extremely difficult to exert success-fully. Such children can present enormous challenges to parents, who can struggle to deal with the child's behaviour, and so the process of parenting can become exhausting. There does appear, where correctly diagnosed, to be a biological basis to ADHD. The evidence from a range of studies indicates a neu-rological aetiology for the behavioural symptoms associated with ADHD in almost all children with this condition (Hynd and Hooper 1992).

Even in less extreme circumstances, temperament, it has been suggested, can exercise a major influence over the parenting process. Kagan (1984, 1989), for example, has argued that temperament can play a more significant part than parenting in child behaviour, particularly in circumstances which can evoke anxiety. Indeed, the strange situations test individual differences in the child's temperament rather than the quality of attachment. Kagan suggests, for example, that temperamentally difficult infants who are uncomfortable with, and resist changes in, routine may be distressed by the strange situation, and, as a result, unable to respond positively to the comforting of the mother. The difficulty, then, resides with the infant rather than the behaviour of the parent.

However, many infants display different attachment characteristics, according to their carer. Infants may be securely attached to one carer and insecurely attached to another. This is not a pattern which would be expected if attachment classifications were merely a reflection of the child's relatively stable temperamental characteristics (Srouffe 1985). Furthermore, the majority of temperamentally difficult infants establish secure attachments with caregivers who display patience and adapt their caregiving to the infant's temperamental characteristics. On the other hand, some babies without such temperamental difficulties may end up establishing insecure relationships with mothers or primary caregivers who experience serious personal difficulties which prevent them from being sensitive and responsive parents (Van den Boom 1995; 1997).

The work of Chess and Thomas (1984) indicates that there is an interaction between child temperament and parenting which is efficacious for secure attachments. This is referred to as 'goodness of fit'. They found three broad groups which defined and described the central features of most children's tem-peraments. They distinguished between those with an 'easy temperament', generally even-tempered, positive in mood and open and adaptive to new experiences, those with a 'difficult temperament', who were active, irritable and unpredictable in their habits, and 'slow to warm up' children, who are less active, moody, and can be slow to adapt to new persons and situations.

They suggested that early temperamental characteristics can sometimes carry through into later life, while at other times they do not. A key factor in this is the 'goodness of fit' between temperament and parenting (Chess and Thomas 1984; Thomas and Chess 1986). For example, difficult children, who are irritable and do not adapt well to new situations and routines, may become more adaptable and calmer in the long run with appropriate parenting. This involves the parent remaining calm, exercising restraint and allowing such children to respond to new situations more slowly. Indeed, difficult children who experience such sensitive parenting are often no longer classifiable as temperamentally difficult in later childhood or adolescence.

Nevertheless, these are difficult children, who, by definition, present parents with a greater challenge than easier children. They can make considerably greater demands on parents, making it far more difficult to respond in a calm manner than when caring for an easier child. It is not always easy for parents to be sensitive and patient with a grumpy, difficult, moody and unpredictable child who resists their bids for attention. Indeed, there may be a deleterious effect on parents themselves, rendering them less patient (where they actually need greater patience), irritable, demanding and punitive, in some respects a mirror of the difficult child (Van den Boom 1995). These parenting behaviours are a poor fit with a difficult child, who is likely to become still more difficult as a response to the parent's demands and punitive behaviour. This was precisely what was found by Chess and Thomas (1984), that difficult infants were particularly likely to remain difficult and display behaviour problems later in life if their parents had been impatient, demanding and forceful.

The parents

The mother is generally the primary caregiver, and, as such, is the most important figure in the parenting of the child. While, of course, this does not have to be the case, and the significance is in the primary caregiver(s) rather than sex of parent, this makes some sense of the emphasis on the mother in the literature.

Mother or not, considerable significance is accorded to the parent's own internal working models of attachment relationships – their mental representations of their childhood experiences. These become part of the 'person of the mother', particularly in the interaction between parents and their children, and are thought to influence parents' sensitivity to their child's attachment needs and behaviour, and hence the quality of parenting that a child receives (Bowlby 1973; Van Ijzendorf *et al.* 1995). These mental representations lead the person to anticipate the manner in which their external relations with the world will be carried out. As the child grows, new relationships are assimilated into existing models, which are largely outside consciousness. As noted earlier, their development will involve a combination of temperament and environmental influences. Over time they build into the person's cognitive structures and understanding of their self and their relationships with others.

Where children are in reliable relationships, they can build up a central subjective experience of the world as not being unpredictable and arbitrary, and of themselves as able to exert an influence over it. Where parental behaviour is inconsistent, it is hard to develop consistent inner working models of the environment. The psychological consequence of this can be feelings of confusion, anger and despair, as well as difficult behaviour. Where parental insensitivity occurs, this encourages the construction of working models of the social environment as essentially hostile and unresponsive, and of the self as inadequate or unworthy of help or comfort.

Parents with secure internal working models have these, it is postulated, either because they themselves have experienced secure attachments, or because they have worked through the negative experiences of their earlier life. They are able to respond to their children's signals and demands related to their attachment needs without experiencing anxiety themselves, and without having to block or distort these signals, which do not, in effect, present a threat to the parent, and hence do not present any kind of inner conflict.

Parents who have insecure internal working models are thought to block or distort their children's, particularly infants', attachment-related signals, because they find these signals threatening. Children can be seen as demanding, and their behaviour can generate anxiety, aggression, or avoidance and neglect on the part of the parent, who is unable, in effect, to cope with the attachment demands of their own child.

However, not all parents who experienced poor attachment relationships when they were children repeat these as adults in relation to their own children. Self-reflection appears to play a major part in overcoming the effect of early maladaptive attachment experiences. Parents who seem to be unable to remember their feelings associated with poor childhood experiences appear more likely to repeat their adverse childhood experiences when parenting their own children. In these circumstances, it seems, they find considerable difficulty in being sensitive to the emotional needs of their own children (Fraiberg, Adelson and Shapiero 1975). However, parents who have experienced problematic relationships with their own parents, but who prove capable of giving a coherent narrative of these experiences when discussing them, tend also to have infants who are securely attached to them (Main and Goldwyn 1984). This suggests that a capacity for self-reflection plays an important role in overcoming the effects of poor childhood attachment experiences.

Quinton and Rutter (1984a, 1984b; Rutter and Quinton 1984) conducted two studies relating admission to residential care to parenting. Both enabled the examination of consequences of serious problems in parenting. In general, women brought up in institutions had more parenting problems when they were themselves parents than women in comparison groups. The first study (Quinton and Rutter 1984a, 1984b) focused on mothers of children who had been admitted into residential care (which was evidence of a serious breakdown in parenting). There were major differences between this group and the comparison group. Women with children in care were more likely themselves to have been in care, to have been subject to harsh discipline, and to have been separated from at least one of their parents as a result of marital discord or rejection. The second study (Rutter and Quinton 1984) was a follow-up of adult women who had been admitted to care when they were children. The 'in care' group were more likely to have been pregnant, and to have been pregnant before the age of 19. Of those with children, the 'in care' group were more likely to be without a male partner, to have had children 'in care' or fostered, and to have had a temporary or permanent breakdown in parenting.

The main problem for these women seems to have been related to what was lacking or absent in the institution, rather than problems in the child's relationship with their parents. The absence of, or limits to, an opportunity for developing attachments, seem to have been critical, and those with the poorest outcome were adults who as children had remained in institutional care from infancy. Nevertheless, matters were not fixed or determined. Positive school experiences, a supportive partner, or some achievement could all have a positive effect through enhancing confidence and capacity to deal with everyday problems.

Mental health state can have a significant, and deleterious, effect on parenting. The more 'severe and enduring mental illnesses', the psychoses, are often associated with a dissociation from reality which itself can be damaging. The greater this lack of contact with reality, and hence the more severe the condition, the greater can be the consequences for the child. For example, a mother's delusions of being spiritually in contact with her infant could lead to neglect, leaving him or her alone all day (Cassel and Coleman 1995). If content of the delusion includes the child, and particularly beliefs about the child, including threatening or evil intent, the risk to the child can include physical harm as well as emotional development (Rutter and Quinton 1984).

Lack of motivation and withdrawal are key negative symptoms associated with schizophrenia, which can lead to parental detachment and feelings of abandonment, particularly in young children (Downey and Coyne 1990). Absorbed as they are in their own thoughts, parents can leave the child to their own devices and neglect even the child's basic needs for physical, as well as emotional care. A parent can become unpredictable and chaotic during acute and florid phases of a psychosis, and as well as being detached from reality, the parent can act in ways frightening for the child. Problematic judgement can involve neglect of the child, and the possibility, for younger children, of accidents occurring (Cassell and Coleman 1995). Some children, for example if the mother experiences pueperal psychosis, can be at risk of death from parents whose delusions leave them feeling threatened by the child itself (Sheppard 1990).

Of all the adult mental health conditions, it is the impact of depression in mothers which has been most extensively researched (Sheppard 1994a). It is by far the most frequent mental health problem, and has symptoms the effects of which are not dissimilar to those of other disorders. Depression can have an effect which undermines the capacity to carry out many of the important tasks of parenting. Among the more serious aspects affected are consistency of care, emotional closeness, responsiveness to the child's emotional needs, irritability and aggression, often unpredictable. Absorbed with their own negative thoughts and emotions, these mothers are often unable to respond to the needs of the child, and indeed may see these needs as a threat to themselves. The needs of the mother may actually be in competition with those of the child, while her sense of desperation can divert her from a focus on the child. The result can be neglect, both emotional and physical, and even violence, which can be sudden and severe.

At the heart of the depression is a loss of hope, a negative cognitive triad about self, the world and the future, and a low self-esteem which deprives the woman of confidence and leaves her feeling bad about herself, so that the child care role, and the demands of the child, can appear overwhelming and threatening, undermining her capacity to rise to the challenges of child care. The loss of hope can leave the parenting role appearing pointless, with an absence of meaning about this role and life in general, and inhibition in relation to the mother's capacity to develop attachments to the child. The result can be the development, in the young child, of insecure attachments, as the child finds the mother unresponsive to its attachment signals.

The two major parenting consequences of depression – the negative consequence of neglect and absence of involvement and the positive consequence of irritability and aggression, often on a 'short fuse' – can both serve to reinforce the depression (because of a further sense of failure in a valued role, exacerbating the mother's low self-esteem), and have damaging effects on the child's development.

In general and psychiatric population studies, depressed mothers have been shown to be more likely to use corporal punishment, to express hostility and ir-ritability towards their children, and to involve themselves less in play with young children. Parents of adolescents are more likely to involve themselves less with children, to have communication problems, and feelings of guilt and resentment (Weissman, Paykel and Klerman 1972). Some evidence suggests that children of moderately rather than severely depressed mothers are at greater risk than other children of child abuse and physical aggression (Whipple and Webster Stratton 1991; Zuvarin 1989). However, detailed studies of depressed mothers subject to social work intervention show that, even compared with the children of other mothers receiving social work support, children of depressed mothers are significantly more likely to be on the child protection register, and to have greater parenting and child care problems (Sheppard 1997a, 1997b, 2001). There is also greater difficulty working in partnership with these women in attempts to ameliorate and resolve these problems (Sheppard 2002).

Mothers' judgement of their children's behaviour is also negatively affected by depression (Sheppard 1994a). There is a tendency for depressed mothers to rate their child's behaviour more negatively than other assessors, such as teachers, or standardised instruments, when they are used. It is probably the case that depression has a direct effect on mothers' perceptions of a child's behaviour (viewing it more negatively) and an indirect effect (through the effects of depression on the quality of parenting) on actual child behaviour.

There is also evidence of higher levels of emotional, behavioural and cognitive problems amongst children of depressed mothers when compared with those of mothers not suffering depression (for a review of literature see Sheppard 1994a). In the pre-school period, these include crying in infants, lower mental and motor development, poor concentration span, delays in expressive language development and more limited involvement in play activities. School-age children of depressed mothers display more somatic complaints, more negative cognitions about themselves, and greater rates of child depression. Likewise, a consistent finding of greater behaviour problems has been found amongst depressed mothers' children of both pre-school and school age. Task competence is generally lower in pre-school children, as well as persistence in carrying out tasks. School-age children are involved in more conflict and fighting (at home and at school), are more frequently withdrawn, and less interested in usual activities. Adolescents tend to have poorer relations with their parents, more behaviour problems at school, perform less well academically, and are more frequently involved in illegal behaviour.

Wider stress and support

The environment plays a key role as the context for parenting. We know that a variety of types of disadvantage or short- and long-term stressors can have a major impact on parenting. Very often this involves a link between the social stressor, the psychological state of the parent and their capacity to care for the child, and so we find, for example, that the extra pressure involved in caring for children with serious disabilities has an impact on both the psychological state of the mother, and her capacity for caring. The same goes for domestic violence, which can have an impact on the child both directly (through witnessing the violence) and indirectly (through its psychological effect on the mother in turn affecting her capacity to cope with child care – Cleaver, Unell and Aldgate 1999).

Amongst the most widespread of environmental difficulties which affect parenting, and which can serve as exemplars, are poverty and the processes involved in single parenthood. Single parenthood is often associated with greater problems in parenting and child care. It is also generally carried out by mothers, who form the overwhelming majority of single parents. Early research by Ferri (1976), focusing on children in single-parent families born in a single week in England and Wales, found that, compared with children from two-parent families, they were more likely to have emotional and behavioural problems, and to be performing less well in their school work. However, some degree of disaggregation is necessary to make sense of this.

It might appear that the absence of a parent would leave parenting more difficult and the child more likely to have adjustment problems. However, there is a tendency for single parents to be on lower income, and when financial hardship was taken into account, the differences between single- and two-parent families disappeared. Similar results were found by McLanahan and Sandefier (1994) in their United States study of nationally representative samples. Here, lower income and the drop in income associated with the transition to single parenthood, was the most significant factor in the underachievement of adolescents from single-parent families. Many single parents are unable to hold down a job, or have a full-time job, because of their child care responsibilities, and this leaves them with a low income. The result is a day-to-day struggle to make ends meet, which can take its toll of psychological and social functioning.

Thus, parenting and child care difficulties in single-parent families are, to a considerable degree, the result of low income and financial hardship associated with lone parenthood. However, most families with single parents begin as two-parent families. The process of divorce and separation is also highly significant in our understanding of parenting performance. Children of divorcing parents are more likely to suffer psychological problems than those in two-parent families (Rogers and Pryor 1998). However, a longitudinal study by Hetherington (1988) showed that matters vary at different points following divorce and separation. In the first year after separation, children functioned less well than children from intact families, whether or not the parents had a good relationship with each other. However, from two years after separation onwards, girls with divorced mothers were as well adjusted as those in two-parent families where the parents had a good relationship. The least well adjusted were girls in families where the parents were in conflict. From two years onwards, boys from intact but conflicting families were least well adjusted, although after six years, sons of single parents continued to show some psychological and behavioural impairment.

The key to this appears to be the degree of conflict between the parents, whether or not the family is intact. However, the worst prognosis of all exists for children in single-parent families where the parents remain in conflict (Amato, 1993; Hetherington, Bridges and Insabella 1998).

There are also significant social class differences in parenting. Working-class parents tend, to a greater degree than middle-class parents, to stress obedience and respect for authority, placing less emphasis on fostering independence and creativity. They tend more frequently to use power-assertive discipline, to talk and reason with their children less frequently, and to show less overt warmth (Maccoby and Martin 1983; McLoyd 1998). This tendency towards more authoritarian approaches has been attributed to the effects of economic hardship. These can involve occupying residences that are crowded and where it is difficult to afford adequate clothing, and even food sometimes. Parents can be persistently tense and anxious living in these conditions. These pressures diminish the capacity to be warm, supportive parents and to be closely involved in their children's lives.

This is evident in the incidence of depression in women of working-class status. Brown and Harris (1978) found that working-class women were four times more likely than middle-class women to experience onset depression over the previous year. One particular vulnerability factor with depression was the presence of three or more children aged under 14. The difference between working-class and middle-class women was largely to be explained in terms of the families which had three or more children aged under 14. Brown and Harris attributed this to the difficulty of performing the parental role adequately with large families, which would affect the women's self-esteem. However, while it is certainly the case that large family size presents a challenge, there is also evidence that the stress of living on low wages translates itself into a psychological state which makes it difficult to parent (Conger *et al.* 1994). Indeed, we have already seen how depression is associated with problems in child care.

An alternative socio-cultural explanation may be provided for different parenting, focusing on different expectations of blue- and white-collar workers (Arnett 1995). Blue-collar workers are to a greater extent engaged in work processes which involve deferring to supervisors' authority. Theirs is a more overtly hierarchical, less consultative world of work. Many lower-income parents may emphasise obedience and respect for authority because these are precisely the attitudes that they view as crucial for success in the blue-collar world of work. By contrast, middle-class parents may reason more with their children, precisely because this approach is central to the white-collar professional world, where such attributes as individual initiative, curiosity and creativity matter in the conduct of work.

As we have seen, social support is a key element in understanding the coping process. It is not surprising, therefore, to find that it is part of the conceptual and empirical apparatus by which we are able to understand parental functioning. Social support can act directly on parenting through help given in various ways with child care, but often also works indirectly by reducing the stress on the parent, arising either from child care itself, or from the social environment in which the parent and family are situated. While it is clear that, for example, maternal depression is associated with greater problems in the performance of the child care task, the high rate of depression among mothers is perhaps not surprising, because of major demands presented in caring for children. It is also not surprising, therefore, that much of the research on the significance of social support for parenting has been carried out with a focus on depression in mothers (see Sheppard 1994b).

The beneficial effects of social support are widely attested in the literature. This is evident among groups of mothers whose social circumstances would be expected to place them under greatest stress and at greatest disadvantage, such as unemployed women, those on low incomes, single mothers and women with children with disabilities. It is the case, regardless of the type of support (for example, expressive, emotional or practical-instrumental). Indeed, when social support is differentiated, as appropriate, into its constituent parts, there is a variety of ways in which it can affect the parent and parenting. Social network and structure, in general, have very little impact on mothers' functioning. The factors related to this include the number of people in the network, frequency of contact, geographical proximity and stability of social relationships. However, where mothers suffer poverty and disadvantage, social network does have significance; isolation has been found a problem for poor unmarried women (Reis 1988a, 1988b), while unemployed women with few social ties have significantly higher rates of depression than low-income, employed women whose daily work routine brings them in contact with others (Hall, Williams and Greenburg 1985). These researchers found that among unemployed women the presence of marital partner buffered against stressors, particularly housing and inadequate income.

The combination of poverty, which limits women's abilities to afford leisure activities, and child care, which limits opportunity for recreation, appears significant. Women who have few people to turn to, when coping with the day-to-day struggles associated with poverty and the responsibility of child care, find their capacity to cope cumulatively ground down. Employment may be beneficial because it brings these women into contact with others, lowering isolation, providing opportunities for discussing problems and aiding self-esteem. Partners may help to improve morale or esteem in otherwise harsh circumstances.

There has been considerable interest in employed mothers. Employment, it is well known from Brown and Harris's (1978) research, can confer protection for mothers against depression, which is associated with parenting and child care problems. Employment can be significant because it can confer protection, through income and contact with others, but it can also, where mothers are concerned, present the problem of conflict between parental and breadwinner roles. Among middle-class employed mothers, the absence of traditional role segregation, entailing support from their spouse with child care and household maintenance, is associated with psychological wellbeing (Holtzman and Gilbert 1987). The availability of a close confidant has also been shown to significantly reduce depression in employed women (Woods 1985).

Support appears significant in particular for employed low-income and working-class mothers. Hall *et al.* (1985) found that the quality of the marital relationship was related to fewer depressive episodes, regardless of additional stressors. Parry (1986; Parry and Shapiro 1986) found that in working-class employed mothers, emotional support acted as a buffer against additional (non-work) stressors. Woods (1985) found similar trends, specifically identifying problem discussion, accessibility and reciprocity in this process. These researchers (Woods 1985; Parry 1986; Parry and Shapiro 1986) found that the absence of instrumental, practical support involved higher rates of psychiatric 'caseness'. The combination of work and child care responsibilities, it was suggested, produced 'stress overload', and this was best combated through non-traditional roles being adopted by both parents. In effect, where both parents undertook both work and home responsibilities, this reduced the effects of stress in low-income families.

In divorced and single mothers, support is again efficacious. Among divorced mothers, Tetzloff and Barrera (1987) found that having someone to talk to about child-rearing problems is associated with lower rates of depression. Except where parenting stress became overwhelming, they found that parenting support reduced psychological distress. They also found that tangible support, in the form of lending money or household items, was inversely related to depression. McLanahan, Wedemeyer and Aldberg (1981) found that for divorced mothers with social networks primarily involving family of origin, kinship ties, and those involving a relationship with a key male, were more effective in preventing depression than purely friendship networks. Thompson and Ensminger (1989) found that lone mothers who, over time, gained and retained a partner had better psychological wellbeing than those who remained lone mothers.

In the case of lone mothers, then, it appears that the absence of an intimate relationship in which the individual is able to express her feelings and gain practical support does make the mother vulnerable to depression and child care problems. The absence of this relationship appears to present a stress in itself, as well as the pressures of parenthood and other aspects of life. However, it is also worth noting that single parents are more likely to be living on lone incomes, presenting additional stresses with which to cope. In the face of these, kinship networks seem most effective.

Parents with children with disabilities are likely to experience pressure from the additional demands of child care. Researchers (Wolf *et al.* 1989; Fisman, Wolf and Noh 1989) found that parents of autistic children had an elevated risk of depression. They found also that social support acted as a buffer against the effects of stress additional to that involved in caring for children. Fisman *et al.* (1989), however, found that these parents suffered lower intimacy (with a close confidant) than mothers of developmentally average children, further reducing protection against depression in mothers of already difficult-to-manage children.

Dunst, Lee and Trivette (1989) found that both familial support, and that from friends and neighbours, was related to psychological wellbeing in mothers of 'handicapped and developmentally at risk' children. However, additional disadvantage hampered their parenting efforts. Poorer, worse supported and more distressed mothers (characteristics which tended to go together) were less able to concentrate on children's educational, developmental and therapeutic needs (where they were troubled).

It is clear, then, that various forms of support can be efficacious in relation to a variety of difficulties and disadvantages experienced by mothers. It is not, perhaps, surprising that these mothers feel the benefit of help with child care and with practical and financial problems, and the availability of friends with whom they can discuss matters, express their feelings, and gain advice. However, it is the enactment of support, rather than its potential presence, that it gains its significance. Henderson *et al.* (1981) distinguished between the *availability* of support, and its *adequacy*, finding that the latter, rather than the former, exerted an impact.

Conclusion

There are clearly a number of overlaps between parenting and coping. One of the more obvious is the significance of social support. This allows an active coping strategy, a means of responding to stressful threat by using environmental resources. It is also a factor in enabling parents to parent more effectively, and in reducing the psychological impact of the problems of parenting.

The literature on parenting, however, enables us to provide a better focus for our research on coping, by, for example, making it apparent that context, particularly wider stresses, are important alongside the specific stresses of parenting and child problems. Likewise, parenting styles, with an emphasis on warmth and sensitivity on the one hand, and child regulation on the other, provide contexts for coping with children. In what senses, if at all, do such strategies come into play when having to cope with particular stressors in adversity? The challenges and needs presented by children, furthermore, vary with age, and provide a further context for considering coping strategies. Our exploration of mothers' coping strategies in adversity, therefore, needs to take cognizance of the traditions of both coping theory and parenting literature.

CHAPTER 4

Context, Study Methods

The central focus of this book is the way in which mothers cope with child and family care problems in circumstances of adversity, and how this links with processes of prevention. At the empirical level it focuses on families in disadvantage, with problems, but whose access to services is limited. The obvious question here, then, is: how do they cope? At the conceptual level it seeks to bring together ideas of coping and prevention, in order that our understanding of both may be enriched.

If we are to draw findings which are widely relevant to this group of families, and hence our understanding and responses to them, we would normally expect them to be representative in some way. In part this is about how they are chosen. How do we get at this group? This partly reflects the social processes by which families come into adversity and are not availed of mainstream services. Our approach was to focus on one group, who, from earlier research (Sheppard 1998), clearly had child care and parenting problems, were in disadvantaged circumstances, yet whose efforts to receive services were 'rebuffed' by the agency from which they sought help. These were families referred, or who referred themselves, to child care social services, but because thresholds for the receipt of services were so high, were nevertheless unable to receive a sustained service. Details of exact criteria for inclusion are given in this chapter.

How can the research site chosen provide for representativeness? In some respects this should be regarded as a case study. This is entirely defensible, since this is the first study of its type, focusing on this particular group in this way, and seeking to bring together major conceptual streams of coping and prevention. Many of the findings, furthermore, were about conceptual development (primarily) rather than measurement of 'scale' (although there were some elements of the latter). We were seeking to develop a range of concepts and empirical data which helped us understand this relation between coping and prevention with this particular group.

However, there were elements which suggest considerable general applicability of findings. The study was undertaken in one particular city, and of course, reflects the particular characteristics of the city. However, the positioning of the subject group in the prevention process – applicants for social service support who did not receive any sustained intervention – is one that is recognisable throughout Britain (and no doubt other places with similar agencies). The broad structures and processes undertaken by social services departments are similar. Indeed, there has been a growing convergence of processes as central government has developed similar expectations to be applied to departments throughout the country. Of particular relevance in this respect is the need for assessment procedures which enable social services to develop eligibility criteria for services at the stage of initial assessment. The social services department involved was similar to other local authorities, in the widely understood application of high thresholds for receiving a service because of the combination of high levels of need and limited resources. Finally, more broadly, all social services are subject to the same legal requirements, and many similar operational expectations as a result of government guidance. Any one social services department child care service is clearly going to have much in common with others, even though much still depends on the operation of services by those at the ground level.

Of course, this study is not centrally about social work intervention, although this forms a part of the study in its link between maternal coping and prevention. It is about high need families with no sustained access to social work intervention, despite seeking support. Thus our focus is on a deprived group with considerable needs in relation to children and parenting. In this respect, it will be apparent that our inclusion criteria enable us to focus on exactly such a group.

The setting

City, at the time of research, was one of the larger urban centres in Britain, with a population in excess of a quarter of a million, but at some distance from other major urban centres. It was a unitary local authority, that is, the administrative authority, and the social services department was responsible for the area coterminous with the city. Some parts of the city were areas of considerable affluence, but others were among the most deprived and disadvantaged in Britain. The city had a large rural hinterland, and was a major focus for employment, both for city dwellers themselves, and for those from rural areas within commutable distance. It had a long association with the armed forces, which, although in decline, still exercised some influence.

The population was overwhelmingly white, in this respect differing from some large multicultural urban areas in Britain. The rate of unemployment was (as a total of workforce) 4.2 per cent on data from the Office of National Statistics. Between a third and two-fifths of the adult population were employed in service industries such as banking, transport, catering and distribution. Nearly two-fifths were employed in other service and tourist industries, and around a fifth were employed in manufacturing and construction. Tourism was an important source of income, both in the city and in the surrounding areas.

Over three-fifth of households with dependent children were owner occupied. Over two-fifths had one dependent child, the rest having two or more, while around four-fifths had car owners. Around one seventh of households with children were 'headed' by single parents. The overwhelming majority of these single parents (all but a tenth) were women, the majority of whom were not in paid employment. Single parents tended to be single mothers, and not very well off.

The social services department, of which more below, comprised three districts or areas which covered roughly equal population numbers. Each was quite accessible to its constituent populations through established bus routes. While, in an initial flush of enthusiasm following the development of care management, there had been moves towards organisational divisions between purchasers and providers, this had encountered considerable opposition at ground level, and an increasing sense of its impracticality meant that the department drew back from such a distinction. Instead child and family care was divided into assessment and long-term teams, the former dealing with initial referrals, and the latter with cases which, following assessment, were considered to require sustained caseload intervention.

The study: identifying the 'in need' group

This was a study of mothers coping with parenting and child problems in adversity. In broad, social policy terms, these would be defined as families 'in need'. What did this mean? The focus of this research, as stated earlier, was on the three broad dimensions of (a) how women coped (b) in adversity (c) with child care or parenting problems. This was in some respects a case study, not of an individual person or organisation, but of a particular area, details of which have been given. However, the means by which the sample was obtained *was* an organisation: these were families not accepted for long-term caseload support by the social services department child care section. To understand this we need to know something of the processes of gaining client status.

Individuals could refer themselves, or be referred by others, for social services support. The nature of the agency was that its primary focus, like all other child care social services departments, was overwhelmingly on child protection. In principle, the duty of all social services departments is in relation to children in need (Section 17, 1989 Children Act). Children are in need if, without local authority services, they are unlikely to achieve or maintain (or have the opportunity to achieve or maintain) a reasonable standard of health or development; or if, without such services, their health and development would be likely to be significantly impaired (or further impaired); or if they are disabled. These are very wide criteria, and have been interpreted in different ways by different local authorities (Aldgate and Tunstall 1995; Colton *et al.* 1995). What is clear is that no local authority is able to provide long-term social work support for all families fitting these definitions, and so City operated a sifting procedure, whereby families referred were assessed for their eligibility for a service. Only those with the greatest needs – those who in fact presented, in the view of the assessing social services officers, children who could be identified as being in some sense 'at risk' of significant harm (see Section 31, Children Act) – went from referral on to caseload.

This was enshrined in an organisational division between assessment and long-term teams. Assessment teams were those who undertook initial assessment of new referrals, undertook some brief intervention, if that was required, and handed families on to the long-term teams for sustained intervention, if that was required. The processes by which these were determined were as follows.

The intervening process involved an assessment, one which was expected of all local authorities to determine the need (and level of need) for a service. The department operated eligibility criteria for assigning priority to referrals, reflecting (a) the nature of problems/needs apparently present, and (b) the time within which an assessment was expected. These criteria were:

Priority One: Safeguarding – 'an immediate response is required'. Children who are suffering or have suffered significant harm, or are likely to suffer significant harm. Timescale – within 24 hours.

Priority Two: Safeguarding – 'an early response is required'. Identified factors exist indicating unacceptable risks to the child without intervention. Timescale – within three working days.

Priority Three: Safeguarding – 'an assured response is required'. Children for whom there is significant concern about their care, health and development. Timescale – within five working days.

Priority Four: Promotional – 'an assured programme of support is likely to be required'. Children who are likely to be moved up to Priority One, Two, or Three unless services are required. Timescale – within seven working days.

Priority Five: Promotional – Cases where advice, signposting (advice or direction to appropriate alternative services), or access to a service is required. Timescale – within seven working days.

These priorities worked as a hierarchy, so that where there was competition between different referrals for social services attention, those with the highest priority would be allocated first. The timescales were intended to be maximum times before families were seen, although pressures of work meant that at times, these periods were exceeded. 'Safeguarding' referred to safeguarding children at risk of significant harm, while 'promotional' referred to promoting the welfare of children and families in need, but without children at risk of significant harm. Although these were intended as clear means for indicating where priorities should lie, the definitions were themselves slippery, involving individual and group judgements. At what point, for example, did a child become at risk of significant harm? Which families could be regarded as being 'in need'?

While, then, the terms indicated levels of problems, the processes by which these were operationally defined rested on interpretations by individuals on the ground. It would be facile to suggest that these were mere social constructions. The permanent damage done to an infant by severe shaking or hitting is all too clear, and rather obviously more damaging than minor chastisement. The roles of key professionals, nevertheless, were very important in deciding which families should be 'processed', and how this should happen. We are looking here at the general rules governing the 'client career', determining which level of prevention would be the focus for intervention.

It was clear that department policy and operation meant that only families who were assessed within priority levels 1 to 3 were to be given longer-term caseload intervention. In effect, this meant that the department had made an operational decision that, of all those families in need, only those who needed 'safeguarding' (that is, those with children considered to be at risk of significant harm) would be the recipients of caseload intervention. The rest would receive one of three types of service: (a) no help at all; (b) some brief help, generally no more than contacting another agency on their behalf, or the work entailed in a few interviews; (c) referral or signposting to another agency.

In relation to the last point, we should, of course, remember that caseload social work intervention was not the only option available, and there were occasions where women were referred, or advised to go, to other professionals or agencies. Most of the time, they were not, but there was a range of relevant agencies to whom the women could, in principle, go (indeed, they were generally eligible to refer themselves). These broadly fell into three groups: informal, formal generic, and formal specialist. 'Informal' included advice or support groups, such as support groups for Attention Deficit Hyperactivity Disorder. 'Formal generic' involved a host of health and other services. These included the GP, health visitor, police and counsellors. Specialist services involved different realms. With mental health, for example, there were mental health centres, alcohol and drug centres and MIND (the mental health charity). With child care, there was a child and adolescent psychiatry unit, family centres, and a youth advisory service. In relation to violence, there were specialist counselling services and refuges. Women's responses to, and particularly uptake of, referral on will form an element of this study.

Criteria for inclusion: the 'in need' group

Our focus was on families which were referred, or referred themselves, but did not go on to receive caseload intervention. We focused on families where the initial appraisal by assessment team workers indicated that an assessment was required, but the families' problems, when examined, were not considered severe enough to merit sustained intervention. In addition, it was necessary that the family should have at least one child or parenting problem. These fell into five areas: child emotional, child behavioural, child cognitive, child disability/health, and parenting. Those without one of these problems identified by the assessing worker were excluded from the study. However, there was a third dimension. When interviewed, the mother herself should identify a problem in at least one of those five child and parenting problem areas. This was done through the use of the Parent Concerns Questionnaire (PCQ) (Sheppard and Watkins 2000). This is a reliable and valid instrument developed for these populations, containing 17 problem areas in its parenting and child sections, and comprising elements of each of the five domains we have identified. In effect, therefore, inclusion in the study required that, in the operational terms of the social services department, (a) these were families in need; (b) they did not receive sustained (caseload) intervention and support; (c) both assessing worker and mother identified at least one child or parenting problem in the family.

The agency undertook to identify the families in the first instance. When they met the initial inclusion criteria, the mothers were contacted in the first instance by social services for inclusion in the project. If they refused, no further action was taken. If they agreed, they were then contacted by the research team, and again offered the opportunity to refuse involvement in the study. If they agreed, a time was arranged for interview, and a location, which, with one exception, was in the mothers' own homes. At the interview, the PCQ was administered early in the interview. In all cases, women identified at least one parenting or child problem, an unsurprising outcome, in view of the fact that they, or another referrer, had considered them appropriate for referral to child and family social services, and the assessing officer had identified at least one parenting or child problem. In most cases, the women identified multiple problems, many of them severe.

These women came from disadvantaged backgrounds. These are evident in terms of their financial, housing, education and psychological circumstances. All these might justifiably lead those making such assessments to conclude that there was a high level of general need in these families.

Overall, 151 women were approached, of whom 102 (68%) participated in the study. This two-thirds response rate was satisfactory when compared with studies of similar groups (e.g. Sheppard 2001). The overwhelming majority (100) were white, reflecting the pattern for the population as a whole. Sixty-five of the sample were single (never married, divorced or separated), and the rest were married or living with a common law partner. This was dramatically greater than the general population of the area. About two-thirds (26/37) of women married or living with a common law partner had a partner in paid employment, as 13 of the women were themselves in paid employment. Single parents, however, were generally without paid employment (51/65). This is reflected in reliance on state benefit. Only 18 (of 102) families relied solely on wages. The rest required some kind of state income support, including over half (56) who were reliant on state benefits alone. Their social disadvantage is reflected in housing status: only 15 were in owner occupied housing, the rest in rented accommodation or homeless.

The women were also low achievers in education. Eighty-seven of them had left school by the age of 16. Almost all (92/102) gained no GCSE 'O' levels, NVQ level 2, or their equivalent, at all, and only five went on to higher education. The families were quite large: 40 (of the 102) had three or more children in the family, creating a significant vulnerability for depression (Brown and Harris 1978). During the crisis, a high proportion (65/102) experienced a transient depression, while a significant minority (27) experienced a sustained depression, as measured by the Beck Depression Inventory, at both the time of crisis and the interview.

The meaning of women's coping actions and prevention

The findings reported here were part of a large study which involved both qualitative and quantitative methods. Although we do report some of the quantitative findings, particularly where they are able to provide some indication of numerical size of particular facets on which we focus, our major attention here is on the qualitative data. We were very much interested in the inductive dimensions of understanding the processes linking coping and prevention in the particular circumstances of mothers in adversity with child and parenting problems. Our focus, therefore, was on how women made sense of what was happening, on the contribution they and others made, and on how they perceived the processes which linked prevention and child care. In short, we were interested in uncovering meanings.

This was because these women occupied the central position linking coping with prevention. Mothers, it is widely understood, generally have primary responsibility for child care. This is certainly the case for women in families subject to child protection processes and child care social work caseload intervention in general. This was also the case with the families in this study. Indeed, over half of the families, as we have seen, were 'headed' by single mothers, who did not have a partner even potentially to share some of the burden of child care. Where, therefore, women played such a central part in decisions which would link coping (by them) with wider prevention processes, it is important that we understand the ways in which they would make those decisions, and upon what grounds.

Of course, no process of data collection and analysis can be entirely inductive, and, as Hanson (1958) has commented, is essentially retroductive, involving a combination of inductive and deductive processes. In this case, we can identify the broader conceptual framework of prevention, and particularly coping, within which our more inductive focus falls. While coping, as we have seen, provides a framework, involving issues like primary appraisal, threat, secondary appraisal and controllability, in the context of our particular concerns this simply provides a conceptual 'space' where the details – theoretical and conceptual themselves, as well as empirical – may be explored. This examination – or perhaps more appropriately excavation – of conceptual and empirical detail was, however, predominantly inductive. Without detailed information, which it was our aim to *discover*, it would necessarily have been impossible to have the knowledge which would have enabled us to develop meaningful instruments for the purpose. We therefore saw our approach as essentially *grounded* in the empirical data collected.

Strauss and Corbin (1998) write helpfully on the importance of an element of induction with qualitative data (while nevertheless not committing us exclusively to their approach). They strongly emphasise the general importance of grounding research in empirical data, rather than approaching knowledge development in a more hypothetico-deductive manner. The problem with the latter approach, they suggest, is that it presumes in advance to know the key issues, and the meanings within which these issues may be framed, before examining them in the 'real world' inhabited by the participants who are the subjects of study. This leads to oversimplification at best, and stultification of theory development at worst. Grounding our ideas in empirical research enables a closer 'fit' to emerge between the experienced, lived lives of participants in the study, and the empirical data and emerging theoretical ideas. Our theory and data become, therefore, more valid and precise in relation to the area of social life that is of interest to the social researcher. In our case, this enables us to develop more precise conceptual and empirical data specific to our area of concern, rather than rely solely on the generic ideas of coping and prevention. In Strauss and Corbin's terms, this leads to the development of substantive theory – concepts particular to a specific area of study.

Schutz (1964) is much quoted on the significance of meaning to the understanding of the social world. Any understanding of social reality must be grounded, he thought, in people's experience of that social reality. This reality has already been interpreted by subjects, so social researchers need to understand the interpretative schemas through which they make sense of the world, and upon which they base decisions for action. The danger of not doing this is to risk creating a 'world' merely constructed by the social researcher. Hence the social actions of individuals and groups are only to be understood where this includes the actors' own interpretations of their actions, and the motivations for these actions. Not only are people arbiters of reality (through their interpretations of it), but they also impact on that reality. Hence we have the famous dictum by W. I. Thomas that if men (sic) define situations as real, they are real in their consequences. In our case, women's coping strategies are only to be understood in terms of the meanings attached by them to their own and others', particularly their children's, actions.

The interview process

As our central concern was an understanding of the interpretative schemas through which women understood and took actions in relation to child care, semi-structured interviews provided the means through which we collected data. The obvious alternative would be direct observation. However, this had clear practical difficulties. It would have required first-hand observation, and hence the presence of the researcher in the largely familial circumstances in which these parenting and child care difficulties emerged and occurred. This was clearly impossible for a range of obvious reasons: how could we know when these problems would occur, so that we were present at the right time? how could we negotiate access to the homes of the families concerned (some were even homeless)? how could we be present at a variety of settings in which many of the problems occurred (e.g. school)? In fact, observation techniques are generally most appropriate to particular organisational settings, such as police, social services or educational departments. However, even had we been able to gain direct access to these families, how would we know that our interpretation of what we observed was, in fact, coincident with their interpretation? We would jeopardise the central focus for the research.

Interviews provided the obvious means for gathering data, as they enabled women to provide an account of their perceptions, reflecting on what they saw, what they did and why. It provided a means for them to provide a coherent account of what had happened over a period of time, rather than a particular moment. The result was a narrative which enabled the exploration of their overall perceptions rather than discrete observations on individual events (although such observations could provide evidential exemplars of individual perspectives).

Interview progression

Where a central feature of data gathering is the meaning attached by participants to facets of their social world, considerable scope is often given to them in interviews to define their own agendas. This is the source of unstructured interviewing processes such as 'rambling' (Measor 1985) – where the participant meanders about, talking about matters that interest them – are, as a result, highly prized. Our approach gave less freedom to the participants to define their agenda, as a result of the use of the semi-structured interview. These gave interviewees the scope to respond in the ways they considered fit to areas of interest to the research team, but those areas of interest were themselves defined in advance. This was consistent with our overall approach: that we were interested in the broad, formal, conceptual areas of coping and prevention, which were designed to create the 'space' for empirical investigation. Within that space we were, however, interested in the emergent and grounded data and concepts which came from the interview process.

We sought to follow a logical process enabling the women to respond to key areas of coping and prevention, in terms of their own experience. Following some initial 'warm-up' questions of social and demographic data, we began the process of identifying parenting and child care problems. This initially involved enquiring about their reasons, or, where appropriate, the reasons of others, for contacting social services. We expected some child or parenting problem to emerge from this questioning, but where it did not, we directly asked if they had found aspects of bringing up their children to be challenging or difficult, and explored this with probes designed to enable them to provide their own account of these issues.

Women were often able to identify a 'problem set' rather than individual problems, and this issue was anticipated. It was important, from the point of view of assessing coping, as Lazarus (1993) has commented, to identify precisely which stressor was the focus of their coping strategy. The danger, otherwise, is that one is confronted with a generalised, or confused, response, which does not specifically relate the coping strategy to the stressor. They were, therefore, asked to identify, from the problems identified, which they considered to be the main, or primary problem. Women were asked to 'expand' on the problem where this was felt necessary. One method used was to ask them to provide one or more exemplar which illustrated clearly what they were talking about.

Having done this, it was possible to make this problem area the focus for our exploration of coping strategies. We then sought to explore the ways women coped with the main problem they had identified. We sought, from their statements, to disaggregate the most significant coping methods they used, and identify these individually. We asked them to explore these further, in a similar manner to the way we explored child and parenting problems. This again featured the use of examples illustrating the features they identified. We again sought to identify from these the single most important coping strategy, as defined by the woman herself, by asking her which she considered to be the main or primary coping strategy.

As we have noted in the chapter on coping, stressors occur in a context. One element of this may be termed contextual stressors. These were stresses which, while other than child or parenting, nevertheless were of significance to the women, and likely to have an effect on their parenting. We again sought to identify the range of stressors experienced by the women, including areas of social instrumental, social relationship and health difficulties. Similarly to child and parenting problems and coping strategies, we sought elucidation of contextual stressors through the use of exemplars. Another aspect of context was the social support which the women were able to use. To a considerable degree, *use* of social support represents a coping strategy. The women were not just passive recipients of support, but actively sought it out. Nevertheless, use of support depends upon its availability, and we sought to explore this. Thus we aimed to obtain information on those who had provided help, in particular, with the main child or parenting problems the women had identified. We asked also what it was that was done, and how, if at all, it was helpful. This was again explored through exemplars through which we were able to obtain more detail.

We were, of course, also interested in the women's experience of formal social and other services, which linked their coping strategies with the apparatus of conventionally defined prevention. Depending on whether they or someone else had contacted social services, we approached matters slightly differently. If they had contacted social services themselves, we asked them about their expectations of the service. We then explored what they felt social services had actually done, and whether this had met their expectations. This enabled us to discover whether the women had felt social services to have been helpful. Where they were referred by others we sought to discover whether they knew about the referral. If they did, we asked similar questions to self-referrers. If they did not, we asked them about their reaction to referral, and then proceeded with similar questions to self-referrers. We also asked them about referral on to other professionals or agencies, whether or not they used these services, and their degree of helpfulness.

Our final line of questioning examined the women's satisfaction with their coping attempts, in the context of all the matters that had been discussed. This enabled us to explore their judgement of their efforts.

The interview and the interviewer

An issue in the interview process was the way in which the women were likely to react to the interviewer. The women were expected to recount personal elements of their lives, sometimes focusing on extremely harrowing events, in which they had invested a high level of their own self-esteem and respect. How far might we expect there to be some distortion, or misleading, to go on in the interview? Of course this is not answerable with certainty: how can we know what we do not have the information to know (by, for example, being present at the event, or even being able to read their mind!)? However, we can at least identify the accounts of women as plausible or implausible, in terms of their internal coherence. A woman who expresses extreme anger at her child for his behaviour, who considers the child responsible for this behaviour, and obviously implies that a strong behavioural response, such as smacking or beating, is appropriate, is going to present a suspicious account if she maintains, without additional reasoning, that she acted purely in an emotionally responsive and supportive manner. It is certainly the case that the overwhelming majority of women presented an internally coherent account.

Another factor that would affect response to the interviewer was the interviewer him- or herself. One, rather obvious, way of dealing with this was to employ a female interviewer. As Miller and Glassner comment (1997), interviewees may respond on the basis of who we are, which may be (in shorthand) identified in terms of the social categories to which we belong. These can involve issues, they suggest, such as age, gender, class and race. We know, for example, from Thoits' (1986) work that people do, indeed, turn to others with similar characteristics and outlooks for their social circle and social support. Our own view was that a female interviewer was vital if we were to obtain the most frank and open accounts from the women. Indeed, as a mother, our researcher (MG) was still more closely identifiable with the research participants. Many of these women had experienced particularly difficult relations with men, and this, we reasoned, would make them more wary of disclosing information to a male interviewer. These women, we believed, furthermore, were more used to expressing their feelings, and generally interacting at a social level, with other women. A female interviewer would most closely approximate these routine social relationships and make the women feel more comfortable talking about themselves and significant elements of their lives. Our belief turned out to be well founded, as we obtained clear evidence that women provided the majority of these women's social circles, and were most frequently turned to when they needed to express their feelings, or seek support.

Some women, however – although still relatively insignificant as a proportion of the whole sample – did not respond to interview as extensively and openly as we had hoped. For example, a small number of women showed a degree of disinterest in the interview, leaving us with less detailed and informative responses than we would have liked. While in one case this almost certainly reflected the woman's learning disability, in the very few other cases the woman was clearly, for whatever reason, reluctant to disclose information which was perhaps just too personal. Of course, the manner of recruiting the sample may have affected some women. Since initial contact necessarily required that we approach them in the first instance through social services, they may have felt that contact between the research team and social services was greater than it actually was. Assurances of confidentiality would have limited currency with some women by whom social services were, at times, feared for their capacity to 'take away' their children (however misguided that belief would have been).

Cornwell (1984) suggested that accounts are most likely to be truthful and comprehensive when contact is made with participants over an extended period of time. It is possible to build up a relationship, even some kind of friendship, through which the level of trust required to reveal personal details can be fostered. It is a relationship more likely to be based on equality, and to prevent exploitation of the research participants. The participant distinguishes between more limited 'public accounts' which will emerge with limited contact, and 'private accounts' liable to emerge when a constructive relationship is developed.

Our own approach was based on single interviews with the women, generally lasting about two hours. This involved the collection of some quantitative data, although the majority of the interview was qualitative. Two interesting points emerged from this. While most women enthusiastically participated in the research, some showed signs of impatience towards the end of the interview, based on its length. A few, for example, asked pointedly how much longer the interview was going to take. Clearly, with these women we reached close to the limit of their preparedness to participate. Their expectations were for a single, limited contact in which they would tell their story, admittedly within the frame of our questions, in the way they wished. A second important point is that in a sizeable minority of cases, women showed a desperate desire to 'tell their story'. Their accounts were punctuated by displays of emotion, often crying, and a need to express their perceptions and feelings about events which were detailed, occasionally involving a kind of 'free flow' of thoughts. This is hardly surprising, in view of the subject matter of the research, but it does provide some indication of the preparedness of many women to tell their story, as they saw it, not just truthfully, but in considerable detail.

The interview in the context of the woman's social world

Our emphasis on meanings meant that we did not see these women's stories as unproblematic accounts of objective situations with which all who were involved would be compelled, if honest, to agree. We did not assume that, for example, the children would generally have agreed with the women's own accounts. However, we do consider that in talking to us they were imparting their perspective on their social world. The interview was not some isolated, discrete endeavour, appropriately the subject of study itself. It was not something which, so to speak, had 'a life of its own', the accounts contained therein only understandable in terms of the interactions between interviewer and interviewee. We do not consider this to be the case generally in relation to well conducted interviews. In this case, the subject matter and responses of the women render preposterous the idea that the accounts were only of interest as an isolated phenomena, rather than a reflection of the women's perceptions of their social world. The considered responses, the expressions of emotion, the importance of the subject matter in their lives make that much clear. These women had, almost to a person, spent long hours, days, weeks and so on, thinking about their situations, and what they were to do about them. Their accounts were clearly based on the deep thinking they had done about these situations. For these women their situations were very real, often desperate, and a primary focus for their attention.

Nevertheless, the ways the interviews were conducted at times affected the collection of information. Interestingly, however, it was the nature and purpose of the interview itself which had the greatest impact on the way it proceeded. Rather, therefore, than the interview process somehow being insulated from the woman's wider experience of her social world, the interview was impacted by her experience of her social world, particularly those aspects which were the subject of our interest.

There were three themes. One, already mentioned, was the expression of emotion, particularly tearfulness. The researcher's notes on one interview, for example, contained the observation that the mother broke down in tears twice during the interview (notwithstanding her wish that the interview be completed) 'because she felt so helpless and hopeless about the whole situation'. She felt she had no control over anything to do with her son, considering his problems to be medical. Another theme, also mentioned already, was mistrust expressed by women who felt threatened by the possible association of the researchers with social services. One woman (for example) expressed outrage that she had been referred to social services by the school, and the interview was punctuated by requests for reassurance that the interview was confidential. A third theme was the way in which women had to conduct their interview in the context of child care responsibilities. This meant that, at times, the children were at home, and the mother could be distracted from the interview by a proper concern for the interests and concerns of her children. Women could be affected in other ways by child care, for example, by tiredness affecting their level of concentration in the interview – which could lengthen it.

It would be misleading to suggest that these factors had a major, particularly distorting, effect on women's accounts. There were some women – a small minority – who appeared to be careful and limited about what they said, particularly where they expressed a concern about the threat from social services, but in most cases (where they occurred), tiredness, distractions or distress simply provided minor diversions from, or added poignancy to, the information gathering process.

Methodological context of research

We are of the view that meaning is an essential element of the explanatory apparatus of social action. We are not, however, of the view that the meaning attached by actors to events and actions, represents the full extent of understanding of social phenomena. For a full explanation, it is not sufficient to ask participants for their views, analyse these and create second order concepts which purport to tell the whole story. The actors' own accounts are not unproblematic. While their accounts can provide us with information about what they saw, what they did and their reasons for acting in this way, we do not have to accept that their accounts represent some 'gold standard' of veracity about the situation. This is a point made by Hammersley and Atkinson (1983) in relation to ethnography and culture as a whole, equally relevant to this kind of study. The accounts given by participants may, for example, be internally coherent, yet still contain information which may enable us to critically analyse their perceptions and actions.

This was the purpose of our case studies (see Chapter 11). These provided some detailed information about the specific relationships between aspects of situations which are inevitably only dealt with thematically when looking at the sample as a whole. However, they also gave us the opportunity to probe whether, despite the internal coherence of the reasoning in the woman's account, she had missed factors of material significance in her conduct of child care. Where, for example, there were major behavioural problems, did her attribution of those problems to the 'character' of the child miss significant losses and disruptions in her own life which could have had an important emotional and behavioural impact?

Nevertheless, these women's accounts, appropriately analysed, do put together a major part of the jigsaw linking coping and prevention in child care. They provide us with clear accounts of their actions and reasons for their actions, which help us understand the whole process, and which can help develop significant concepts and models through which we can gain a greater understanding of this process. We see this study, therefore, as a hopefully important element in our development of understanding.

To understand better the status of this study it is useful to refer to Layder (1993). A focus exclusively on the accounts of participants for the generation of concepts and empirical data tells us little about the wider context in which their actions occur; they are unconcerned about the broader processes and structures of the social world, which go beyond these actions. This does not at all invalidate such research, it just emphasises the importance of recognising its place within the broader social processes and structures operating. Our focus, in particular, on prevention, as a context for understanding the actions of these women, provides us with a wider canvas on which to place our study. Hence the conceptual framework, linking coping with prevention, is very important in lifting the research beyond the immediacy of these women's lives, understanding them as part of broader social processes. Meaning provides an unavoidable requirement for social understanding – and is a complex matter to investigate on its own – but it cannot purport to present the whole picture.

Our research focuses empirically on the cusp between two realms of social understanding which Layder terms 'the self' and 'situated activity'. He comments that in practice, the self cannot be easily separated from the situations in which it is embedded. The notion of the self points to the individual's sense of identity and perceptions of the social world as they are influenced by her social experience. With situated activity the focus moves from the individual's response to various social situations, to the dynamics of interaction itself, in those social situations. The concern with the dynamics of interaction stresses the way in which encounters between individuals tend to produce outcomes that are a result of the interchange of communication between individuals rather than the behaviour of constituent individuals viewed singly.

On the one hand, we have very much focused on 'the self'. The woman's perceptions of her social world were at the heart of our research, but also how she perceived herself, the impact of that world on her, her sense of hope, of loss, of self-worth and despair, all permeated her accounts of her interaction with her children and family (and, indeed, wider groups and institutions). On the other hand, these perceptions and interactions were contextualised. She was reporting interactions in which at least two, and mostly many more, individuals were taking part. Indeed, the contexts were also significant, involving social situations and institutions. These women were generally quite disadvantaged, and their disadvantage provides a context for considering their perceptions and actions. They also operated within a number of social institutions: their families, schools, social services, health settings and the like. In these respects we are also examining situated activity.

Moving on

We now have a clear idea of context, of key conceptual dimensions, and the methodological issues which set the stage for our study. Our next stage is to look at the findings, and we shall begin with the ways in which women constructed their parenting and child problems – the focus for their coping.

PART II
Problems and Stressors

CHAPTER 5

Women's Construction of Problems

Coping theory points to the stressor as the logical starting point for analysis of the processes involved in managing child care problems. Here we are concerned with women's primary appraisal of threat, upon which her focus for coping will fall. This involves some form of harm which women perceive as happening, or liable to occur towards them. This, though, also requires that we have specificity – the particular problem which concerns them is the focus for the particular coping actions they undertake. These formulate into particular 'threat meaning's, and our concern is to understand these threat meanings. These were formulated as problems in three areas: child behavioural, child emotional and cognitive and parenting.

Child behaviour problems

Egocentricity

At the heart of many of the referrals was a range of behavioural problems presented by the children. Women identified child behavioural problems as their main problem in over one half of cases (52/102). Indeed, in three-fifths of cases (62/102) women identified the presence of severe child behavioural problems, whether or not they were considered primary. These were felt most immediately by the women at home. The women complained of the immense stress placed on them by their children's behaviour, and the difficulties they had containing both the behaviour and its effects. At the heart of the women's reports was a sense of *egocentricity* on the part of the children. They were, according to the mothers, very focused on themselves, little concerned with others, and expected, to a considerable degree, to be able to do what they wanted.

This often expressed itself in terms of wants, which frequently bore no relation to the possibility of their being achieved. One 15-year-old whose general behaviour was very aggressive, both towards people and objects, generally responded badly if he could not get his own way. In this case, his focus was on money, and his response to refusal was aggressive. As with other cases, where attempts were made to set boundaries, escalation could be the result.

> Just if he can't have his own way, if he can't have his own way like if he's sat here and he just 'I want some money', 'I ain't got [son]'. 'Oh yes you have got money' and then I say 'Don't start [son] leave it go I haven't got no money, don't go on', and he just goes up and plays his music, I tell him to turn it down and it just triggers him off... All my furniture, he moved it over, took all the holders off the kitchen wall. I had to paint the passage, because he done it to my passage, it was a right mess.

The egocentric focus meant that the children were in many cases far from being aware, or even concerned, about the impact of their behaviour on others in the family. Women often complained of the 'knock-on' effects of children's behaviour on other family members. Worst of all, perhaps, was when younger, more impressionable children began 'copycat' behaviours. This was the case with the brother of a teenager whom the mother considered 'vulnerable'.

> He's mentally impaired and it strains against [son] because he thinks that's the way it's got to be, like, because he's copying what [brother's] doing, and when I tell him off he'll have tantrums and he'll punch the doors, but he's going to a special school that can help him but it's not helping him while [brother's] doing it. Because [son] will do exactly the same thing as [brother's] doing, but I keep telling [brother] at the end of the day what he's doing is gonna rub off on [son]... I've got two adult girls of 17 and 16 and they have a tough time with him. It's putting a lot of strain on them because they've got boyfriends and they don't like bringing them here because of [brother's] attitude. So at the end of the day he's affecting their relationship as well as me and my husband's, and he's just got to realise that he can't do it.

This egocentricity was a general facet of women's accounts of many, particularly teenage, behavioural problems. Where associated with a diagnosis of

Attention Deficit Hyperactivity Disorder (ADHD), the women had an explanation of the problem which left them less critical of the children. Understanding rather than criticism might be the theme:

> I've actually got some books out from the library so I can know more about the condition. It's to do with the signal to the brain, they are not actually getting to the centre core as quickly as ours do, so it's bit like having a fuzzy reception on the television or switching from one channel to the next.

Routine disruption and younger children

Many of the children and young people were described as routinely creating mayhem both within the home and outside, with habitual defiance. Attitudes described as 'difficult', tendencies towards aggression, and living on a 'knife edge' were ways in which these routine problems were described.

In some cases, children did not go far beyond relatively low-level dismissiveness and social ineptitude. Where this was the case, it was most frequently with younger, particularly pre-teenage, children. Among the youngest children, egocentricity would not be a surprising trait. Young children often displayed attention-seeking by all kinds of disruptive behaviour: shouting and screaming, naughty behaviour which steadily escalated and demanded the mother's attention, constantly being 'in your face' (as far as the mothers were concerned). Some mothers – as was the case in the following example from the parent of a two-year-old – felt they could get no respite from it.

> Attention-seeking. That's one thing, her attention-seeking. She won't like, her lying there just then, kicking that off, because I'm not paying any attention to her. Like if I want to watch something on telly, she will like come in and distract me or make, like, noises, or I want cartoons. I just put the cartoons on to keep her quiet, you know what I mean. She will want things, she will want it straight away like…if I'm sitting having a conversation with one of my friends, she will just do something to make me tell her off, you know what I mean.

Some young children were unable to understand the limits to their behaviour. This, of course, is a problem frequently encountered by parents of young children. However, tantrums, in these referrals, generally took on a more pervasive and extreme form. They were not so much relatively sporadic outbursts as frequently encountered problems. The women, at times, felt worn down by them, and also embarrassed when they occurred in public. Yet they sometimes gave way, for the 'quiet life'. These were comments by the mother of one two-year-old girl.

> The tantrum bits… She can't get her own way, she just thinks that she can go in a shop and pick up what she wants. She'll have a big scene, and I'll say, well, no, no. It's difficult when you haven't got the money though, you can't do it, you know what I mean…when she is around other kids. She has a problem with sharing… And with sharing is quite hard for them, do you know what I mean, so you've got to get them out of that.

Hyperactivity and sleeplessness were further problems identified by mothers. These were often associated with the need to 'get their own way'. Children could constantly seek new experiences, never settle, and always want what they found. One woman commented about her two-year-old: 'he never settles down at all, he's constantly on the go into things that he shouldn't'. The need for a break was common to many women who had young children. What they suffered from was the *remorselessness* and routine nature of the child's behaviour, which, for them, lifted it above the 'ordinary' problems of other mothers of young children. The children often wore the women down. Such was the case with one woman of a two-year-old who reacted badly to the birth of a rival baby brother.

> She never goes to bed, she very rarely sleeps, actually. She's got a bedtime at eight o'clock and she'll keep coming downstairs. She goes to my bedroom, sleeps in my bed. I take her up in her own bed, and by half past six in the morning she's back in my bed. She's awful, it's like a security thing. She doesn't like being on her own or that sort of thing.

Where children were older, but not teenagers, the problems described by the women bore some similarity to those experienced with young children, while taking on a more urgent and severe nature. The underlying theme, reflecting the overall theme of egocentricity, was that of disobedience. Women complained that they often could not get the child to do what they were told. There was a sense that the women were close to being out of control of the children. One woman described, for example, how (with her three children ranging from 10 to 12 years old) they would take practically no notice of what she said, and that responses such as 'grounding' them had no effect. They simply walked out of the door and came back when they wanted.

Some of the behaviours were serious for their shock value as much as the disruption they caused. Women could be extremely distressed by the language used by some children, particularly where they were young. This was the case with one nine-year-old boy:

> I mean, this morning if you'd been here at half past eight you wouldn't have believed what was coming out this little boy's mouth. Do you know what I mean, he's obscene, running around, screaming, and then ten minutes later he's sitting there and he's being all nice. So I don't know why it happens or why he does it, but one of those things with him.

What was perplexing for this mother was the changeable nature of her child's behaviour, from one extreme to another. Others would attack the home, if not people, and, as one woman described it, 'physically trashed' parts of the house. The kinds of things described were stabbing at walls, stripping the wallpaper, ripping the curtains, damaging the carpet, kicking the door, and even attacking the dog!

'Problem' behaviours and experiences could become much more pervasive during the teenage period. These included stealing, both in the home and at school, and bullying. The sums of money or value of objects were not generally very large at this age, but mothers frequently feared that matters could get much worse as the children became older. Bullying, at this age, was not very frequent, and the children were generally the victims of aggressive behaviour by others. Bullying by the child was described in such terms as being 'spiteful' and 'aggressive' to peers, suggesting it was a less premeditated 'picking on' children than an outburst of belligerence. However, as shown in this example of an eight-year-old, victim status could have serious emotional effects:

> He's sat in a playground thinking, they don't like me, they're all talking about me, they're all talking the mickey out of me. They are, I've seen them doing it and I don't want him to grow up and end up like that guy, thinking it's him, like, you know, I'd rather take him up the school, put him in a[nother] school. …At that school he's got [only] one friend, but bullies him now and again when he feels like it and then goes off and takes the mickey out of him with the rest of them.

Some children, admittedly rarely, showed behaviours as severe as those of teenagers with behaviour problems. In these cases, the women experienced a gamut of problems, ranging from the routine refusal to do what they were told, through obscene language to theft and violent and aggressive behaviour. The few women with all their children behaving like this were at times at their wits' end, with a sense of despair that they were completely out of control of the situation. In one case, a woman with three children aged 10 to 13, all of whom manifested extreme behaviour, frequently contemplated suicide. The behaviours could manifest themselves in serious threats to the mother, as in this case of the mother of four boys aged 7 to 13:

> Well they, they beat me up. Two of them literally. My eldest one beat me black and blue, like a man would hit you... I won't hit him back, 'cos I've got to lead life after that. And the other one is, I'm getting same things, like hitting me, wanting to kill me. And, like, it is getting out of hand... And I don't know how far it's gonna go before I lose it. 'Cos I would have lost it ages ago, I think. Probably I would have damaged him or killed him... One of them was out completely, gone.

> *Researcher*: What was he doing?

> *Woman*: His behaviour, like shouting all the time, laughing at me, 'How's your bad leg', 'I wanna kill you, we are better off without you', and all this. It went on for hours. And I mean for hours.

Teenagers

The largest number of behaviour problems was found in the teenage group. Many, but not all, of these young people were aged 15 or 16, and the failure by social services to respond with longer-term intervention reflected their age: they were soon to reach the point of adulthood, and so were less of a concern for child care services, particularly where their antisocial behaviour was the problem, rather than some immediate threat to them (such as sex abuse).

Egocentricity, as with younger children, was at the heart of the women's perceptions of their problems, yet, with age and greater social sophistication, such egocentricity appeared often to indicate immaturity. They were, it was felt, operating with the sensitivity (or lack of it) of much younger children. These were *rebellious*, defiant and self-centred youngsters, 'running wild', like this 15-year-old young woman:

> She was in my opinion running wild… It was basically down to my daughter
> being a teenager… This was about drinking and partying down town and not
> doing as I wanted her to do, basically. I thought, well, then she left home, she
> went to stay with a friend and she refused to come home… I want to know
> where I stand or she stands. Is she coming home, is she staying, and where do
> we go from here?

In this case, there was a tussle between the mother and daughter about the
degree of freedom of decision-making the daughter was allowed. 'Being a
teenager' may have been part of the woman's description, but the situation was
actually breaking down, with the daughter refusing to follow her mother's
expectations.

The worries about teenage girls frequently involved fears about their vulnerability. Mothers feared they could get pregnant, or be physically or sexually
assaulted, and hence did not want them out late. This 'teenage rebelliousness'
often involved a thorough disregard for the mother:

> She said, I'm going down town, well I'm going, end of subject. Well, will you
> phone me? No. Can you tell me where you're going? No, I don't know. You
> know, it's just that open that disrespect for me really, I suppose, at the end of
> the day. Then if I try to stop anything, she becomes stroppy. She pushes past
> me. I mean, I've had locks put on the windows, 'cos she's tried to get out of the
> window, and tantrum…like the terrible twos [laughing]. But it's like open
> defiance.

This concern with vulnerability was less evident in mothers of teenage boys.
Drugs and alcohol came more to the fore as an indication of 'running wild' by
teenage boys, although this did not mean that this was their exclusive
prerogative. Drugs were not only dangerous in themselves, they could lead to
dangers from association with violent criminals, a fear voiced by one woman in
relation to her 16-year-old son:

> He won't go out now, he used to go out, now he don't go out. And that's the
> only thing I can think of, but, 'cos he used to go out selling drugs or mixing
> with people who got drugs since we moved here he won't go out at all now,
> that's the only thing. I mean…he was still doing drugs… That's what he was
> doing, mixing with them over there still. Told them about it but they don't
> want to know nothing about it.

That such behaviour was not exclusive to boys was evident from the comments of another woman:

> She lives up the road. With a lady because there is no way you could keep her here. She just kept going, and I kept saying that she's just gonna go, and any minute she's gonna wind up dead. We're gonna find her somewhere dead because she was drinking and all the rest of it. We were up the hospital one night because she had drunk herself unconscious.

Drug use was not the only illegal activity of these young people. The major issue was theft, which at times could be associated, by the mother, with drug use. One woman described how she had to get a safe in the home because of her 'light-fingered' daughter, who stole £600, while another linked theft to drug use and association with older, undesirable peers.

Aggression was a frequent facet of teenagers' behaviour, and it could emerge in a variety of ways. This, of course, was evident in younger children, but in teenagers it represented a considerably greater threat. Violence, or the threat of violence, could enable the young person to dominate their familial situation – a control mechanism – or merely to demonstrate their disaffection regarding any attempts to set boundaries to their behaviour. One woman described the systematically destructive behaviour manifested by her 16-year-old son:

> I was getting on with things, trying to do everything, trying to get the house sorted out… Now I can't even do any of that. Anything I try to do, he ruins. I put wallpaper up when he moved, before he moved back in here, he's ripped all that down, he's catching the curtains on light, net curtains in fire. Lighting fires in his room, chucking them out of the window, that's why I said I can't do nothing with him.

As she described it, this behaviour had a calculated element to it, and specifically focused on the mother, suggesting the intent to demoralise. The woman herself was profoundly depressed, and attributed this largely to the sense of entrapment she experienced as a result of her son's behaviour. Forced to suffer this vandalism, she nevertheless felt powerless to eject him from her home.

Aggression could be directed at people, and involve considerable ferocity. As one woman said, 'Violence. Violence and beating the kids. He can't have what he wants, then he'll take it all out on the kids.' At times this involved instant actions, in which the young person was simply considered to be 'losing it':

> [Son's] a very quick-tempered kid…he just goes blank and he would just,
> well, not being horrible, but he would end up doing damage to somebody…
> All I wanted [professionals] to do was just come and have a talk to [son], like to
> tell him how serious it is. But…they won't talk to him at all. They have just
> told me to phone the police.

This woman was concerned that her son would eventually find himself in serious legal trouble, a concern characteristic of a number of women, particularly when they saw the young person's behaviour to have transcended any normal level of aggression and became outright violence.

Violence could be directed at the family and mother, and could be shockingly extreme. In one case a traumatised mother described the behaviour of her 15-year-old son, who had, in the past few months, changed from being reasonable and fairly well behaved, to a self-centred, aggressive, abusive individual. She recounted an escalating situation of increasing demands on his part, and a growing atmosphere of abuse and aggression, until this exploded into violence.

> He'd actually pushed the door in my face, he didn't let it go… I wasn't expect-
> ing it. It hit me in the face, full force, and he's still got the handle, so all his
> weight's pushing on it… It caught my lip and it caught my cheekbone and I
> actually stood there in shock because it really hurt…it was all purple, red,
> black and whatever. And he actually stood there laughing, and 'so what are
> you looking at me like that for'?

Another woman commented on the persistent violence of her 16-year-old and that 'I had just come home from hospital and he just hit me in the chest, and I had stitches and everything'. In one case a 16-year-old was damaging the house by knocking nails in the floor. When asked to stop he started swearing:

> [he] picked up the screwdriver and stabbed me in the leg. And I said, 'I don't
> believe you've done that, [son], I can't believe that you done that,' and I said,
> 'and I'm going to have you charged now with assault.' 'Please yourself.'

Trouble at school

Frequently the problems described were focused on the school. Nearly a quarter of women (25/102) described such problems as severe. Behavioural difficulties could make for poor relations at school, impairment of education, and, in the end, suspension or even exclusion from school. Exclusion, in particular, could become a problem in its own right, and exacerbate other problems.

At times the behaviours manifested in school were simply translated from other settings. One mother of a 15-year-old girl described her general rebelliousness, her verbal aggression and stealing within the home, and her determination to have up-to-the-minute clothes regardless of the consequences (of theft) for others. She commented on the efforts made with the school to curb the girl's behavioural excesses, but agreements made in meetings were disregarded soon afterwards. The consequence was aggression by the girl towards her teachers:

> Yes, she was very bad with the teachers. Bad language, I mean she…had no respect at all…and she still hasn't now. She finds that very difficult. You know, being called at the school and sat in front of the teachers and had meetings and all different things, you know, and when I'm there, she's very good, oh yes I'll try, oh yes I'll try, and they're all saying, oh very good, well done [daughter]. And then as soon as she walks out the door everything she said is gone.

However, poor behaviour had consequences: schools had limits to what they would accept, and were likely to respond firmly to continuously violent or aggressive behaviour. In one case of an 11-year-old, suspension followed upon repeated, uncontrolled loss of temper by the child in the school, which caused as much distress to the mother as the child. The mother tried to be supportive, but feared he was 'going to get into…trouble with the police in a minute'.

Other behaviours gained particular significance because of their importance within the school setting. Where, for example, concentration was a problem, this was likely to be especially important in school. Failing to concentrate properly on work could also be associated with disruptive behaviour within the class, as well as a reduction in confidence about the possibility of successfully completing academic tasks. It could lead to alienation from the educational process. This could be exacerbated by the negative attitude of teachers:

> I mean, he has difficulties concentrating on learning and he's often upset, distressed and depressed… He's quite bad in school and last week we had a parent evening and the school didn't have one good thing to say about him, you know, which in a way is quite upsetting. But then I find with schools, and

that, they tell you all that's bad about him but they never praise him when they're good.

Other school-specific behaviours frequently included truanting. This, again, reflected alienation from the culture and expectations of schools. Mothers, however, associated this with the risk of further deterioration in behaviour, which could lead to serious, or more serious, trouble with the law. They felt that non-attendance at school could have wider implications, impairing the young person's future opportunities, while currently leaving them vulnerable to other risky behaviour, including drug taking and offending generally. Non-attendance at school often involved deceit:

> He won't tell me why, I mean, I didn't even know he was truanting to begin with… It wasn't until…in town I bumped into him and he was with a couple of mates and I said, 'What do you think you're playing at?'… [Teacher] said, 'He hasn't been here for weeks'. But the school didn't bother to let me know… and now I just give up. 'Cos he's what, 15 in May, I mean, I can't drag him.

Bullying was a particular problem at school. The child was sometimes the bully, but more frequently the victim of bullying. When this happened it could leave them reluctant to attend school. The bullying could be quite violent, as with this child of only eight years:

> Last week…this girl's come up to me and she says, 'He's just hit your kid,' and I turned around and [son] was like doubled over like that. He'd kneed him between the legs, he'd just gone up to him and kneed him between the legs and walked off, so I went up to him and I says, 'Excuse me,' I says, 'over there, Ms…wants to see you.' 'I'm not going.' 'You move your arse over there now,' I says, 'I'm not pissing around with you, you don't touch my kid,' and he's gone over and he's like that.

The emotional impact of this could be great, an issue which will be examined further later.

Emotional and cognitive problems

Just under a quarter of women (29/102) cited child emotional and cognitive problems as primary. It is interesting that some women identified their children primarily as manifesting behavioural problems, while recognising emotional upset (often as a facet of behavioural problems), whereas other women considered emotional problems to be primary, while at times recognising poor behaviour to be a facet, or consequence, of emotional problems. Where emotional problems were identified as primary, however, they tended to be in children in the pre-teen period, whereas where behaviour problems were most severe, they were generally in the teenage group.

This may have a lot to do with age. The notion of teenage rebelliousness sits comfortably with the egocentricity which lies at the centre of women's understanding of behaviour problems, and the capacity of older children to wreak damage was far greater than that of younger children. The behaviour might, therefore, simply overwhelm consideration of emotional distress. Where children were younger, this imbalance between experience of emotional distress and behaviour would be rather less, and the notion of rebelliousness would be more difficult to sustain. It would appear, then, that the women were drawing on more generalised constructs of age and stage, which helped to inform their definitions of the situation. The example of tantrums in the 'terrible twos' further bolsters this idea.

However, if egocentricity lay at the heart of women's construction of behaviour problems, so *sensitivity* lay at the heart of emotional problems. It was the perceived egocentricity of the children which led the women to label them with behaviour problems, even where they were upset. It was likewise sensitivity (of the child) which enabled women to label them primarily with emotional problems, even where behavioural difficulties were present. The children were reacting sensitively to adverse situations and stresses, and if they had behavioural difficulties, it was as a result of the upset.

The distress was manifested, according to the women's descriptions, in a variety of ways, and differed according to age. Women with younger children saw persistent and repeated crying as indicators of emotional problems. Others were aware of subtle ways in which distress could manifest itself. One woman described how differently her three young children responded to stress and manifested their distress:

> Oh, em, [son]. Always [son] (4½), he shows it so outwardly. Em, he will have tantrums, he will throw things around, he will start fighting and kicking with anyone who comes close by. [Son] (7½) is the quiet one that holds it all in, and he became much more…And it's very easy to forget the one that's in the corner, em, but I specifically look out for [son] and think, right, where is he,

what's he up to, em, not because he's going to be in any trouble because he's going to be sat there mulling things over and worrying. [Son] (2), thankfully, is young enough to be able to take anything on the chin. It's all a big adventure to him.

In older children, the emotional distress showed itself in different manifestations of depressed mood. One woman spoke of the lethargy in her son, who was only eight, which manifested itself in a reluctance to get up and dressed in the morning. For her everything became difficult because she was a single mother with three children, stating that 'it's like looking after five' to look after just one of them.

In another case the mother described the difficulty her 12-year-old daughter had getting off to sleep, and her wakefulness during the night. This not only reflected her depressed mood, in response to her fears at school, but made her tired and more lethargic during the day. She was, said her mother, frequently exposed to criticisms of her mother by her estranged father (when she visited him), which, together with the separation itself, took its toll on her emotions. She became quite withdrawn:

> So he's like come down and then he has said to my daughter, my eldest one, in front of her 'You see this is what my mum does,' you know, he tells her I'm horrible and things like that so she sort of, like, looks at me like that. You know, and she just withdraws into herself so the sort of things like that all the time, so he is very much against, putting her against me, if you know what I mean. But she hasn't been, she's never been before, she's always been quite close to me and now it's like, we're like apart, you know like she's, I don't know, like she doesn't want to be here or be near me or anything like that or be near the girls. Or anything, so I don't know, she's never been like that before, it worries me so.

In school-age children, bullying provided a significant context for these emotional problems. Bullying could contribute significantly to emotional problems, and range from teasing to major assault. Children reacted really badly to the bullying, becoming fearful and withdrawn. Children could fear the very idea of being at school, which was not a safe place, as was the case for this girl, aged only ten years:

> Yeah, because she's just returned to school in after two and half years and every morning is a nightmare, she doesn't want to go to school because of the fear and anxiety that's inside her. And she throws things try and be there and hold onto the dog and you know, that kind of stuff. Bullying, she's kicked me and that sort of thing, so she doesn't have to go to school, and that's every day, five days a week… It feels like you're a bodyguard, you've got to be her bodyguard because she's terrified of children. Terrified of teachers, terrified of anybody.

Bullying also involved verbal attacks, diminishing and undermining the child, leaving them short on confidence and the capacity to involve themselves with other children. This could take a racist form. One girl, aged 12, was drawn into retaliation, which was likely to get her into trouble:

> And then she gets called names because of her colour, she can't deal with that at all. It's insidious bullying, it's like pushing, they will push her when nobody is looking, and she will turn around and whack them. You know I said, don't, walk away, ignore them, she's says no, I've had enough, I've had enough of it… And then she gets into trouble you know, through retaliating, and then she gets all sulky and throws tantrums in the school. She is just not dealing with it at all.

The impact of the emotional problems could be marked. Children often reacted to their emotional distress with frustration and aggression. Tantrums and violence were identified quite frequently as the accompaniment to emotional distress. In this case, the mother accepted that her eight-year-old son was not nasty (nor essentially egocentric). He was upset rather than bad, even though she feared a violent future:

> I mean he is not a nasty or neglected kid, but he has his problems. When I say no, you are going to do that, if you don't do that you don't get what you're wanting… And that's like every time, that causes temper tantrums, don't go there, go in your room. And then it's like, 'Mummy it's not fair', moan, moan, moan.

Psychosomatic problems – tiredness, headaches, sickness, bedwetting – were at times the accompaniment to emotional distress. One woman drew attention to her seven-year-old son's eneuresis, which had been exacerbated by the family's eviction from their house. While she tried not to make too much of it, she found this difficult in the stressful circumstances of bed-and-breakfast. Other aspects included effects on education through a lack of concentration at school, becoming more socially tentative and inept, stealing and lying. One woman commented on the fantasies of her 13-year-old daughter and the ways these could create trouble for other children. It could be difficult to tell what was fantasy and what was reality:

> Sometimes she'll make up things that are not true and I caught her out in it and I said to her 'Come on, this is not fair, you were trying to get somebody into trouble and they haven't done it.' But other times she says things that are true, but then you don't know whether to believe her because she tell, not doesn't tell the truth, and it's very confusing sometimes. Trying to figure out when she's telling the truth and when she's not telling the truth.

Cognitive problems were less frequently identified as primary, generally related to learning difficulty and underachievement at school, but were in turn associated with emotional and behavioural problems. These could include being statemented, problems relating to other children, becoming more socially withdrawn, and becoming hyperactive. The link between many of these issues was apparent in the case of one 12-year-old girl who had emotional difficulties adjusting to the move to a new school:

> She's having a lot of problems at school... She has always had a learning difficulty, but never behavioural problems. But now I am very concerned and so is the school about her behaviour. She's just graduated to comprehensive school, and she isn't dealing with it very well. She's being cheeky at the school, she's swearing, she's hitting out an awful lot and she's retaliating, but she always gets the worse end of the stick you know. She's always gets caught. She is not mentally or capable of her peers. I don't think she can cope with the things that are being said.

Parenting

The third major area troubling these women was parenting, considered the primary problem by just over one sixth of women (18/102). At the heart of this was a sense that the major problem lay not with the children but with themselves. While child egocentricity and sensitivity were the keys to understanding, respectively, behavioural and emotional problems, a *sense of failure* was at the heart of cases where the women saw parenting as the key issues.

The feeling base for this came out in many accounts. This is illustrated by this woman, who had a three-year-old son, but castigated herself for her lack of attention to him, despite recognising that her basic physical care was satisfactory. Her sense of guilt at the lack of involvement came out throughout her interview in high levels of self-criticism and self-doubt:

> We'd give them all their meals and always clothed and bathed them and looked after them in that respect but we didn't give them any attention. We just let them get on with it all the time and they just used to fight all the time and we just used to just scream at them for fighting all the time. And I feel really guilty, I've cried a lot over this 'cos I do feel really guilty for just ignoring him. He needed me so many times in those like five months that I was doing it. But I neglected him, I didn't listen to him, I wasn't there for him when he needed me.

Women also expressed a sense of failure when they could not cope on their own with their children. This was the case with one woman, who had four children, and was ill, and found it impossible to cope with her husband away:

> Well, my husband was in the Gulf…and I wasn't very well…and I did ask my husband because he was going off, and I said I don't know whether I'm going to cope…and he went to, and he said you're the one who's going to have to make the contact, and I couldn't do that because I felt like a failure… But in the end I did see the doctor and the doctor contacted the naval social services or the naval family services and they brought [husband] home.

Senses of guilt and failure are ever-present elements of depression, and it is not surprising to find this in many women. However, rather than poor child care leading to a sense of failure, some women considered the depression as part of the whole process of parenting. One woman, with two children under three, commented that she 'was really depressed and I found it difficult to cope', while another, with five children, described the detail of what this meant for her and her children:

> I just dissolved and cried every time we walked in the room. I was just a bit of a mess. Em, and then I thought, this is not going to get any better if I just sit there crying… The children were more upset by me being upset.

Many of the women were single parents, and they saw this as an integral part of the difficulties they had with parenting. Single parenting itself was a parenting problem, because there was no back-up (although this woman, with two young children aged six, was ambivalent about any involvement with a man):

> It's different, difficult to be a single parent, 'cos you haven't got that back-up. But then again, saying that, I don't know whether I'd want someone now. But at the time I used to wish I did. Like they [were]...out of control and I'd be screaming and shouting at them. All mums scream and shout sometimes, but this was just like all the time, constantly. And they'd be like 'arrggg', jumping around. I just couldn't control them.

Other women commented that even young children 'got no respect for me, even the oldest one', and they were not scared of her, which made control difficult. The problem was made worse when there was more than one child, one woman describing herself as having to 'split myself into three for all of you', meaning that she could not be there for all of them all of the time. She was constantly faced with choosing one over the other, especially when they wanted comfort or reassurance, which led to arguments and jealousies between the children. Children, particularly young children, found this difficult to understand, while the women found themselves stressed and spread too thinly. In the light of this, one of the key issues for some women was the need for a break from what became the daily grind of parenting, particularly of young children, even when there was only one.

Many of the women, whether single or not, described their parenting behaviour as problematic. One of the key problems was the degree of interaction with the children. Under pressure, or through distress, or merely disinclination, the women often felt they did not have enough time with the children:

> I think the main problem is not having time to spend with the children because there's always other things to do and... It's hard. It's hard. I'm trying to get them both interested in the same things, or at the same time, but there's conflict between them, because if I do spend time with [daughet], then [son] says, well you haven't spent time with me, and then if I spend time with [son], she seems to get upset because I'm not spending time with her, and unfortunately I can't split myself in two.

Where there was more than one child, as in this example, women at times described themselves as 'piggy in the middle'.

The other main dimension of parenting behaviour considered problematic was *control and discipline*. One woman described her own difficulties in setting boundaries:

> …disciplining kids, I can't always make myself to do it you know, I mean…I find it hard to discipline them and stick to it you know, be continuous with it…and when they are that age you don't know whether to, you know, you don't know how to, how to discipline them. I know I'm not perfect mother you know, but I try my best to keep them straight and narrow but it's difficult you know, when they are, you know.

Women often asserted that smacking was both an appropriate and necessary part of child care, yet some feared that their response was too strong for the misdemeanours committed. One woman's solution was to imagine that her daughter was someone else's child, to temper her behaviour. Others asserted the right to retaliation – even violence – when children misbehaved. One woman stated, graphically, that 'I gave her a good hammering. For smoking, considering that she is only ten'. Others became concerned by their potential for violence against their children: 'Cos he was going through a really bad patch, I said I'm really scared I'm gonna end up hurting him in a minute.'

Some women cited *affection and bonding* as the issue, always with younger children. One woman felt that the involvement of her family from the outset in care of the child meant that 'I haven't got that bond', a fact that continued to upset her. (Her son was now three.) Another described how her failure to bond (to her seven-year-old boy) stretched back to birth:

> When he was a baby yeah, I couldn't, when he was born. I had a caesarean when he was born. My husband didn't know how to tell me that, we had a little boy, 'cos I didn't want a little boy,' I wanted a little girl. I was devastated when he was born. I couldn't hold him or anything like that… So I love him as much as I can, do you know what I mean, show him as much affection as I can. It might not be as much as I want but I got to stop somewhere.

The final area did not focus on the woman at all, but on the parenting by her partner. Here, either the *partner (or ex-partner's) behaviour* was inadequate, or there was conflict between them about parenting, which affected its continuity. Even here, the woman could feel a sense of failure, as with one case of separation:

I took away his dad which was, he had two main pillars of stability, his dad and his mum and we split up, it's like a, it's only me left.

In some cases, the parenting difficulty was the overt behaviour of the partner. One woman actually telephoned social services because 'my boyfriend had been hitting my son', while she nevertheless commented 'I was feeling like incompetent'. Another commented on the violence of her husband, even though she felt he was goaded:

It's with his rages, I mean I can really get resentful and angry towards my husband… It's difficult because sometimes you have to turn a blind eye to his behaviour but it's very difficult for a man to have his son swearing at him and not doing anything.

Another dimension was the *differing expectations of parents*, particularly when they were separated. This could lead to conflict when the children took behaviour acceptable to one parent to the home of the other.

They see their dad weekends now, he lets them get away with murder you know. Their dad just doesn't discipline them. I mean they come here punching and farting and they haven't got no manners, you know what I mean, they are really horrible to me. I say, look don't come from your dad to me, giving me all the grief, do you know what I mean?

Summary and conclusion

There was, then, a wide range of situations, for which we can nevertheless find thematic meanings, recounted by these women. All, however, focused on the particular area of child care.

1. Coping theory indicates that in this, as in other, areas, we should focus first on the stressor, and do so with some specificity. However, we should also be looking for underlying meanings.

2. There were broadly three types of problems which were the focus for these women's concerns: *child behavioural, child emotional and cognitive,* and *parenting.*

3. At the heart of child behavioural problems was the perception of *egocentricity*: a self-regarding way of behaving in the way the child wanted, combined with a disregard for others.

4.   Child behavioural problems *varied in severity according to age group.* In younger children they could take the form of social ineptitude, being demanding, tantrums and sleeplessness, and were marked by remorselessness.

5.   Older (pre-teen) children's problems were generally more urgent and severe, with an underlying theme that they were close to being out of control. Behaviour began to emerge which was more pervasive amongst teenagers, including *violence.*

6.   The largest number of behaviour problems was in the *teenage group.* They were perceived as rebellious, defiant and self-centred. Women were more likely to fear vulnerability in girls and violence from boys. Illegal behaviour, such as theft, and drug use were also concerns.

7.   Trouble could be focused on *the school.* At times this was just an extension of troubles elsewhere. Other problems gained significance from the school setting, including non-attendance at school, bullying, and behavioural problems related to poor academic performance.

8.   At the heart of emotional and cognitive problems were perceptions of the child's *sensitivity* in reaction to adverse social circumstances.

9.   Emotional problems were more frequently seen as manifested directly by younger children, for example with crying, but could be more complex in older children. Some women recognised the emotional origins of behavioural problems.

10.   In older children, emotional problems could manifest themselves in lethargy, difficulty in sleeping, and direct displays of distress, as well as poor behaviour.

11.   In older children, bullying was sometimes the context for distress. This could involve physical attacks, but also esteem-reducing verbal assaults and psychosomatic problems. School phobia could result.

12.   Parenting was characterised by a strong sense of self-blame and guilt, very unhelpful for the woman's emotional state. This was of

particular significance because of the centrality of performance in parenting for the self-esteem of the large majority of these women. Such women consequently frequently recounted feelings of depression.

13.   Many women were single parents, and for some this itself was a parenting problem, because their single status meant that so much of the parenting responsibility fell upon them alone.

14.   Problematic parenting behaviour included a failure to spend enough time with the children, control, as well as affection and bonding, which could involve considerable inner conflict.

15.   The partner or ex-partner's behaviour could be an element of this problem. Where this was the case, although the focus was on the partner or ex-partner, women frequently also felt blame and failure by association.

While there were clear meanings to the range of child care problems, these are insufficient on their own to gain a full understanding. To grasp this more deeply we must look at the way women attributed responsibility and blame for the problems.

CHAPTER 6

Ascribing Responsibility and Blame

The mothers' coping strategies were intimately associated with the way they saw the situations. One aspect, we have already seen, was their ascription of the nature and 'site' of the problem. However, the mothers were seeking to explain the situations, in order to act on them. Problem ascription and explanation were central to their response. Women did not simply seek to explain, they sought to ascribe responsibility, or even blame. Blame could be ascribed to people ('it's all my fault'), or to circumstances (such as material circumstances, like poverty). The notion of blame has a clear moral dimension. One key dimension of the meaning attached to these situations, therefore, was the idea that some person, or circumstances, were to blame.

We may also distinguish between primary responsibility and secondary responsibility. Primary responsibility was the main reason given by the women for the particular problem with which they were confronted. However, the women frequently had a multi-dimensional understanding of their situations. There could be a number of 'sites' for their blame, but generally they would have one which they regarded as primary.

Some women made further distinctions, between blame (even where multi-dimensional) and the contribution of causal or influencing factors. Causal factors, where this happened, would be one level removed from blame. It might, for example, be possible for the woman to blame a child for behaviour problems (which they often did), while recognising that some factors in their lives, such as an unstable environment of some sort, had contributed to the child's behaving in the way they did. This kind of distinction would involve a subtle recognition of the degree of individual autonomy and self-directedness available to individuals. Some negative events might have influenced the way the child had behaved (would be the implicit analytical statement), but nevertheless the child could be blamed for his or her behaviour. 'Influence', in other words, does not mean 'determine', and these women were not generally determinists.

Blaming the mother: guilt, anxiety and depression

Many mothers, it is widely recognised, are deeply involved, at both the cognitive and social level of identity and self-worth, in their performance in the maternal role (Sheppard, J., 2000). The context is provided by the social construction of motherhood, where the dominant ideology is of the woman whose primary role remains that of mother (if she has children), and where adequate performance of that role is the *sine qua non* of motherhood. It is not surprising, therefore, that some mothers should blame themselves for the problems which were being experienced. Blame could, therefore, be attached by mothers in two ways: by identifying the problem as parenting itself (rather than child care), or by identifying child care or child problems as the result of their own poor or inadequate parenting. According to the latter they were 'reaping what they sowed': poor parenting led to child emotional and behavioural problems, with which they now had to cope.

Ineffective mothers and self blame

Some women saw themselves as *ineffective parents*. Sometimes they saw their past parenting as a lost opportunity, and the situation as beyond redemption. However, this did not always involve some enlightened notion of nurturing and care, but a more resolute approach. This was the case with one mother of a 16-year-old male, who was violent towards her and other people. When commenting on the responsibility for his behaviour, she said:

> It's the way he was brought up, because if I was allowed to hit him we wouldn't be having half of the trouble now... I mean, not being funny, but if my parents was alive, my father, he could kill, knock it out of him no matter what you lot (sic), the social services say...we wouldn't be getting any of this trouble... Because that's what all the kids needs.

She did not seem to consider whether such violence might contribute to further violence, rather than resolving the situation.

With other women, bewilderment was the main theme, one woman commenting on the tantrums of her three children (all under five) that 'when you try to tell them off they don't seem to listen, and I think that really upsets me, yeah'. Another woman's bewilderment was matched by her severe depression when confronted by her older three children, aged between 10 and 12. No matter what she did, indeed no matter how violent she became, she felt unable to gain control of the situation:

> They don't do what I say. They try telling me. If they wanna go out they just open the door and go. I say, right you are grounded, they just go out the door and say we are not grounded, you don't tell me. And their language is disgusting... This morning [daughter] said I need a pound for school or I'm not going. So, when she was gone I asked what she was like in school, she's a completely different child. So, when it's here they are fighting, they are arguing, they are swearing and I just can't control. I just go upstairs and leave them. 'Cos I said to my husband, I said to him, I will kill them.

Threats and violence did not work for her, and in the face of that, she had no alternative.

Problems with causes

In other cases women could, on the one hand, blame themselves, yet on the other recognise some influencing or causal factors in their behaviour. Generally, these did not serve even as mitigating factors in their assessment of self: they still considered themselves responsible. However, these factors could serve the purpose of making sense of why they were as they were. In some cases, the women saw themselves as having been restricted by the interference of a 'nanny state', particularly if they saw corporal punishment as the answer to their problems. One woman felt she had given her teenage son too much leeway:

> Er, 'cos you are not allowed to hit your kids, that's the way he turned out like it really is mine, as a parent fault and that's the truth. I mean, as soon as you hit them they phone up the police and tell them you are hitting them. But if the parents phone up the police and say the kids are hitting you back, they don't want to know nothing about it.

One woman firmly blamed herself for the problems she was experiencing with the care of her two children (aged five and seven). She was aware of neglect and poor parenting and associated that with their poor behaviour and problems at school, particularly in participating in the learning process. Nevertheless, she recognised factors which had a major impact on her capabilities in all aspects of her life. At the heart of it were very long-term influences of relationships with men, including abuse by her father.

> Well, the sexual adv…adv…one, my dad used to do things to me when I was little and that, and that's affected the way I am. And the violence happened, my ex is quite violent. Not violent violent, but verbal violent, verbal abuse and that, and lot of violence in front of the kids and that.

These interactions clearly affected her, including the way she conducted her life in general, leading to poorer parenting. In this case, it was not that the environment directly affected the children, but that it affected her, or that *she* was responsible for environmental factors which in turn affected the children. She took drugs, and this impaired her caring capabilities. The drugs blocked out the more painful feelings, but they also stopped her parenting adequately. Likewise, her choice of men as partners was poor. Instead of supportive, she found her relations with men emotionally draining, drawing attention away from the children and creating stress, which made child care more difficult.

A number of women felt that they were not involved sufficiently with their children, or had not bonded well enough with them. This could be about simply giving the children 'sufficient time and attention'. In one case, the competing demands of her two children meant that the mother could not win. She commented:

> … not having time to spend with the children because there's always other things to do, and… It's hard. It's hard. I'm trying to get them both interested in the same things, or at the same time, but there's conflict between them, because if I do spend time with [daughter], then [son] says, well you haven't spent time with me, and then if I spend time with [son], she seems to get upset because I'm not spending time with her, and unfortunately I can't split myself in two.

In both cases there were factors which influenced the situation, but this did not prevent the women from blaming themselves for the problems. In the first case, the woman suffered with the 'claustrophobic' conditions of her tiny, unpleasant flat, her general poverty and 'problems with men' – a persistent theme for these women, often involving violence. In the second case, marital break-up affected the woman's ability to focus on her children as effectively as she might.

This recurring theme could involve traditional notions of bonding – not having as much affection as they felt they should for the child. One woman, herself only 20, for whom this was the key issue in her care of her two children (aged two and three), attributed a lot of this to the overbearing, indeed overwhelming, involvement of her mother-in-law from when her children were very young. She was aware of a lack of confidence on her part, frustration and anger, which made it difficult to care for her children as well as she would like. She felt the children, in turn, were more difficult, clingy and whingy, and were more likely to be 'distressed and stroppy':

> I just haven't got that bond with [son]. And that's quite upsetting 'cos I can't get that still, you know what I mean… I just wished I hadn't had that taken away from me when he was born… I mean, I'd wake up in the morning to give him his bottle and she'd be there feeding him already and like changing him and giving him a bath. Totally took over.

Reprehensible fathers

Fathers were blamed, particularly where estrangement had occurred. Rejection was sometimes a key issue. In these cases the women felt aggrieved that the father was no longer prepared to act with responsibility towards his own children. This was the case where some fathers 'dumped' their children. This was worst, in some ways, if, despite estrangement, they had previously stayed in contact, and cared for the children on a regular basis. This was the case with the father of one male, aged 15, who became dramatically more difficult in his behaviour. (He had been far from perfect for some time.) Commenting on the cause of the problems, his mother said:

> We're not sure… When he's been living with his dad…everything was fine, then he started getting in trouble with the school, he was being expelled, in trouble with the law down there. So my ex-husband rung me up and said can you take him up there… Brought him up here. He was fine and it's just gone wrong. But when I've rung him and asked him for advice, 'I don't want to know,' he said, 'they're not my kids. They're all yours now…' Because he wants to go down for weekends and holidays, they won't let him have them

down there. I've said, at the end of the day you've got to realise that your dad don't want you, but I don't think he's accepted it, to be honest… He [father] hasn't got the guts to tell him.

In other families some kind of violence, perpetrated by the father on the mother or the child, was, according to the mothers, the trigger for child problems, as with a violent relationship a child had witnessed between her mother and father before they separated:

> No. I know it is not easy, like, with all the violence and that she's seen throughout her, like, her little life. She has got a bit abrupt in her voice, she is demanding, she, but I mean she needs to get a mix of other kids to calm her down a bit. And she has been, but she has herself been through a lot, but she has seen a lot.

It is not surprising, in view of the cohort, to find that sexual abuse was occasionally an element in the situation, even though these were not cases which were taken on to social work caseloads. In one family, with adult children, the mother of an eight-year-old girl was told by the adult children that her estranged husband had sexually abused them when they were children. This followed a description of inappropriate behaviour by the father when the daughter visited him. Her daughter

> first told me that my ex-husband which is [daughter's] dad had been interfering with her when she was about 11. So and because he had part control with [daughter] and she used to sleep there for so many days a week, I thought that just for her own interest, so I gave them [social services] a ring. I actually rang them up and said this has happened.

The consequence, for the eight-year-old, of her own 'interference', was greater emotional and behavioural instability, although she was calming down now that she was not allowed to return to her father's home.

Blaming both parents

The children's emotional and behavioural problems could be put down to the behaviour of, and relationship between, both parents. The emotional environment created by relationship difficulties led to the problems for the children, as they reacted to the instability and aggression. A number of mothers cited separation as bad for the children, particularly where they were young.

One woman had ongoing problems with her three-year-old's sleeplessness, severe tantrums and aggressive behaviour:

> Well, we were together for four and a half years. We've always had a quite violent on-off relationship and…he's always lived with us until sort of last year… And obviously now she's that little bit older, she's more aware of our arguments, more aware of an atmosphere between the two of us and picks up a lot of what we say… But it's more a…although we split up we haven't let go and we haven't made that clean, proper clean break… She sees…me doing myself over it. She sees her dad doing himself over it. And she's sort of, you know, trying to be there, bringing it together and it's not working… She's very aware of what's going on around her…about the violence, she's obviously very aware of that… At the moment she's very destructive and…it's gonna take a while to solve.

Blaming the environment

In some cases the environment itself was viewed by the women as the primary causal factor, and, although they may have been distressed, guilty or unhappy about their own performance as parent, they recognised the overwhelming influence of factors which were not directly under their control. Where there were parenting problems, the women felt these were fundamentally a 'knock-on' effect from more fundamental environmental difficulties.

In one case where the *material environment* was significant, the woman, with a large family, was overwhelmed by the impact of homelessness. She was a student with five children, three of them aged under five, who suffered, she felt, the brunt of the problems. She was evicted from her privately rented house because of a 'cock-up with social security' when she became a student, and was forced to go into bed and breakfast. Her description of the impact of this material problem was graphic.

> …all six of us were living in a bed and breakfast situation throughout the summer where we were literally in one room, four beds, six of us and, em, no cooking facilities, no washing facilities, nothing at all. We were able to have our breakfast there, but nothing else, so there were no meals or anything for the children, I had to try and work it all out… Well, being in the bed and breakfast was an absolute nightmare – they had no toys, they had no television, they had none of the normal family routines that we would have. Em, there was no room for any play or interaction between the children them-

selves, because literally there were four beds in the room and you could just about tiptoe around the beds. Em, I think being separated from their friends, because of course where we lived before, there were friends that we could go out to play with, so none of that was available to them. I was constantly stressing on whether we were going to get a house, when it was going to be, who I could attack next to make this happen sooner. So I was not necessarily there for them and their emotional distress, because I had enough of my own. And so it was really, really difficult for all of us to cope with.

Medical issues could be considered responsible for the problems. These were generally some kind of long-term disability which affected the woman's capacity to parent, or the child's emotional and behavioural state. One family had to live with the difficulties and dangers of the disability and pain suffered by the father.

I mean with my partner, his arm, he's paralysed through a motorbike accident. He still gets severe pain in it but they're like spasms, they come and they go. He's terrified, as am I. I know he wouldn't do it on purpose, but if he is going through a spasm whilst going down the stairs with [daughter] in the pram, he'd automatically let go of the pram, it's the first thing you do.

Where there was a diagnosis of Attention Deficit Hyperactivity Disorder (ADHD) the women generally attributed the behavioural problems to the ADHD, hence it was not the responsibility of the child. One woman's comments exemplified this trend:

He suffers from ADHD and he suffers from secondary behavioural problems to that... I mean even at school he doesn't break like the major rules at school, it's the little rules, he doesn't listen... He's always on reports and it's just silly the behaviour... I mean he's got a medical problem but it's the secondary behavioural problem. He's not just naughty, I mean he's a lovely kid, but he's got a medical problem.

Alongside the more practical environment of medical and material factors were relational issues which could be held responsible for the child's problems. In some cases, it was the relationship with peers, outside the home, which was considered responsible for the child's problems. As one woman commented on her 13-year-old daughter's isolation from her peers:

She doesn't mix very well, she tends to play with younger children, and older children than people of her own age. I try to get her to mix but she doesn't seem to do it very well... [Some children] take the mickey out of her 'cos she has special needs, and I think that's what's knocking her confidence.

The issue of bullying, as a primary problem, has been considered in the previous chapter, and it was considered a key factor in attributing responsibility for the emotional and behavioural problems of some children, particularly those approaching, and in, their teens. However, it was at times the *inaction of figures of authority* which was considered to be responsible for the problem. In one case, the mother commented on the way the school had done almost nothing to deal with children bullying her daughter, and she had felt very reluctant to allow her to attend:

> I was constantly going down the school complaining of people hitting her, pushing her, and I even asked them to move her from one class to another out of the way of the children that were being the bullies. You know, they refused to do that, they left her in the same class on the same table and I don't know, for about maybe two years maybe, going down asking to deal with these children and then it all went, you know, too far... I believe if they'd have sorted out at the beginning, moved her from one class, kept the children under control, then this would never have happened.

Blaming the child – the mother as victim

Blaming the child was almost entirely a characteristic of families with teenage children, and exclusively of families with children aged over eight. In these cases, furthermore, the women, while allocating the primary responsibility and blame to the child, rarely attributed to themselves more than a marginal place in the origins of the problems. They were, implicitly or explicitly, the victims of the situation. In pursuing this route to responsibility, the woman did not exclude possible influencing factors, for example, past experiences. Like the mothers who blamed themselves, however, they did not consider these experiences and events as causal. Children still had a choice.

They showed, furthermore, less 'systemic awareness', within the family, particularly less than those who blamed the environment, but also less than those who blamed themselves. They tended to isolate the child from their familial context, in the sense that current familial factors were not even mentioned as significant aspects of the situation. However, they did display a wider 'systemic awareness' in the sense that, peer groups, in particular, were at times considered a vital factor in understanding the child's behaviour.

It's just the way they are

The cornerstone of these women's conceptions was generally (though not exclusively) an attribution which involved identifying the 'person of the child'. In one example the mother felt there was no give and take, no compromise, and this led to a constant series of battles between the two of them. This teenager was 16, the oldest of four children, three of whom were also teenagers. The mother focused on her, and none of the other children: 'If she can't have her own way, when I said to her, no you are not doing that, or no you are not going there, that's it. That's the whole thing. And she goes out of the window, goes out of the door to get her own way.' Where such perceptions existed, of course, the opportunity for dialogue was limited, and the woman described an ever escalating level of conflict. However, another implication was that the onus, and responsibility, was not on the mother. She was both innocent and a victim.

Other women took a similar, hardline, position. One woman commented on her 15-year-old daughter's awareness of her actions, which she (the daughter) nevertheless thought were fair and right.

> She knows what she's doing, she thinks what she's doing is right. And she doesn't understand why I think it's wrong. So, she gets not depressed so much, she gets upset and very distressed with me and throws tantrums. Aggressive…openly defiant and has tantrums, but aggressive to a point, not so much aggressive towards any of us as to things.

Others talked similarly of the 'willed and wilful' nature of the young people's actions. In this case of a two-parent family with two children, aged 8 and 13, the mother drew attention to the capacity of the 13-year-old to choose to behave badly or to choose to improve:

> And there was nothing I could say or do to stop what was going on. The only person that could have stopped it didn't want to and that was [son]. You know he could have stopped at any time. He could have sat down, thought to himself, right, this is not worth it, I'm being really naughty, I pull my socks up, I'm not gonna give anybody else any more grief. Then it would have stopped, but [he] wasn't prepared to do that.

Isolating the responsibility

Some women, in these cases, drew attention to how they could not be held responsible for what happened, actively *excluding* themselves from blame. To be fair, this attitude could be accompanied by bewilderment. The very fact that they referred to themselves indicated, perhaps, that they had asked themselves about their own involvement and responsibility. This was certainly the case with the single mother of a 15-year-old who had apparently quite suddenly become extremely violent towards her.

> I've never been violent, do you know what I mean… A lot of people have been abused, sexually, mentally or whatever, usually become abuser themselves, but no, they were protected so [son] was never brought up with violence…you know when it's all little yeah…you tell them off and you give them a little smack on the hands, but when they all got bigger, I mean I was more like a friend…also their mum but also their friend.

In some cases the exclusion of self from blame could take on a 'self-justificatory' tone. This occurred, for example, in cases where the mother's own attitude to the child was challenged, and this challenge was rejected. In this case, the rejection involved what appeared to be a rather self-righteous comparison with her own former self.

> I got a friend, got a lot of friends, and Mum is next door, next block of flats. And just asked them, well my mum (laughing) I do think she tried to give me support but she said, 'Well you were that age once, don't you remember what you were like?' No, I don't. I was never that bad. But she was just saying, well she's coming home at the end of every night so you know, she's all right.

The implication of the maternal grandmother was that the mother was rather overreacting to her daughter going out, and that hence there was a parenting issue – an issue of, in view of the girl's age (16), being rather over-controlling. The mother would have none of it.

There were times when mothers gave cause to doubt their account of where blame lay. In these circumstances, just as some women who blamed themselves may have been internalising responsibility, so it is plausible that these women were *externalising* blame. One woman objected strongly to her 16-year-old daughter going out drinking and nightclubbing with friends, which reached a peak when she went to town and punched her daughter in the face. She nevertheless regarded herself as having been provoked and blamed her daughter for the situation. Yet she admitted feeling jealous of her daughter.

> I do feel alone sometimes. I mean, a lot of my friends have got partners. They seem to have a better social life than I do. So I get depressed about that then, [daughter] goes out and has a social life and I get jealous of that, I suppose. 'Cos I'm sat here seven days a week and I rarely go out, rarely, now. So, I do get a bit depressed about that sometimes. I've been on my own for ten years as well. Not that I need a man…but that bugs me sometimes.

Causes and influences

STAGE AND AGE

While the women blamed the child, they were generally not so naïve as to view the child in isolation. There were influences on their behaviour – influences which the children or young people could nevertheless have chosen to ignore or reject – if not causes which determined their behaviour. The notion of 'teenage problems' pervaded the ways the women understood the issues. This is evident, for example with one woman with three children over 13:

> Yeah, because of my middle daughter, the 16-year-old, I've had problems with her over the last two, three years. Got to a stage where it was unbearable to live together… Her behaviour was uncontrollable. Temper, language, foul language, just refusing to do anything we asked her. We had certain rules, just basic ones, she doesn't accept them. She wouldn't accept nothing that was said or done. And very unreasonable, became very unreasonable.

Closely associated was the notion that the young person saw themselves as more mature and capable than they actually were. In these circumstances, conflict could emerge from a clear desire to protect the child from themselves, as was the case with a 13-year-old girl, one of four in a family with both natural parents, involved with a violent 18-year-old boyfriend, who reacted strongly to parental attempts to prevent her seeing him.

> And when it was going on it was, she was very aggressive towards us because, as it happened she's a thirteen-year-old, but in a thirty-year-old relationship, and still trying to be a thirty-year-old while she's at home. Us knowing that she's a thirteen-year-old, not realising that she was having a thirty-year-old relationship, there was a lot of, we didn't know what was going on, and she was a pain in the arse.

FAMILIAL RELATIONS

In one case, the daughter was one of three children in a reconstituted family. Her mother and stepfather were the natural parents of only one of the children, who was the youngest. The mother was aware that her daughter felt that both parents favoured her stepsister, but rejected this as mere jealousy or manipulation. It was, she felt, a way of trying to get her own way, and receive favourable treatment:

> I mean, I suppose, what she would say if she was here is that she feels jealous towards her younger sister. They are half-sisters if you like, because [daughter], my son and daughter are both from my first marriage and I got married and had [daughter] and there is an awfully lot of jealousy that comes out through all these little rows. 'Oh you do it for [daughter], oh she gets more than me,' and it's absolutely not a question, we've always given them equally at birthdays and Christmas and even pocket money.

The mother was also aware that the separation caused some strain for the daughter, especially when she was not able to see her father: 'She hasn't seen her dad, not at the moment. She's spoken to him on the phone so it helps her a little bit.'

WIDER EXPERIENCES

In some cases, it was the wider peer group who influenced the child's behaviour, or experiences which they had outside the family. In some cases, changes involved in the process of growing older, such as attending a new school, were given as factors influencing behaviour. In one case of an 11-year-old, the sole child in a family with a stepfather, seems suddenly to have become disruptive soon after starting at a new school. She had tried to jump out of a moving car, had a knife with which she threatened to harm herself, was disruptive and abusive, and phoned Childline and the police without stating anything substantive. Her mother contrasted this with her former 'angelic' demeanour: 'she is so angelic normally'.

> I believe it started, the extreme behaviour started when she started her new school... It started off as cheating and it turned to bad behaviour. That's when it started and the behaviour included like, she was running away, trying to jump out of the window, we had to physically restrain her. She was verbally

abusive towards us, kicking the furniture, throwing things through the glass panel… Extreme behaviour caused by fear.

The account shows that the mother did not consider her daughter's fears sufficient justification for her behaviour – 'I don't think it's serious' – so that the influencing factors did not, in her view, exonerate the girl from blame.

Peer group influence could also be a significant factor. Peer groups could be considered to undermine parental authority by encouraging children to 'disregard parents, to give young people the wrong ideas about what they should or should not do…encourage them to stay out later than they should, and drink or take drugs'. At the worst, this could lead to direct and violent behaviour towards the mother herself. Violence, as we have seen, was a feature of some teenagers' behaviour towards their mother. In one case, for example, the woman felt that her teenage son got the idea directly from a friend, and subsequently re-enacted the violence with his mother:

> But [son] come over this particular night and he just said…'he's over there and hitting his mum'. Now I'm shocked. I looked at him and I went, 'What did you say?' And he went, 'He's over there hitting his mum'. Well, with that I just said to [son],'Well, what do you mean, hitting his mum?' He was like, 'Well his dad is working away,' he said 'I didn't tell you this before, but he is doing it to her all the time when he's not allowed to smoke. With his mum he's not allowed to smoke in front of his mum. He, this other boy, said, called his mum a fucking slag. Called her a fat bitch.'

Conclusion

The circumstances, as we have already seen, were highly fraught. These were women already in families which in many respects were often characterised by disadvantage and exclusion. The immediate problems with which they sought to cope generally, if not always, placed considerable strain, or additional strain on them. The issue of blame, therefore, with its moral dimensions, became very significant. Blame could serve either to vindicate the woman in an interpersonally explosive situation, or to induce strong feelings of guilt alongside responsibility. If she could identify the child, for example, as being responsible, then, at the same time, she could exonerate herself, in circumstances where she could, in principle, be considered responsible. Blame, therefore, could act to deflect attention (including her own attention) away from herself.

Likewise, however, guilt could be tied up with their perceptions of their own 'failed' performance. Again, this reflects perceptions. It is, in principle, perfectly possible for the women to have been in intolerable circumstances, and, as a result of environmental pressures, to have failed to parent to the standards they expected. They could, indeed, set standards which were unrealistically high. In some cases, this would not prevent them from allocating blame to themselves, with the consequent negative and condemnatory emotions attached to such judgements.

Thus, women's understanding of the problems and situation can be understood at a number of levels. Overall they sought some sort of understanding of the situation, ascribing meaning. This in turn involved ascribing responsibility or blame, which specified both a 'culprit' (an individual, relationship or situation), and a moral judgement – this situation or person was in some sense bad. This could involve a primary ascription of blame, – to the main culprit – and secondary ascriptions of blame – that is, to other elements which bore some responsibility, but not the main one. Beyond this, the women understood some causes which they could analyse separately from blame, but which contributed in some way to the actions or circumstances to which blame could be ascribed.

To sum up:

1. Women did not simply define the problem or stressor. Their construction included an *ascription of responsibility or blame*.

2. They were able to distinguish *influencing factors* (which affected behaviour, but for which responsibility was not ascribed) from *causal factors* (which were blamed for the problems).

3. Some women blamed themselves, and this affected their sense of *self-worth*. They saw themselves as ineffective parents and were at times bewildered by the complexity of child care.

4. Women could blame themselves, yet recognise that there were influencing factors, such as past life experiences or environment, affecting their behaviour. A recurring theme was the problem of *bonding*.

5.   *Fathers* were blamed, particularly where estrangement occurred. Rejection of the children, violence to the mother, and abuse were amongst the reasons for blaming them. Both parents could be blamed where there was conflict between them.

6.   The *environment* – particularly social and health – was sometimes blamed. Homelessness placed a particular strain on all members of some families. Medical issues could be seen to exert long-term strain, as well as relational issues.

7.   When the child or young person was blamed, the women often saw themselves as *victims*. They displayed less 'systemic awareness', particularly of the influence of familial factors.

8.   Where the child was blamed it was often attributed to *personality*: 'It's just the way they are'. Women may, at times, have been externalising blame.

9.   Among factors influencing the child's behaviour, stage and age, *familial relations*, and wider experiences, such as *peer group*, were often attributed as causes.

CHAPTER 7

The Context for Coping: Associated Problems

It is clear from our review of coping theory that the stressors with which these women had to cope occurred in a psychosocial context. This context could provide a means through which problems could be either alleviated (through, for example, social support, of which more later) or made more stressful. The psychosocial environment could itself be a source of stress. The stress could exist independent of the child care problems the women confronted. It could also interact with these problems, affect the problems or their coping capacity, and make it more difficult to manage them.

Likewise, the literature on parenting shows clearly the ways in which both environment and past history are significant for the quality of parenting on the part of the mother. Social disadvantage, problems with support, conflict, and problematic life history can all have an impact on parenting. This chapter focuses on stressors experienced by women, specifically those they considered to be *most* significant in affecting their capacity to cope with the immediate problems they had in relation to their children. These, it should be remembered, were not the *central* child care problems, but stressors which were impacting on the women's coping, by affecting either them or the children.

Financial and housing stressors

These women lived in disadvantaged circumstances. Many were living in poverty. Over half were solely reliant on state benefits, while nearly 30 per cent received income support to supplement their wages. Over two-thirds reported financial problems, which were considered serious by nearly one-fifth. They experienced this in terms of debts, or difficulty in managing their money. They often felt that their income was just enough for food and bills, but that there was no money for recreation. This was bad enough for the effect it had on their own social lives. However, it also had an impact on their children, and it was easy for the mothers to feel a sense of guilt for not being able to provide for them as well as other (better off) families. They were often not able to take the children out for the day, or buy them new or fashionable clothes. Some wanted the children to attend nursery or after-school clubs, but could not afford to do so. The source of the more serious financial problems was at times loans that they had taken out, but which they had not been able to repay. At times this involved 'sharks' who loaned for short (initial) periods at high rates, while the women, unable to repay, were sucked into ever more debt.

One woman had financial problems, having had to leave work, and this was affecting her son because of the degree of stress she was feeling, and the distress she was manifesting. The following quote shows how interrelated the problems could become. Her poverty arose in the context of lack of work, and was associated with psychological distress and acute embarrassment, all of which made it difficult to care for her child in the way she would have liked.

> Yeah, I had no money for three months. I was at my wits' end, I was about to have a nervous breakdown about it… I mean, if social services hadn't given me that money I would have had no electric, no food, no anything, so yes, I was really concerned… When it got to the point where I had gone to social services it was very bad, and I felt like if it had gone on for another week, it would have affected his health and it would have affected, you know, every-thing… I was looking into the next week ahead thinking there isn't going to be food in my cupboard… I was feeling a tremendous…felt like I had failed, like I'd just got myself into a big pit of desperation… When I was phoning people and going down to Income Support I was feeling really embarrassed.

Financial difficulties did not arise just because of unemployment. Women described how the breakup of their marriage had left them impoverished, or how the failure of their former spouse to pay maintenance following separation had the same effect. Others were single parents who had never been able to develop sufficient financial stability. Although many were used to having to manage on a shoestring, it was still an unhelpful context for child care. Like the woman above, they could become depressed, which affected their relationship with their children. Where there was a big drop in income, children were deprived of opportunities to do the kinds of things which were formerly commonplace for them. This could be all the more frustrating for the mother, if she saw the primary cause of their poverty to be the father (not paying maintenance), while she had to take the brunt of the children's frustration at the restriction of their recreation.

For some women, the pressure came from more than one direction. They might, for various reasons, have a low income, but then be pressured by the expectations of the children for particular commodities. This was most marked with 'brand' clothing, which was frequently too expensive to afford. However, the children, with strong peer-group pressure, sometimes demanded brand clothing, particularly as the consequence of not having this clothing was to stand out, and even be the subject of ridicule by their peers. Women were caught between the rigours of financial constraint and the distress of their children. This was illustrated by one mother of an 11-year-old girl:

> She demands a lot, named gear. She's always after the, er, then she feels I'm picking on her if I can't afford it. 'You never think of me, you never buy me anything!' Which is untrue. She tells me what to buy her. And if I haven't got the money you can't buy it can you? So she thinks that money grows in trees and it doesn't, we get just enough off the social security and that's it. But she thinks that I get more and I don't. I tell her 'What we get is not for expensive clothes, [daughter], to keep the roof over our head, something nice and warm in our belly at night, nice cup of tea.'

Women described how they often felt the lack of money most at Christmas. No matter how hard they saved, they often felt they were not in a position to give the kinds of presents that other children received. They felt for their children, and felt a sense of guilt and failure themselves. Other women spoke about the way financial difficulties directly affected their opportunities for limiting their child care problems. Unable to afford after-school care, or children's clubs, some mothers felt they had no option but to let their children play in the street, often with children from whom they would rather they steer clear. Bored, and under the influence of 'undesirables', their children were more likely to get into trouble.

The routine nature of financial limitations, and the equally routine effect on children, was described by one mother on income support. For her, money had the biggest impact on her capacity to care for her children.

> There's things I'd like to do with the children but it's having the money to do
> it. If you have five children, you take them out just for one day, it would cost
> me a fortune, so I know that for sure because, I mean, I've tried it (laughing)…
> I tried that one day to see if we could go up in the Hoe and you could imagine,
> it was like, 'We want this, we want that', you know, ice creams, and you just
> know that you got to have money to do it with children, you know.

Housing presented another major contextual stressor. The overwhelming majority did not own their own house: 55 per cent lived in council accommodation and 28 per cent rented privately. Just under one half experienced problems with their housing and nearly a quarter rated them as serious. Housing problems could have a variety of aspects. People could have accommodation that was too small for their family's needs, they could have substandard housing which was unhygienic or dangerous. They could live in areas which were plagued by vandalism, or where they felt in fear of moving around. Often, but not always, problems involved council housing. However, problems with private accommodation could involve unscrupulous landlords, or properties not being properly looked after.

Many women complained about wishing to move from council housing, but the council took a great deal of time to act upon this, if at all. This was the case even when children were considered to be at risk, because even here women often did not get priority. Problems, furthermore, were multi-dimensional. Where there was poor housing, and unhygienic conditions, the health of the family could suffer, particularly where there were very young children involved. Where there were high levels of dissatisfaction with poor housing, or housing position, relationship problems could emerge, as the family became more frustrated. Furthermore, it could have a psychological effect in the form of distress, anxiety and depression.

Some women felt the stress arising from actually moving house, which could have an effect on the children. One woman with young children, who was subject to domestic violence, moved to get away from her violent partner. However, the new housing was far from perfect. The woman had been used to a rural environment, and found her new urban environment noisy and impersonal. She missed the 'communal type living' and found that the flat restricted her, and the children, because it had no garden. Another woman moved because the lives of her family were threatened by her nextdoor neighbour, with the additional, consequence that her partner became depressed. This had unfortunate consequences for her relations with their children, as she commented:

> They threatened my children's lives. She threatened me with a knife and her boyfriend, a 21-year-old, threatened [partner] with a revolver and a knife, so we were forced to move. But she [daughter] doesn't like it here and that's when it started. And all I wanted was somebody to come out and talk to her and now I've got to deal with it my own way, and I'm the biggest bitch and I'm the rottenest mother going, there you go, as according to her and that... She wouldn't take it from me, she wouldn't listen to her father either.

Other women complained about not being able to get away. Women complained about the restrictive or inappropriate nature of their housing. One woman with a physical disability was living in a block of flats without a lift. Having to negotiate stairs, she could not get out and felt entrapped within her accommodation. She described herself as a 'prisoner', considered it a nightmare trying to get in and out, and said that she was 'constantly getting really upset'. This in turn affected the way she cared for her children, making her more short-tempered and less tolerant with them. Another woman described how she wanted to escape from the undesirable peer group with which her daughter was involved, as she was truanting from school, and generally to prevent her daughter from getting into trouble: 'for safety reasons'. Again, she felt considerable frustration from being unable to move.

Another woman was desperate to move, because her son had 'been abused' by a neighbour. Although the neighbour had moved, the area had very bad associations for her son, with consequences for his emotions and behaviour:

> Since the abuse my son's behaviour has been very bad, behavioural difficulties... I think because of the housing and that, he doesn't feel safe here and it's not gonna change until they move us, him upstairs he only moved out last weekend... And it's because he doesn't feel safe... But here he's just constantly, it's just a constant reminder of what happened.

Problems with partners and ex-partners

Relations with partners and ex-partners was another key factor identified by the mothers as having a crucial impact on children and child care coping. Seven women identified negative interactions with partners, alongside 17 with ex-partners. Many mothers felt strongly about negative aspects of their relationship with their partners and ex-partners, and its impact on the children. One of the key facets of these women's situations was the high incidence of separation from the fathers of their children. Separation provided a whole series of opportunities for conflict in a relationship which was already likely to have descended into acrimony for that separation to have occurred. This was formulated around contact with the children, responsibility for child care, and rivalry for children's attention and affection. In other circumstances, though less frequently, where a woman lived with a partner (whether or not the father of the child), this could be the trigger for child problems related to these partners. Very strong emotions emerged where these kinds of conflicts occurred.

Conflict with partners could either have a direct effect on the children, or provide the backdrop which made proper care of the children more difficult. Arguments with the partner provided the most frequent backdrop. This was a particular problem if the partner was not the natural father. While the mother had to take the brunt of the child's difficult behaviour, the stepfather could feel angry, but have little authority actually to prevent the child abusing the mother. Oddly, this could serve to create conflict between the mother and partner, arguing about whether the partner should be allowed to respond. Tension could also exist where the partner was part of the nuclear family, and yet his authority had no or little legitimacy among the children. Stepfathers could be an easy target for challenge by adolescent children, particularly of the 'you're not my father' sort. In one family the difficulty with the children was attributed to a transference of anger from their natural father to the stepfather.

> [Daughter] has got disrespect for [him], it's no way around it and it's to do with the blood father and the upset. And his input in the family life was virtually nil when he used to have them. When he had them it was a relief, but now he's not having them no more, like there's no where for them to go at all, he's cut them off completely. He really hurt them bad, really hard for them to understand why he's doing to and he's their real father.

Domestic violence was a serious danger to both the mother and the child. While the woman remained with the violent partner it could create a frightening environment with major implications for coping with the child, and, indeed, affect the child's behaviour. Generally, where it was mentioned, however, it related to the past, and mother and child had left the violent partner. Some mothers felt caught between their partner and the child, and had arguments with the partner in support of the child. Women could also be very angry if they felt they had been left with most of the burden of child care. One woman described the way the father was never around when she needed him, and how, over the years, this built up to a fury which affected her relations with the children:

> You know, I'm a very strong person but I'm just losing it with the kids... It was just I could feel all this rage inside... I thought, I don't really need this emotion... And phoning their father I just got 'Sorry I'm busy', and he's going to be a teacher.

There was a whole range of issues relating to estranged fathers. Women sometimes resented the father and his behaviour towards them. Some women felt resentful that they had had a relationship with the child's father at all, feeling that it was a mistake, that they had wasted part of their lives, or that they had suffered unnecessary distress. They occasionally felt they had been dumped with the children. Others felt resentful of the affection the children felt for their father, especially if they perceived him as having put little effort into caring for the children. One woman put it this way:

> It just, it pisses me off... I think that's the bottom line and [daughter's] emotions with their father... I get all the stress and beating or kicking from her and slashing out, I'm doing everything and then it's 'Oh daddy's brilliant' and I'm the bad one as well. He's amazing and I'm awful, it hurts... I feel like it's really difficult dealing with her.

One woman was so frustrated that she smashed in her estranged partner's car with a hammer, only to find that her children had been watching, and drew their own conclusions about her behaviour.

Some elements of problems with partners were cited in the previous chapter. Women also complained that estranged fathers did not behave responsibly towards the children. The central theme here was the way in which fathers placed their personal interests before the needs of the children. The result was inconsistent behaviour towards the child or non-participation in child care:

> Her dad, her dad is not around, it's always been her and me. There hasn't been a man figure in her life; it's just been her and me. She is asking about her dad now, she wants to go and see him. She is old enough now to understand. Maybe that will make her better, with her dad. It will give him some responsibility too. I have had her 15 years without him about.

Other fathers substituted money for contact and attention to the child. This could be particularly galling for mothers, who were themselves struggling financially, and could not hope to provide the presents the children received from the fathers. Women felt that they did all the important but unappreciated tasks, while the father received all the praise. On other occasions, children were used by fathers as 'go-betweens' communicating between warring parents – 'Tell your mum I'm gonna have this from the house, tell your mum I'm gonna have that, you know? Well, he was six at the time... He's gone through a lot, and still does with his dad.'

Problems were often related to contact arrangements, and the perceived disinterest, or deliberate awkwardness, of the natural father. Women complained about the irresponsible behaviour of estranged fathers, particularly the unpredictability of their contact with the children. Fathers would fail to see the children as much as the mother thought desirable, would only see the children sporadically, inconveniently rearrange contact, and, perhaps, constantly cancel contact at the last moment, when the children's expectations were at their highest. These problems were exemplified by one woman:

> Now he doesn't even stick to once a month, does he? He would phone up on the day he was coming down or the night before and say, 'I can't make it through work'. And I used to get uptight because I used to say, 'You know, you know your commitments to the children and so do your workplace, so they shouldn't expect you to do that weekend when they know it's your time with the children,' so...he really put the kids through a turmoil.

Women complained that children found contact with the father upsetting, or that the process of separation had deleteriously affected the children. Women described how the children could become angry, how their mood changed following periods when they had contact with their fathers, how they upset children when they were with the fathers, and how they frightened children by saying they would be removed from the mother. Women also complained that children's behaviour deteriorated following contact with the father: 'When he goes up there...you can guarantee you're gonna have a couple of days of moodiness or sulkiness.'

Personal and interpersonal issues

A range of personal and interpersonal issues, in the form of the mother's psychological wellbeing and her social relations, were considered to be major factors impacting on child care and coping. Women were, as we have seen, frequently depressed, and alongside this had considerable feelings of anxiety and being generally 'stressed out'. This could be a reaction to child care problems, but could in turn impact on the child, and the woman's functioning as a mother. They also had a range of social relations problems – difficult relations with adult family members (not just the partner) or friends, or social isolation, indirectly affecting their child care.

Depression was identified by women, along with housing, as the most important problem affecting their capacity to cope with children. Around a quarter rated this as a problem, and one in six named depression and extreme sadness as the main problem impacting on their child care. Women described themselves as being ground down by the relentless routine of child care and other problems in their adverse social circumstances. This was particularly the case where they felt that there was no one, or few other people, to whom they could turn for help with child care. Some women were on antidepressants in an attempt to deal with this, and were even referred for specialist help. It had a profound impact.

Where depression struck, women felt that they had to live with this problem as well as the problems engendered by coping with, at times, difficult children or situations. Women would say that they just had to learn to live with it: 'I just have to cope. That's just how I feel, I have to get on with it.' However much they tried to live with it, though, they were not easily able to neutralise the effects of depression, or its impact on the children. One woman commented:

> My depression and feeling anxious, both of those. I think they really affect my feeling with [son] and he picks up on it, and he gets stressed when I'm stressed, and he's quite sensitive when it comes to how I'm feeling. You know, if I'm feeling really down he seems to act really badly because he doesn't cope with me feeling bad so. I don't actually help him do I (laughing)?

This sense that when the mother suffered mood fluctuations, so did the children, was evident in the accounts of a number of women for whom depression was a significant factor. Some women felt it became circular: they became depressed, the children were affected, they felt guilty and became more depressed, and so on.

Women had problems in their relations with friends and family, with arguments and conflict being at the fore, while troubles affecting the family or friends could have a 'knock-on effect' on the women. Over one third cited problems with their adult family, and 13 (of 102) considered them severe. Fourteen cited problems with friends, of which seven were severe. These were the main problems impacting on child care for ten women. One woman, for example, talked about the fact that she did not see her family anymore. In particular, her sister, to whom she was close, 'has her own problems' and was now taking antidepressants. Occasionally women talked about sexual abuse by their father, which had a long-term impact, both on their relationships with family and also on their own sense of psychological robustness when seeking to cope with child difficulties or the challenges of parenting. Illness was another factor which could create problems with the family. One woman identified multiple problems in her extended family.

> My brother and sister, well my sister used help an awful lot, she's not there anymore… She's got six years before the [Huntington's] disease sets in, she's not had children, so she's not here anymore. My mum's not here, my mum had been really ill for ten years since the disease started and my dad's not really there. And their father not really there apart from once every two weeks.

Women complained about being isolated, without others to turn to. Sometimes this was associated with a defiant assertion that they were coping (nevertheless), even though it was affecting them and her children to some extent. A few women said they felt on top of everything, and that they felt strong and in control of their lives. Others (the overwhelming majority) felt the impact of being on their own. It left them lonely, exhausted, sometimes desperate, without reassurance about their child care efforts, and hence more uncertain about what they should do. Simply having someone (adult) to speak to would have been welcome. As one woman put it: 'I'm alone – I'm on my own the whole time. I'm on my own the whole time, there's nobody to help me, to talk to.'

Women felt similarly about loss. This was generally around bereavement. For some women it could lead to a reappraisal of their lives. Mostly, women spoke very negatively about the impact of loss. Women spoke about the pain of losing their parents, particularly their mother, and the way it could lead to them becoming irritable, anxious and withdrawn. At times the losses could be multiple, and this could impact on their wider behaviour:

In May I lost my mother-in-law, she died (crying) and my mum. And I thought, oh good, I've got my mother-in-law who I'm really close to, and then she dies within five weeks, she got diagnosed cancer. And then next week my partner left who I've been with for two years, and that's when I...said I think I'm actually having a breakdown... It's sort of like it changed me, you know. I closed off so that I couldn't see anyone. I'm just trying to deal with everyday and I don't wanna be a burden to anybody.

Social and health context

Women considered that a range of social and health issues had an impact on their capacity to cope with parenting or child problems. Health was a problem for many of these women, and in some cases it had an effect on their coping capabilities. A few women were diagnosed with a mental illness, and involved with mental health services. The fact of their diagnosis sometimes made them concerned about the effect they might have on their children, and that these effects could be long-term. The label may (or may not) have helped the women themselves, but it could create anxieties over their parenting. Mental illness in close adult family could also take its toll. One woman described how the dementia suffered by her mother got her down, and how this led to arguments with her partner and more turbulent relations with her children. Alcohol and drugs were a significant factor in the parenting of some mothers. One woman described how a series of personal catastrophes led to her drinking heavily, which in turn impacted upon her children:

I really got into a hole really, and I started drinking really badly and my mum... So when my dad passed away... And well, when I found out he had cancer, I got into really heavy drinking, and my mum started drinking really heavily as well, really heavily because of it. In the end she killed herself when my dad went... I was getting into drinking and I was going to pick him [son] up when I was drunk.

Women had a variety of health problems, some of them long-term and serious (ten cited these as severe). Women suffered cancer, heart and respiratory problems, and one was paralysed from the waist downwards. More routine difficulties included asthma, which could leave them feeling tired and breathless. Migraines could have an impact, as women were unable to provide the children with the care and attention they needed. Women could sometimes take to a darkened room for extended periods. One woman identified the connection between her illness and the feelings of insecurity that developed in her children:

> I think they are stressed out because they know I am ill. Last night [son] came down worried because I wasn't at all well last night. And I think they are worried because I have been in and out of hospital for the last couple of months, it doesn't help them, and it doesn't help. They think it's all a joke, they don't realise how much it is a nightmare for me.

Inevitably, home management became a casualty when the woman's ill health made it difficult to move around or accomplish everyday tasks. However, it was a problem which could exist independently of ill health. Many women admitted to having home management problems, and sometimes (perhaps inevitably) this was related to the disruptive behaviour of the children:

> Well, I mean, my boy, when he has a tantrum he wrecks the place and I mean it, everything goes and I mean really goes, I mean he nearly got the telly down and he knocks me about (laughing) he's quite a strong boy... If I try and tidy up then the children sort of untidies it and they makes a mess, and once I do it they untidies it all the time.

However, this was very rarely a factor which women considered impacted on their capacity to cope.

Women sometimes experienced stresses in the public arena which negatively affected their coping abilities. Employment could be a problem. Where women had a partner who was employed, or they were employed themselves (which was the exception), strains could emerge from work, which affected their coping. Worries about the loss of a job, or an overbearing supervisor, could lead to the experience of tensions at home. One woman described the strain of working for the bus company. Her husband came home, she said, shattered, both mentally and physically. He was also subject to routine threats and violence. He was himself stressed out, so the mother could not talk to him about her stress, or about the problems of coping with the children, with the result that she was less able to be stoical when they misbehaved.

Racism could make life much more difficult, both for mother and child. One woman felt strongly protective towards her son, yet felt powerless to prevent the constant racism he experienced, not just from the general public, but from authorities, like the police and education departments:

Er, well [son] was expelled from school for the crime he didn't commit, because he was found not guilty in the court. Er, and he was expelled as well before he was tried… And he tried to take his life because basically he just couldn't stand the pressure anymore… And [son] from the age of 14 I suppose…he's experienced a lot of difficulties, like racism and things like that. Er, from the police as well as, er, the community, and he tends to lash out and then of course that causes trouble for [son] because then the police will come down and they arrest him.

Conclusion and summary

The context for child and parenting problems, both according to coping theory and in the light of these data, is of considerable significance for these women. There were a range of important connctions between environmental stressors and coping capacity.

1. Coping theory emphasises the importance of psychosocial context for coping strategies and capabilities. One aspect of this was the stress women experienced in various spheres of their lives, which, they felt, impacted on their coping with child care.

2. Most of these women lived in deprived circumstances. Many experienced *financial problems*, impacting on the things they were able to do with their children. Without the capacity to offer their children that which more affluent families took for granted, their financial difficulties could leave them feeling guilt.

3. Poverty was closely interrelated with other problems. It could occur in the context of *unemployment, family breakup,* failure of *ex-partners* to pay maintenance. The children themselves could feel deprived when compared with others.

4. *Housing* was another stressor associated with poverty. Women were subject at times to a stressful environment plagued by vandalism, violence, overcrowding and threats of violence. Interpersonal problems could emerge in this context, as well as difficulties with health. Housing could be restrictive and inappropriate.

5.   *Relationships with partners and ex-partners* could provide a significant contextual factor. Separation provided many opportunities for conflict in an already difficult relationship. Partners who were not natural parents could feel a lack of authority with the children.

6.   Women complained that *estranged fathers* did not behave responsibly towards the children, or resented the past relationship itself often as wasted time. Unpredictable contact, and the substitution of money for affection, were other issues cited.

7.   The women's psychological state, particularly *depression*, was cited as the single most important factor affecting their coping capacity. Depression, of course, occurred in a context of difficulties and disadvantage, and was closely associated with these. It also had an impact on child care.

8.   Problems with *family and friends*, particularly arguments, provided another significant background factor. Women complained of being isolated and lonely, with associated feelings of exhaustion and desperation. They felt similarly about loss.

9.   *Health problems* could make child care more difficult. Some women had severe and long-term problems, such as paralysis or cancer, or drank heavily.

10. *Employment* (or lack of it) was a problem. Many women were in a difficult position, as single parents, with child care responsibilities. This could, particularly with younger children, make obtaining and holding paid employment more difficult. This, of course, was associated with financial difficulties.

PART III

Direct Coping

CHAPTER 8

Child-controlling Strategies

One obvious and key issue of child care challenges was the way the women tried to cope *directly* with the children. At the heart of this was their appraisal of the situation. This, as we have seen, involves the issues of threat and controllability. To what extent did the situation present them with a threat? And how far was the situation itself controllable? The circumstances of the mothers diverged widely from each other, and according to the women's own accounts, the challenges presented to them varied widely. Variations in the children's ages and family circumstances were associated, for example, with differences in the nature of the problems, and attributions of responsibility and blame.

The women, in general, saw themselves as a major, generally *the* major, factor in relation to managing the child. Despite the wide range of direct actions undertaken, they can be distilled into two basic orientations.

The first involved actions through which the women sought to gain control. These *child-controlling* actions were generally aimed at the child's behaviour, which they sought to change, or reduce in range, severity or intensity. They were not simply aimed at the child's behaviour, but they also operated at the level of behaviour.

The other broad group of direct coping actions was *child-responsive*. Although these too could be aimed ultimately, in part or whole, at controlling the child's behaviour, they were generally actions which centred on enabling the child to feel more secure, stable or understood, or to help them understand their own circumstances rather better. The focus was, therefore, primarily on the cognitive–affective aspects of the child's situation, with rather less action focusing on behaviour. These two groups did not have to be mutually exclusive – it was possible for child-responsive and child-controlling coping actions to be undertaken with the same child. Nevertheless, there was a tendency for women to take predominantly one form of action or the other, which, as we shall see, reflected their perceptions of the problems.

Behaviour-oriented coping

Behaviour-oriented coping sought to work directly on the child's behaviour rather than their understanding or feelings. It was behavioural in that it involved consequences for actions. These were based on behavioural principles of rewarding that which the mother considered to be desirable, and penalising or punishing the child for behaviours they considered to be bad or undesirable. Behaviour oriented coping related to the creation, maintenance and enforcing of rules of behaviour. There were two main dimensions: positive oriented actions and negative oriented actions.

Positive-oriented actions

Positive-oriented actions sought to create a virtuous circle by rewarding behaviours the child was already manifesting which were considered positive or good. Given the nature of the situation, these were likely to be exceptions rather than the rule within the child's overall behaviour pattern. Nevertheless, women very rarely talked of positive-oriented actions, indicating that a major characteristic of this group was their negative orientation to direct coping.

By rewarding the positive, the parents were generally hoping to chip away at the overall behaviour pattern, altering the balance between undesirable and desirable behaviours. There were two distinctive elements of this approach: first, that the mother was able to recognise positive behaviours within an overall negative behaviour pattern, and second, that they were prepared to consider encouragement and reward as powerful motivators to change behaviour positively.

In one case, where the mother felt she had a headstrong 13-year-old, she found him alternating between very good and very poor behaviour. At times he could be quite aggressive towards other children, or destructive, yet at other times he could be quite affectionate. While the professionals had diagnosed Attention Deficit Hyperactivity Disorder, the mother was unwilling to accept this, and had not sought services for this problem. She felt it was attention-seeking, and sought various positive ways of reinforcing positive behaviours:

> A lot of the time he was seeking attention, but, er, we tried everything. We tried, like, lucky stars, like if he was good all day, we'd give him a lucky star and at the end of the week he'd have seven stars, or so many stars. If he even got two we'd got him a little treat, nothing big, go to MacDonalds or something like that. But er, that didn't work, 'cos he just didn't care after a couple of days.

The problem, the mother felt, was because he was obstinate, 'he want to do something and there's nothing no one's going to do to stop him, you know. "I'm doing it, tough, I don't care what you say."'

In other cases, the mother used positive encouragement alongside negative discouragement (carrot and stick). If he behaved badly, things were taken away. If he behaved well, they were reinstated. This attempt to exert control could take the form of confiscating some desired object, such as a Playstation or other toy. The advantage, as with this example in relation to a nine-year-old boy, was that this strategy could be part of a more flexible way of mixing positive and negative approaches.

> Punishment, I've got, like, taking things away from him, but then if he behaves I give it back to him (she laughs). This is wrong, you know, and I should take everything away and say 'That's it for today, you're not having it or you're not doing this', but then I think if he behaves and try to improves I say, 'Alright, you can have it back now', I don't know.

Negative-oriented actions

Much of the confrontational interaction occurred when negative-oriented actions were undertaken by the mother. Negative-oriented actions sought to change the child's behaviour by instigating unpleasant consequences for negative behaviours. Such behaviours, because of their tendency to work on the negative *with* the negative, ran the risk of being self-defeating, particularly, as was usually the case, if the mothers did not adopt any positive reinforcement as a coping strategy alongside this negative reinforcement. The relationship itself could be damaged, leaving the child disinclined to 'follow the rules' particularly when they were old enough to take alternative actions (for example walking out), the child could ignore and undermine the efforts of the mother.

The prospects for behaviour-oriented coping, therefore, were in some respects age-related. To be sure, women who used this approach, particularly with young people in adolescence, often did so when the relationship was very poor and their degree of control over their child's actions quite limited. Furthermore, the more the child or young person was able to subject the mother's actions to critical appraisal, and the more they felt able to defy her, the more likely these negative-oriented actions were to break down.

TAKING AWAY PRIVILEGES

Women sought to control behaviour by taking away privileges. These commonly involved the deprivation of some desired state on the part of the child. Taking away privileges was a conscious strategy to deter the child and punish him or her for misdemeanours. This comes through from the mother of a nine-year-old boy:

> How can you punish him? Do you know what I mean? I mean…when he does silly things, he needs to be not punished but, like, say 'that's naughty, sit there and calm down'. The rest of the time you punish, you are taking away privileges, like 'you won't get sweets if we go to the shop'.

'Privilege deprivation' could take a number of forms, which were usually at the lighter end of possible punishments. For teenagers, (and on occasions younger children) pocket money could provide some leverage. This could also have the effect of preventing them going out, because they had no money, as with one 15-year-old.

> We ain't been giving him his money, like his dad sends over his pocket money every week, he ain't been having that. He wants money off me, I told him not to until you start behaving yourself. So when he sees the boys and that going pool and in town and that, and he can't do it, he really hates that, being punished that way because he can't go with the boys.

One of the most frequently used behaviour-oriented actions was 'grounding', particularly used by parents of children in their teen or immediate pre-teen years. Grounding involved not allowing the child or young person out for a specified time (a few days or a week). It could be used for any particular problem, from arguing to theft, but was most frequently invoked when a child was out when they should not be – contravening any time limits set by the mother. The key to the effectiveness of grounding was whether or not they wanted something badly enough. In this case the 14-year-old daughter was desperate to go to a concert, and the mere threat of grounding had the desired effect:

> Yeah, because she wasn't allowed to go out to the cinema with her friends because she had a bad report from school. And she had a report from the school saying that she was good, so I let her go to the cinema... So that's helped. Yeah, so the fact that she can go to things she likes, taking away her privileges, you know like grounding, not allowing her to speak to her friends, not allowing her to go out. And it doesn't work straight away; it will only work if you absolutely stick to it. That's the hardest thing.

One approach occasionally used resembled the behavioural method of extinction. This is a fairly straightforward approach whereby undesirable behaviour is ignored. The assumption underlying this approach is that simply providing attention, even if it is negative attention, has the effect of reinforcing the undesirable behaviour. Hence, by ignoring it, the mother takes from the child any form of encouragement unintended or otherwise. One woman, the mother of a violent 15-year-old, sought to create some space for herself amidst the turmoil caused by his behaviour, commenting on his penchant for 'gobbing off and throwing things around'. This had the double virtue, not only of creating space but of discouraging his behaviour. She simply 'blanked him':

> I puts the telly on, picks up that foot loader and just sits there and listens to the telly so I can't hear his mouth, that's what I do. Just completely blanks him and that's the best way to be with [son] because if you answers him back he thinks got to have the last say, you know, you might think 'well I've got to have the last say'. So if I just blanks him, turns the telly up louder or I even put the music up a bit louder so I can't hear him and he's just talking to himself. He don't like being talked to himself so I just lets him go, got wise to [son].

Extinction was not just for awkward teenagers. In another case, extinction was attempted with a three-year-old with behavioural difficulties. Here the young mother required no professional advice, but found it hard to follow her own advice. Her approach, she recognised, required patience and determination, which she was finding hard to summon, if it was to be successful. Ignoring the child may seem straightforward. However, using extinction in stressful situations clearly was not necessarily an easy option.

> The worst thing to do is to shout at him because, like I said, he's not listening to me but he knows that I'm listening to him. The best thing to do is to ignore

him, I know that so much. When he is doing it, ignore him. I can sit down and try to explain to him, he won't listen, he's screaming his head off. So all I can do is ignore him, but I don't in fact if I'm feeling stressed, I snap at him. Which again won't work, so I got to learn just to ignore him and he will shut up eventually. He cannot scream forever.

CORPORAL PUNISHMENT AND THE DESCENT INTO VIOLENCE

Corporal punishment was another means used to discourage poor behaviour. This was an approach, however, which could, and did, easily slip into violence (some would argue that any form of corporal punishment is violence) and some of the accounts demonstrate this vividly. To the extent that this was part of a behaviour oriented strategy, the actual coping strategy arguably contributed to the problem itself, by undermining trust when children were not 'cowed' into conforming.

Some women, it should be said, regarded any form of corporal punishment as inappropriate. This could be, as one woman put it, because it was simply ineffective: 'I try not to smack them because…it's not particularly helpful… We try not to do, but, you know, these things do happen.' It might be ineffective, but she did not entirely rule it out. For others it was a moral as well as strategy issue, one woman evincing a concern that it was larger people simply pushing around smaller people:

> …'cos I don't smack the children, I've never, I don't believe in smacking, because I just see it as a form of bullying. And people think I'm really soft, and [daughrer] thinks I'm really soft because I don't hit the kids, as she puts it. But I just, [that's] the way I deal with it.

Indeed, most women would have stated that not smacking was 'soft' and even 'spoiling' the child. 'Non-smackers' were an exception, and it raises the question: to what extent were the coping strategies a response to the problems, and to what extent were they a cause/contributing factor?

Corporal punishment was a widely used technique, indeed, it extended to all ages, not only teenagers. Smacking was a routine method of gaining compliance from very young children; as one woman commented in relation to her two-year-old, 'Some of the time he gets a smack for it [naughty behaviour] and some of the time he gets sat on that chair, that is the naughty chair.' This was a major means by which mothers sought to wrest control. Indeed, the worse the behaviours of the child, the more likely that corporal punishment became a feature of the situation. In this case the mother referred herself because she could not control her children, who simply never, as far as she was concerned, did what she asked of them. She was bewildered by their behaviour, which involved violence and threats towards her, and constant abuse, calling her 'thick' and 'fat'. Her response was to hit them:

> And I won't give it to them. They start, well they do start a riot in here. I've had people knocking on the door saying 'Are your kids alright in there' I say, 'Yeah, I'm hitting them, if you don't mind'. When I phoned social services, I told them the same. Yes, I do hit my kids. I told them I had nothing to hide… They said, 'Oh, there is not many parents that phone and say you hit your kids.' I said, 'Well I'm honest, yes I do hit them.' Rather than someone knocking on the door saying we've had a call from the social services, I rang them myself and told them.

An unusual case, it appears of contacting social services about (possible) abuse, while maintaining the right to act in this way. Her terms, such as 'hammering', interestingly shared by some other mothers, indicates times at an alarming level of violent intent. This woman, furthermore, on her account at least, seemed not to have thought of possible actions to reinforce the positive, although the situation, from her perspective, was almost entirely gloomy. This may have reflected a rigid, aggressive parenting style. She displayed a fine distinction between 'hammering' and 'beating up' when discussing her response with a neighbour: 'Well, I said, I did not beat her up. I did give her a good hammering for smoking.'

Many of these cases were pervaded by differing levels of violence, which could be quite routine. The violence often proved counterproductive. Indeed, these were often crisis situations, so these actions were frequently not calm, considered, proportionate responses to the child's behaviour. One mother of a 16-year-old whose daughter was staying out at nightclubs later than she wanted, sought, against the advice of friends and relatives, to 'draw the line' at a level which was clearly not working. Drunk, she went to town and attacked her daughter:

> Because I stopped her going to town, I told her she wasn't going. What happened. I did this on a, stopped her going in town on Friday night, she stayed home on Saturday, this is after I've beaten her savagely. And then she

left on a Sunday after dinner (laughing). There's no working her out, really isn't. Then she decided she wasn't going to live here any more.

This glib response was in relation to a case where the girl was found by her teacher with cuts and bruises on her face and arms, which was then reported to social services. Another women also recounted an alarming penchant for aggression on her part. Here she recounts, in relation to a daughter whom she described as depressed, 'going after' her because she was not happy with her smoking. We can only speculate how this made the daughter feel, in the light of her depression and the relationship between the depression and smoking.

> I can influence her quite a lot. She's only fourteen but she smokes. She knows when I mean it. If I get up and run for her, she knows I mean it. I did once and I ran for her and I got her all by the hair and I flung her by it, and she knows if I really wanted to I would get her all by the hair, and I would really get her and pull her hair and drag her. But I've got to drag her, even if it's up home, I've still dragged her. She gets such hysterics it drives me mad, screaming, because she knows how to get me, but in the end I just say, 'Do what you want, do what you like, go on.'

The pointlessness of the exercise is evident, despite the initial statement that 'I can influence her quite a lot', because such coping behaviour has no effect.

ESCALATION

Some women, while using negative-oriented actions, identified an escalating response to child behaviour, which meant that they would respond to repeated poor behaviour with ever more severe actions. This involved a cycle whereby poor behaviour led to a negative response, which had no effect (or made things worse), which then led to a more severe negative response, poor behaviour, greater negative response, and so on. The woman was, at times, left with an ever narrowing repertoire of possible responses, with the consequence that she might run out of alternatives, while the child remained behaviourally problematic. They could, in other words, become trapped in a negative cycle of behaviour and response.

At the 'lighter' end of such responses (one might suggest 'enlightened') the woman sought to tell the child the consequences of their actions. This could exclude parental response, but simply focus on outcomes the child was bringing on him- or herself. This was the case with an 11-year-old male whose problems included poor school behaviour, where consequences, but also positive outcomes, were discussed.

> I tell him the consequences of his behaviour if he keeps going, I said his education is suffering and you're missing school because your being excluded, so he needs to have a good education behind him… And we have an agreement with the teachers, if he behaves then we get a certificate to say he is behaving.

For others, the consequences, in terms of the mother's response, of continuing poor behaviour were rehearsed as a warning. This was the case with a 12-year-old girl, where the woman consciously held back from more draconian responses:

> If it's something really bad I try not to threaten the really bad things, in case she doesn't do it and then I can't cope with it when she's done it. Like once, she goes to Girls' Brigade down the road and she loves it. And one day I said, she didn't lay the table, because I have a rota to lay the table, that's about all they do, and she refused to do it and I said, 'Look, [daughter], if you don't do it you won't go.' I kept trying to say 'Please (laughs) lay the table because you'll get really upset if you don't go,' and she said OK and she didn't do it, because she's very stubborn. Of course it's hard trying to carry it through because it hurts you more than it does them (laughs). Yeah, well, getting to bed early, not going to bed early, we've got and she doesn't like that, so that's a good one.

Other women described the ever escalating response if initial controlling actions did not work. Here the woman points to quite severe threats which would be the ultimate outcome of poor behaviour by her five-year-old son. Her facetious tone suggests some embarrassment about the potential severity of her response to a child that age.

> Lock them in the cupboard (laughing), no, I shouldn't have said that. Er, I have smacked them, you know, you'll not tell my social worker, I've smacked their bums, you know. And like I've talked to them, but if they don't listen to you the first time I say it again. No, I ground them, if they are naughty they get grounded, er, don't have their videos on, take their Playstations off their bedroom or send them to bed. When [son] was upstairs he smashed some things but I've got, this might sound horrible, but I've got, I wouldn't use it, but I've got wooden spoon in the cupboard, all I've got to do is to say, 'Right, do as you're told', and bang on the stairs and they all go up the stairs and they

are quiet as mice you know, and I think – yeah, you know, but I shouldn't have told you that (laughing).

No matter how much these women escalated their response, however, they were often, by their own admission, not very effective. One woman only went as far as grounding, but found her strategy to be self-defeating because it annoyed her (the mother) more than it did the daughter, who was always 'under her feet'.

> Basically grounding her. Stops her doing the things that she wants to do, like when she like goes to a club with her friends, stops her going there, stops her going out after school hours. Basically she has to be in the house at half past four, bedtime nine o'clock, which she got used to it. Wouldn't let her watch television in bed and then still got used to it. It's like, I'll ground her for a day like, a day or two like, went for a week, got to well, I'll ground her for six weeks, didn't bother her, didn't bother her at all. Nine times out of ten I'll give up because she's getting on my nerves being under my feet and she knew it, so she's won again.

The strategy seems not to have been very intelligent. In another case – where the 16-year-old male was diagnosed with Aspergers syndrome – it really did not matter what the mother did, how things were escalated, because the punishment did not matter to him. She took his television and computer off him, or sent him to bed early:

> Nothing mattered. It didn't matter that we did that. You know, like he just took it in his stride and he just got on with his life. Nothing mattered, you know, I mean he'd be in bed at half past seven, just sat there on his bed, but it didn't matter, you know.

Some women reached the point where they were violent to the children, having tried other approaches, but they were still ineffective. Situations could degenerate severely, and in the following case, the woman went below her own standards of behaviour. Asked, in relation to her 15-year-old, whether she had had any effect, she commented:

> No, none at all. Couple of months ago we had a really, really big argument and I just let loose on him. I mean, I really hit him, and I hit him and hit him and he just got up and he laughed at me, and he said 'That didn't hurt.' But it hurt me, 'cos I'd never ever hit kids, but he just got me so really angry that day I just blew and my husband pulled me off him. He told him, '[Son], you've got to

learn to keep your mouth shut and when to keep it shut.' But he doesn't, I mean he can stand there and call me a bitch, cow, and everything, but it's not the way to talk to anybody.

In many of these cases, the behaviours appear to have been self-defeating. They could well have made matters worse: negative behaviours seemed to feed off each other, rather than halt the slide. The cycle seems to have ever more marginalised negotiation, with the consequence that conflict deepened. Rather than create a more positive situation, the women simply ran out of ideas of what to do.

DISTANCING

Another form of coping was distancing. This involved in some way creating distance from the problem, so that the problem was removed. This could take two forms. One would be the mental or physical separation of the child from the factors creating the problem. This was possible where the problem was in some way external to the child (although it did not need to be exclusively external – the child could be involved), so that the child and the problem could be separated.

This happened in one case where the mother was very concerned about the influence of an older teenager on her 13-year-old daughter. In this case, the boyfriend (18 years old) had had unlawful sexual intercourse with the girl (she was under age), had been taking her money, and had been physically violent towards her. Despite this, according to the mother, the girl remained loyal to him, and became increasingly aggressive towards her parents. Their solution, since he lived nearby, was to take her entirely out of the situation (and the vicinity):

> It was to get her away from the problem… The problem was the lad downstairs, and to get her to be able to think clearly without the interference of, of anybody who was directly involved down here, to talk to someone objectively that could just sit there, be there for her, go out, learn to be a 13-year-old again and see what other 13-14-year-olds are doing, and get her mind settled. So she's been getting back into a social circle of her own age, rather than being with older people, which was what was happening down here. Plus she'd got her sister there, we're here, we're sort of one-sided to the problem that was happening. So sending her away, and reassuring her that we weren't sending her away because we didn't want her – we do want her, we

missed her terrible while she's been away, but the only reason that she's been away is for her own safety and to get her head sorted out, which is what happened.

She was sent to a sister in a town a few hundred miles away, which took her entirely out of the situation. The mother, it should be noted, was careful to try to avoid any negative connotations, aware that the girl might feel rejected.

A similar situation emerged with a woman, made homeless, and in bed and breakfast. Although she wanted the younger children in the family to stay with her, her teenage son felt unable to stay. Here the mother agreed to his wishes, because she was aware how strongly he felt, and felt also that he would go to a safe destination.

> [Son] was so upset by it all that he actually left the bed an breakfast to go and stay with his father, and at this point still hasn't come home. So that was the reaction of a teenager, was, er, 'I'm just not going to go through this, I'm going to take the option I've got and I'm going off with my dad.'

While the mother agreed to this 'distancing', the longer-term effect of this was a distancing, not just from the problem, but also from the family. Both examples show that distancing, even for the best of motives, and to resolve an immediate crisis, can run the danger of its own effect, of distancing the child from the mother, or, more widely, from the family.

The second form involved distancing the *mother* from the problem – getting the problem away. This most frequently involved the problem being (in the mother's eyes) the child him- or herself. They would, in short, throw the child out, which would generally occur when the mother had failed in setting and maintaining boundaries, and generally involved (see below) the threat of throwing them out, before actually doing so. One mother called the police when her son became very aggressive outside the house.

> They could see that this child was a bit of an arsehole. Then the police man wanted to speak to me, the policeman said to me, 'That's your child outside.' And I went 'Yeah.' 'Would you let him back in the house?' 'No.' 'Why would you not let him back in the house?' I said, 'Because a few weeks back he gave me a black eye, he abuses me, and I'm sorry but you can think whatever you like of me, I've passed the stage now, I don't care what anybody thinks of me as a parent, I'm not a bad parent, it's not him being abused, it's me that's being abused, and I'm sorry I'm not taking the shit no more, now get him away from

my door.' He said, 'The only thing that we can do, is to put him down the cells.' 'Do it.' 'Look, can't you just let him back in ?' 'No, I don't want him in my house. Get him away from my door.' He actually didn't believe that I would go through it. But sometimes you got to have luck, that's how I look at it.

Another example, very similar in consequences, occurred after a 13-year-old boy attacked his mother, and this was a step too far. Unable to take any more, even she could hardly believe what she was saying.

So on this Monday, this is three weeks later, I've said to [son], 'I want you out now,' because he has drove me insane, I think I was on the verge of a nervous breakdown. And I have nobody to turn to and I said, and I said to him, 'I can't believe I am saying this to you after all these years of looking after you, caring for you and being there for you.'

Summary and conclusion

1. Women's direct actions with children were very important to women's coping strategies. Women generally saw themselves as the major factor in managing the child.

2. There were two basic orientations to direct coping with the child. *Child-controlling* actions were aimed at the child's behaviour, which they sought to change. They operated at the level of the child's behaviour, on crude behaviourist principles.

3. The other orientation involved *child-responsive* actions. These were generally actions centred on enabling the child to feel more secure, stable or understood. The focus here was primarily on the cognitive-affective aspect of the child's situation.

4. *Positive-oriented* actions sought to create a virtuous circle by rewarding behaviours that the child was already manifesting, which were considered positive or good. Rewarding positive behaviour was designed to chip away at overall behaviour, gradually to produce more desirable behaviour.

5.   *Negative-oriented* actions involved a range of themes. These involved taking away privileges, ignoring behaviour, and use of corporal punishment or worse. However, these could be self-defeating since they involved responding to negative with negative. This was particularly the case with older children.

6.   *Corporal punishment* exemplified this, in that it could involve initial hitting and then the development of considerably more violence. This could arise from an emotional response, rather than a careful and proportionate response to perceived misdemeanours.

7.   *Escalation* describes the process by which women moved from one to another, more severe response to child behaviour, as each one failed to work. Escalation could arise from the failure of imagination on the part of the mother, in relation to thinking of alternative responses.

8.   *Distancing* was a response by which the child was mentally or physically separated from the problem, or the circumstances engendering it. Another form involved the mother removing the problem from herself.

CHAPTER 9

Child-responsive Coping

While child control strategies reflect, to a considerable extent, some of the dictums of a more behaviourist philosophy, child-responsive strategies, again not entirely, but to a considerable degree, reflect some of the insights associated with attachment theory. The responsive dimension involved cognitive dimensions of assisting insight and understanding (on both sides, mother and child) and using direct, physical and affect-related actions to provide a deep sense of care for the child. These women, in crisis, saw the importance of reassurance, clear communication and understanding, and physical care, and used them positively in coping with the situations with which they were confronted (or involved). Child care strategies which are advocated as appropriate to general care of children were also pursued in situations of some difficulty.

Instrumental-oriented coping

Instrumental-oriented coping involved strategies designed to develop and maintain routines of behaviours and expectations, together with physical safety of the child, both of which could contribute towards a sense of security and reliability for the child. Although instrumental, they could have affective consequences. Maintaining routines could, of course, help foster calmness, through a sense of security, in difficult situations.

Protective commitment

A basic child-oriented concern was for the protection and care of the child. This could involve seeking to avoid placing the child in dangerous situations (or children placing themselves in dangerous situations), or dealing with crises which were already presenting dangers to the child. This could occur even where relations were strained. One woman showed the extent of her ambivalence towards her daughter, when she described her as having created a 'problem' by taking an overdose, even though she saw herself as protecting her daughter (from herself, in this case):

> She caused the problem this summer [!], when she took the overdose, I had to rush her to hospital. Telling me I didn't care enough of her. I was with her every step of the way. Went to the hospital with her, they managed to get rid of the stuff 'cos this it would have killed her in three weeks... And then they kept her in for a few days after the incident 'cos what had happened. I was with her all the time.

Another case was of a 16-year-old whom the mother saw as a disruptive, defiant and argumentative teenager, while the girl herself, according to the referral, felt that she was treated less well by her mother and stepfather than her brother (who was the child of both of them). This was disputed by the mother. On one occasion, when they had been on a day trip, the girl got out of the car when she was not allowed to stop for chips.

> She sat in the back of the car and she refused to put her seat belt on. So, we've come up out, parked to the lay-by, I said, 'We can't drive all the way home, it's quite a way from [town], you put the seatbelt on, it's against the law, we need you to do it.' 'I'm not effing doing it,' 'cos that's what we got. We sat there for about an hour, trying to talk her into it. We got out of the car, got the flask out, started having a cup of tea, thinking, well, she'll get in sooner or later, but there was no way she was going to. And in the end me husband drove me younger daughter back [home] and let us just sat there. And I punished myself really, I should have got in the car with them and said, 'Right, bye, find your own way home.'

Normalising

One way women sought to deal with abnormal situations was an attempt to normalise family routines. This, in short, involved seeking to set in place the normal ways in which the family would operate, had the crisis or the problem not existed. This was based on the idea that it encouraged a sense of security, by giving some sense of certainty and expectation, and by enabling the children to do or participate in activities in which they had invested some interest. This, of course, would be desirable in routine circumstances, but became doubly important in times of crisis. This is apparent in one case, of a woman made homeless through eviction, with a family of small children:

> Em, I've just tried to instil the family routine here as quickly as effectively as I can… Em, the boys got, you know, all their new Pokemon quilt covers, and you know, things to make it seem special, and their bikes and things again, and I've just tried to establish that bit's over with, we've got a nice house now, we're going to do the garden, and just try to gee them along with some optimism for the future and know that it's a lot more secure than it's been for the last three or four years now.

Another woman described the normalising efforts she made when her daughter returned home, having previously walked out under, she felt, peer pressure (she had been picked on by her peers):

> Get her home, get her sorted, get her back into school. Get her back into normality. She's got to come home… Once they know that she's back, see if anything does start up. If it does start up, take a course of action then. If it doesn't it'll be fine.

Cognitive-affective coping

Cognitive-affective coping strategies were designed specifically to impact on the internal emotional or cognitive state of the child, in a beneficial way. These strategies would be designed to help instil a sense of personal confidence, of being able to direct and control one's life, of being a valued individual, of having the interest of significant others, of being the subject of real affection.

Proximising

Proximising entailed greater involvement with the children in their activities and interests. The aim of this was to create a greater closeness with the children concerned, and give them a sense that the mother was interested in them and their interests. The underlying affective dimension is obvious, in that it provided, implicitly (or explicitly) an indication that the mother cared about them.

An example of this occurred in the case of a woman whose two pre-teenage children had reacted disruptively, defiantly and sometimes aggressively to her separation from her husband, at the same time as they moved from one part of the country to another.

> I think if I continue to try and spend more time with the children, and try to get more activities that we can do together, then I think we'll resolve the situation... [Daughter] gets very involved with things when she's interested. It's like now she's expressed a wish to join the Leos ... so we'll find out about the clubs, and if they're not too far away, then I'll start taking her to meetings, and she can start doing the charity work that they do.

The parents of a pre-teenage girl who was becoming seriously behaviourally disruptive, aggressive, threatening suicide, similarly sought to involve themselves more. In this case, it was not just in the child's interests, but seeking to involve the child in *their* activities:

> And we did try together. I said this yesterday as well, initially we tried to do positive things with her like swimming, walking, watching movies, buying a video maybe, and trying to think about something else to think about really.

Proximising could also entail involvement with the child, not simply in some instrumental way, but seeking to gain a 'closeness', even empathy, through attending to her experiences, wishes and feeling, especially when the child was suffering some trauma. One woman talked about the way she had responded to her daughter's possible sex abuse at the hands of her estranged father. She tried to get closer to her, something she found harder than usual. The whole demeanour of the child had altered.

> She was very, very quiet. She used to come back and just go into her room and I found it hard to have a conversation with her. She just wouldn't talk to me like, you know, with, with all the kids we are quite open, we talk about anything, we laugh, but she wouldn't, if I tried to make her feel better she just

said, 'You are all horrible', and go to her room so, very hard. But I just thought it was to do, her dad.

Caring-affective nurturing

Caring-affective nurturing strategies involved a range of actions in which the mother sought to reassure the child emotionally or instrumentally or to provide a structure through which the child might be enabled to feel more secure. One key area was providing *physical* care for the child. This was a basic parenting task, but became part of their coping actions when faced with child care crises or problems, as with a mother in bed and breakfast who had a child with eczema:

> Yeah, yeah, of course, you know, because there was no bath there for him. I'm lying, there was a bath at the B & B, but it was absolutely disgusting and I wouldn't, I probably wouldn't bath the cats in it to be honest, let alone the children. So, em, I still maintained all the creams and things that he has to have, and obviously, but yes, the bathroom thing, it's so important for him to have the emollient 'cos it's what provides the moisture in your skin to stop the dire irritation. Em, so yeah, it did suffer a bit, em, and that is always a concern to me because I know how painful that is for him.

The nurturing response was often more affective. Some women, particularly with young children, were particularly concerned about their children's emotional state, either as a result of perceived deficits in their parenting, or because a disruptive situation was affecting them negatively. Their nurturing response was not associated with care in routine situations, although it might resemble it. Emotional warmth as a response to insecurity was a characteristic of some mothers with young children, if they felt the children had become neglected or insecure in some way. One single mother expressed this, in relation to her two six-year-old twins. It was, she felt, necessary to treat them with respect, as people first, rather than just as children, and through this, she was trying to create a more positive response from the children. One of her twins had been wetting the bed and sleepwalked, a matter of some concern to her, and they were 'generally just shouting, looking for attention', and she was neglecting the children: 'I didn't want to be involved really'. Her efforts had already made her more upbeat:

> Basically they get more respectful towards you, they are just like anybody. I don't care what anybody says, they are young adults, that's all they are, they are young people. And you got to respect them before they respect you and we have come a long way. Before, I didn't have no respect for them, and they didn't have no respect for me, and stuff like that.

The demonstration of affection could also involve reassurance to the child of the mother's love for them, particularly where the child was in an insecure or fear-inducing situation. The key here was how to re-stabilise the child in the face of this instability. In one case, again, of a young single mother, brought up in care, she and her child had experienced a violent, unpredictable relationship with her partner, which had recently led to separation; she attempted to reassure her young three-year-old daughter. Additionally, they had experienced eviction and temporary homelessness, and a 'new' five-month-old brother. Her three-year-old had, she felt, been traumatised by these events:

> She's very rarely asleep actually. She's got a bedtime...and she'll keep coming downstairs... She's awful, it's like a security thing. She doesn't like being on her own or that sort of thing. She goes to my bedroom, [I let her] sleep in my bed.

Encouragement through firmness

Encouragement through firmness was undertaken by mothers who sought to develop competence and confidence in their children, but recognised that this could only be achieved by providing boundaries to what would otherwise be the child's chosen behaviour. Of course, boundary-setting was an aspect of child-controlling strategies, but in those cases it was primarily about preventing inappropriate or aggressive behaviours, or getting children to enact appropriate behaviours – i.e. it was more about external considerations of child action and interaction.

Encouragement through firmness was aimed more at 'internal' considerations, primarily involving more positive attitudes, confidence and the child's sense of being able to achieve certain things. The 'firmness' dimension involved the notion that this could only be achieved through setting boundaries or barriers to their behaviour, because if this were not the case, the child would pursue actions which would increase his sense of alienation from the possibility of achievement in, and control of, his life.

In one case, the purpose of boundary-setting, 'ensuring something happened', was clearly psychological. Here the mother identified in her teenage daughter a tentativeness which was undermining her self-belief and encouraging a pessimistic, even depressed, outlook on life. Her robust response was to encourage confidence:

> Making her taking control of herself… I try and, if she's not doing something that I want her to do, then I say, 'I've told you twice now, come on, get it done,' then I say, 'You can't do something *you* want to do if you can't do what *I* want you to do'… Er, she's meant to do her own underwear and she has accidents, so she's got to do it 'cos it's not my job to do it… So I'm making her to take control… I said, 'If you go away like, I can't be there to do it for you,' and that's how I'm trying to get her to be more confident about herself.

The firmness was based on a perception of doing a kindness. Instead of learning to be helpless, the girl was learning to be in control, and this needed, as far as the mother was concerned, to occur with mundane and everyday activities, not just in periods of crisis.

A similar process of encouragement occurred with a 12-year-old girl who had been, according to her mother, bullied at school, with serious consequences for her self-esteem. In this case, the mother was not dealing with routine issues of control of life, but with the consequences of a crisis. Where, before, she had been involved with other children and played easily with them, the girl was now much more introverted and socially isolated. Here the mother tried to encourage her to be strong:

> Just talked to her, say, 'It's not your fault,' you know, and try to encourage her to be strong again, because her she's terribly quiet, terribly shy now. Well, she was out going with loads of kids and stuff, playing with them, and now there's nobody, she doesn't play with them, she won't. The chance of something like that happening again, she won't let it go.

In a similar fashion, one mother was concerned about helping her daughter feel good about herself, after being told by her estranged father that he was no longer interested in her. The mother reflected the feeling (true enough for any number of single parents), that she was the only one there who could actually help the child in this way. She very much felt that others had been of no use:

> Yeah, that was mainly just to help [daughter] get over what had happened to her and to make her feel good about herself, because nobody else was going

to do it. Because there was no help for her and you know, there was people she was supposed to see but they didn't talk to her, they talked to me, and it's no good talking to me, I'm not the one who's had it happen to me, it's her.

Insight-oriented coping

Insight-oriented coping was child-responsive in that the mother sought to facilitate understanding, either (on the part of the child) of her perspectives and reasoning, or (on her part), of the child's understanding and perspectives of the situation. This form of coping essentially sought to improve communication, but also understanding of the other's position. In a situation characterised by conflict, it was possible for relationships to deteriorate to the point where neither was prepared or able to hear the views of the other. Of course, listening to the child did not necessarily mean taking their view seriously, nor did it necessarily mean that the child felt that their view was taken seriously. When carried out seriously, however, this approach had the potential for reducing tension, by, for example, opening 'channels' for negotiation, with the implicit message of taking the child seriously, of providing the child with a sense of being valued or cared for.

The woman in the following example shows an awareness of all these dimensions. Confronted by persistent arguments with (and between) her two children, she decided to change tack and seek their views. She sought to develop a dialogue between them so that aggression and stress were replaced by (relative) reason and calm.

> You have to see it from their point of view, which I know is hard, because it's a long time since I was that age… I try to have a discussion with the children, if one would have an argument, em, to get their point of view about it, because they see it different than I see it. I mean, I'm older, they might think that I'm always telling them to do this that and the other, so if I can get their reaction, and why they reacted the way they did, then I can try to explain why I reacted the way I did. And then, if we can understanding where we're each coming from, then hopefully there's a middle ground and we can talk about the problems, instead of me just getting stressed out and screaming at them, and then they don't understand why.

Some mothers did not simply seek to discover the child's understanding of the situation, but also how they felt about it. In one case a 12-year-old girl had two estranged parents who were in frequent conflict with each other. Her anxieties may have been related to skin problems (a psychosomatic response), and the mother sought to get at her feelings, although it seemed to make things worse rather than better:

> Yeah, I have tried. Both times that I have tried she's like, started crying so I just don't…do it anymore… I know it upsets her and things, so I just try and, I don't know, try and make her a bit happier while she's here, sort of thing, and try and not put her under any of the stress from that… I won't speak about it [now].

The feelings, it seems, were so 'raw' that a sort of supportive avoidance became, for her, the best strategy. Sometimes, mothers felt they could not get an answer from the child, possibly because he did not know himself, as with one mother who commented that after frequently trying to talk to her son: 'He won't sit down and tell anyone why he's doing it'. At times, as with this 15-year-old, the mother felt that they would go from one thing to another, and there was always a further, deeper issue, to deal with.

> We sat down, we tried to talk to her, me and my partner… 'We can sort it out if you can just tell us what your problem is, we can help you. If you don't tell us we can't help you,' and she would just go from one story to the next story, to the next story. Like changing schools was a way of getting out of that school up there, and then she'd say, 'Oh, I want to see my real dad.' So I'd try and arrange for her to see her real dad and then it would be next problem. You know, it just went on and on and on, and you never ever got to the bottom of what was wrong and, like, I say we still haven't now.

Seeking to explain the mother's position to the child could also be beneficial, by enabling the child to understand better the reasoning behind it. It also invited the possibility of dialogue, which could aid the possibility of some negotiated settlement. However, it could also take the form of a more rigid presentation of the mother's position, with less intention to negotiate, with the presumption that it was right and the mother knew best. This is perhaps less about creation of insight than simple, rigid presentation of view, as is apparent in one case, where the mother of a 15-year-old who had walked out of the house and was actually camping outside the house, about 40 feet away, sought to talk to her about this. This approach, while appearing to be insight-oriented, was, in fact more rigid and controlling.

> I tried to go out and see if I could talk to her, calm her down…to see if I could get her to come home, explain things to her. Didn't get anywhere with that…but that was the only action I could take to get the situation put in proper, not let it expand and get worse than what it would have been.

Not all mothers sought simply to present the child with a non-negotiable positions. To mothers who sought to explain their position, the success of this action could depend on the child's capacity to listen. This, it would seem, was most likely where there was a reasonable quality to the parent–child relationship, despite the problems. This was the case with a mother who was severely disabled, and those problems affected her capacity to parent. Talking to her teenage daughter in a calm way was an important part of her strategy for making a difficult situation work. Here they sought to resolve their differences about visiting a friend.

> I do still feel I have an effect, I mean the way she spoke to me, she…wasn't shouting, she was listening to what I was saying and… She agreed with what I said about perhaps having a week at [friend's], have some time out and then for her and [friend] to come and stay. And she agreed to that, so and that's what I wanted. So obviously if I go round it the right way I can have an effect on her behaviour. Yes, as long as it's not confrontational, which it wasn't happening.

Where, however, the child was not open to reasoning, mothers felt they were 'banging their head against a brick wall'. One woman counselled against the dangers of getting too close to the child, because he might be less likely to take notice:

> What to do when he's having an outburst? Well, try and calm him down. Try and reason with him… I think maybe we are too close, that sounds a ridiculous thing to say but we have, er, we are more like buddies, I suppose, than a mother and son. I talk to him like an adult more than a child.

One approach was to seek to develop the child's own capacity to develop insight. Here, rather than explain the parent's position, the mother sought to get the child to imagine what it would be like to be the victim of his behaviour. The mother in the following example was, in effect, trying to encourage empathy, and to do this to develop in the child (a 13-year-old) a motivation to change his behaviour.

Yeah, so I'm always saying to him, 'What do you think?' or 'How would you react if you were a dad and you had a child that would have just done what you have done to me, what would you do?' 'Ground him, put him into the bedroom', or 'I don't know', would be the next one 'I don't know'. And like you say to him, 'Why did you do this?' and it's like, you either get the blank, silence and the look, or he just, it doesn't look as if anything is registering. Or you get, 'I don't know'. I think at the time he doesn't know why he's doing it, he's just doing it because it's something to do.

Parent-oriented coping

A further dimension of active coping with the child was the way the mother sought to undertake actions or processes which were fundamentally oriented to herself, yet directly affected her interaction with the child. These kinds of approach were essentially facilitative to the actions which she would directly undertake with the children, and fell into three groups: reflective consideration and planning, setting boundaries to herself, and suppressing competing activities.

Reflective consideration and planning

This area involved the process of thinking about the situation. In one sense this is an obvious dimension – in stressful situations the women were clearly seeking to identify the best course of action, from their perspective. Yet the response of some women appeared to be primarily one of bewilderment. The stress of the situation could actually make it difficult to reflect and plan in a constructive way.

Women could find themselves groping for answers, seeking to identify the best course of action to take with children who, for them, were extremely testing. One woman spoke about her son, aged ten, who was already threatening his parents, stealing money from home, and behaviourally problematic at school. She was constantly seeking to find a way to deal with these problems, but was not getting very far.

I mean, I try and to find out why he's like that but at the moment I just don't know, I don't know, I mean I wish I had an answer. So I could work on it, and try to work out why he's like that, but I don't know, actually. So maybe it's got something to do with my past, I don't know, I don't know.

At times, the women were undertaking constantly changing strategies in order to respond to the child. The problem was that, once one strategy had been tried and worked, the child might no longer respond to it, so an altered strategy was required. One woman drew attention to this:

> They always change, I have to keep changing them, because he adapts, he adapts with it, I mean these here are done because he lost his temper with me and I was getting him to do something that he didn't want to do… A big sock-puller-upper was I gave him a book and he says, 'Oh this is a nice book,' I says 'yeah, I was reading that book at your age.' 'Oh.' I says, 'Yeah.' 'Oh, okay, I've read five pages.' 'That's very good [son], thank you.' 'So every time you feel like crawling on the floor and meowing like a cat,' I says, 'you pick that book up and you remember I was reading that at eight, not doing that, I was reading that…' So it's kind of like trying to turn the light on and say like, 'You know your behaviour's it's not acceptable here and I don't know if it's acceptable anywhere else, but not here,' so that changes.

The reflective thinking also frequently involved planning, and when this was the case environmental factors were often the focus as well as the child him- or herself. One woman of a nine-year-old boy who was frequently aggressive blamed the school in part for this and commented that, 'I'm always ticking over what to do', stating also that, in terms of possible schools, she had 'made plans – already his name's on waiting lists, I spoke to the headmaster, I spoke to the teachers'. Working on the environment as well as the child, together with the difficulty of thinking clearly, is well illustrated by the comments of one woman. In this case, the woman was trying to make sense of behaviour of her 11-year-old, which was completely out of character, how she should react personally to this, and what outside services might be helpful.

> Yeah, at the time, 'cos we were under a lot of stress I couldn't really think clearly, you know. I was really thinking of which way forward, sanction-wise for her, maybe it would be the school, was she mentally disturbed, what you know, trying to think out different ways. How to deal with the school, what professionals to get into touch with… We felt really, at the time couldn't get any help really initially from social services, nobody you know, therapists or counselling, none of them were talking to us.

Reflection could help the woman avoid acting precipitately, particularly where problems were occurring with more than one child. In this case, the woman was both trying to hold herself back, yet also figure out why the children might be behaving as they were:

> If I go to the bedroom, and I find them arguing and screaming at each other, I don't rush in straight away, because nine times out of ten it's either [daughter] gone into [son's] room or son has gone into [daughter's] room. And I think, 'Well, why was it quiet before they were together? Has [son] come home from school in a bad mood?' Because if [son] comes home in a bad mood, everybody knows about it. Well, I do tend to sit there and think, 'Come on, has something happened, or, is he just doing it to annoy her?' before I go storming in.

Reflection and planning were also contextual, with women focusing on environmental factors, particularly where they were considered the primary factor behind the child care problems. In the following case, the woman was being stalked and threatened by a former partner, and lived in a flat which she felt was far too small for their needs. She felt desperate.

> I thought about moving. And I thought about having improvements there. I kept thinking, 'What can I do?' I thought I got to move and I thought, 'We can go anywhere. I can't live there with the bad memories, we got to move, before I get anywhere... You got to move into a different environment. You got to start again basically.' That's what we did.

Setting boundaries to herself

Just as it was important to set boundaries to children's behaviour, so some women felt that it was important to set boundaries to their own behaviour. This contrasted strongly with some women who took violent actions against their children, or 'snapped'. Where women set boundaries to themselves, they recognised their potential for overstepping the mark and frequently considered themselves responsible for the problems.

This was the case with one young mother who felt it was her inconsistent parenting and overreaction which underlay the behavioural difficulties of her three-year-old. She was concerned about her own 'adult temper tantrums':

> ...like me smacking her. I have obviously reduced the smacking and shouting... You don't shout and scream at them, you deal with them in a calmer, different sort of way. So you look at your child and think 'OK, so just for ten minutes you are not gonna be my child,' try and deal with it that way.

> It's very hard to train yourself into thinking like that…'cos obviously you lose your temper with your own child more than anybody else's. And so basically I think it was more about training me than training my child.

On other occasions the boundary-setting involved not succumbing to the overbearing influence of others, drawing the line on their behaviour and on her submissiveness to it. One woman sought to resist the interference of her mother-in-law. Having received health advice from her health visitor, she refused to respond to her partner's mother when she asserted that it was wrong.

> And she was like, 'Oh, no you don't do that in my day, you've got to like feed them up, you know, and give them milk, they get angry otherwise.' I said 'No,' I said, 'this is what they told me to do.' She wouldn't have none of it… She just wouldn't listen at all. But I tried like, and I said to my health visitor, 'She's trying to take over,' and my health visitor came round to talk to her about it and she sat there going 'Oh, yeah, oh yeah.' And she'd gone out of the door, 'She don't know what she's talking about. I know, I've brought up two boys.' She didn't take any notice of her.

Suppressing competing activities

The final form of parent-oriented coping involved making sure, when under pressure, that the mother was not distracted by other concerns. This could be particularly important where the child care problems were experienced in the context of, at times, considerable adversity. Many of these mothers had multiple problems, and conservation of coping resources could mean ignoring other problems in order to deal with those which were most significant. This was exactly what was described by one mother. She decided that supporting her former husband could no longer be her priority.

> Em, things were really difficult. And so my physical and emotional wellbeing was severely depleted – that's where I had to go on the anti-depressants… So, my wellbeing was severely depleted, and consequently, em, I was not a stable influence on the children, em, I found them more an irritation than a joy, em, it obviously got worse as we were faced with the bailiffs coming, and knowing that we had nowhere to live… I begun to perhaps, tackle the main issues and concentrate, you know, and I did let go a lot of things, em, like whatever [former partner's] problems [alcohol] were at that point 'cos he'd already relapsed, I let him go, you know, he had to deal with that.

Summary and conclusion

1. Child-responsive strategies involved cognitive dimensions of assisting insight and understanding, and using direct physical and affect-related actions to provide a deep sense of care for the child.

2. Instrumental-oriented coping involved strategies designed to develop and maintain routines of behaviour and expectation which could contribute to a sense of security and reliability for the child.

3. *Protective commitment* was a concern for the protection of the child – avoiding placing them in dangerous situations, preventing the child from doing so, or dealing with the crisis which already presented danger to the child.

4. *Normalising* was an attempt to normalise family routines, particularly in ways the family would have operated had the crisis or problem not emerged. This was based on the idea that normal routines, adopted in abnormal situations, would help instil a sense of security.

5. *Cognitive-affective coping strategies* were designed to impact beneficially on the internal emotional or cognitive state of the child – to instil a sense of confidence, of being able to direct and control one's own life, or of being a valued individual.

6. *Proximising* entailed greater involvement with the child, with the aim of creating a greater closeness with them.

7. *Caring-affective nurturing* involved a range of actions by which the mother sought to reassure the child emotionally or instrumentally, or provide a structure enabling the child to feel more secure. This included physical care, emotional warmth and reassurance to the child.

8. *Encouragement through firmness* was undertaken by mothers who sought to develop competence and confidence in their children, but recognised that this could only be achieved by putting boundaries on what would otherwise be the child's chosen behaviour.

9.   With insight-oriented coping, the mother sought to facilitate understanding, either (on the part of the child) of her perspectives and reasoning, or (on her part) of the child's perspectives on the situation.

10.   *Parent-oriented coping* was a strategy by which the mother sought to undertake actions or processes which were oriented to herself, yet directly affected her interaction with the child. This included reflective consideration and planning, setting boundaries to herself, and suppressing competing activities.

CHAPTER 10

Emotion- and Self-focused Coping Strategies

It is well understood that crises and problems exert an emotional toll. The situations in which these women found themselves clearly caused great strain to them personally, as well as stress in their relations with their children (and others). The women, therefore, did not simply need to react (or not) to the problem, but needed also to react to themselves. They were acutely aware of the challenge these problems set them, both in dealing with their own emotions, and in considering their own capacities to deal with them.

There seem to have been two groups of self-focused coping strategies. The first was a group of strategies which were about avoidance, and separating themselves from the problems. These *avoidance strategies* included various forms of denial and disengagement. Denial involved women refusing to accept a problem, pretending it did not exist, or refusing to accept its seriousness. Disengagement involved women seeking to separate themselves from the problem or situation. This could occur physically, literally by taking themselves out from it, or mentally, where they sought not to focus on the problem or issue. It could also involve the use of alcohol or drugs.

The second group were coping strategies designed to help them better deal with the situations, or those they were likely to confront (*adjustment strategies*). Acceptance indicated that the women were prepared, or recognised the need, to come to terms with the situation, in particular that the situation was unlikely to change. Positive reinterpretation and growth involved drawing upon the situation, and the challenges it presented, to change the way they viewed such situations, and/or, as a result of their experiences, to develop as a person.

Denial and disengagement

Some women found the whole situation to be so stressful that they undertook avoidance strategies. One such strategy was *denial*. This is, in some respects, a difficult area to identify since, according to psychoanalytic theory, denial is a defence mechanism, of which people would themselves be unaware. It would follow that they would not be able to identify it during interviews (or at any other time). It might be possible to surmise some form of denial, from the degree of incongruity between different aspects of a woman's account of the situation (for example, when blaming an adolescent for 'rebellious behaviour', justifying a violent response, while also stating elsewhere that she was jealous of the young person's age, youth, looks and involvement with friends).

A wider notion of denial would enable women to identify their attempt to deny the occurrence of the stressful event, and to be consciously aware of it. This would involve some sort of recognition of dissonance between the experiences they were having and their recognition of these events. Even defined in this way, denial was very infrequently identified by these women, perhaps because doing so, particularly when blaming the child for the problems, would imply that they were not being truthful to themselves, and were guilty of placing the responsibility on the wrong shoulders. Not recognising denial would also be a guilt avoidance strategy for many of the women.

On the rare occasions that women recognised denial, it entailed somehow pretending to themselves that the event or situation had not happened. In one case the woman felt that she experienced serial repetition of the same, highly stressful, rebellious behaviour by her daughter, including unwarranted abuse, disobedience and staying out without permission (placing her, as far as the mother was concerned, at risk). In between these events, the woman pretended that they had not happened, as a means of reducing her own stress. A facet of these situations, exemplified by this woman, was the failure to be entirely 'taken in by themselves', so that, while they fantasised that nothing had occurred, at the back of their mind they did know the truth. This may have been part of a necessary 'self-preservation exercise'.

> So many times in my mind it hadn't happened at all. And I used to think to myself, 'Well hang on, it has happened and I was thinking it hasn't. Why have I got to go through all this again? And go through all this suffering and all these problems?' I didn't need it, but I ended up having it, because it felt to me

that it wasn't there, but it was, and I just didn't know what to do... I was at the end of my tether... And I just didn't know what to do with myself.

In another case, a woman whose daughter had died simply refused to accept this fact, and half expected her return. The pain of the event was affecting her relationship with others, and non-acceptance, even if a pretence, was a way of reducing the pain. Nevertheless, this led to descriptions of both accepting and never accepting the event:

> I will never accept it. Or I will accept it, but not fully, 'cos I can't. And even now it's still comes out, you know, but mmm, I suppose when [son] was about, I don't know, he was a little toddler, I suppo...you know, about from 18 months onwards, I started feeling better about [son] and myself. I suppose from back then. You know, I've lived with it and I do accept that I can't change that and it's got to stay like that.

Mental disengagement

A second area was mental disengagement. This was where the woman separated herself in her mind from the problems she was confronting. One type of mental disengagement could be termed *mental escape*. It was a form of 'escape' from the situation, without necessarily leaving it. Some of the disengagement was completely involuntary, a consequence of the extreme stress effects of the problems. This could be termed 'mental escape through negative involuntary disengagement', where the disengagement was, in a sense 'forced' and anything but pleasant. One woman commented on exactly this effect:

> ...he was having a lot of behavioural problems. I was particularly low at that point as well, I was on anti-depressants and just wandered around, already pregnant with the sixth child, which, you know, my marriage was on and off, but mostly off and, em, so I came in tough with social services at that point through my health visitor at the doctor's surgery, em, to see if there was anything they could do basically to give me some support.

Although she was able to seek some help, it was only after a period of disengagement related to stress, depression, and possibly anti-depressants.

The impact could also leave the woman incapable of responding to the problems, characterised by inaction. This was clearly the consequence of the stress, in this case leaving the woman overwhelmed when she went into bed and breakfast, having been evicted, with her children. Her state is clearer for her comparison with her children:

> Em, the first three or four days we were there I just dissolved and cried every time we walked in the room. I was just a bit of a mess. Em, and then I thought, 'This isn't going to get us any better if I just sit here crying about where we are.' The children obviously were more upset by me being upset, whereas…at the beginning…they just thought it was a great big adventure. I mean, they thought it was great, that we were all sleeping in the same room, and they could jump on everybody's bed, and that the trains rattled past the window every 20 minutes or so, and the whole room shook.

Some women disengaged in a more positive way, by focusing on the possibility of positive change – whether or not there was any evidence that such change was occurring. In these cases the women were essentially fantasising by imagining themselves in entirely different circumstances. This, then, could be termed 'mental escape by positive fantasising', as in the case of this woman, who said she was able to disengage by:

> Smoking (laughing). Smoking and thinking that things will get better, because I will be soon better. It will all take time. Just having a vision of the children. Like a happy sort of vision, like a dreamlike vision. It wasn't over the top, it wasn't a vision that it couldn't be. It's just like feeling happy.

A second form of mental disengagement was not just mental escape, but *mental disengagement through actions*. Here the women sought to distract themselves by immersing themselves in some other activity, or simply doing something else. One woman distracted herself by doing the housework, but this provided the basis for her also to think about other things – allowing her mind to wander:

> Ymmm, yeah, I find sometimes in some evenings if she's really bad, then all I would think about is, how I'm gonna deal with it. How I'm gonna…and I just find myself a distraction, I go and do the housework, think about something else or, you know. What I'm gonna do at work tomorrow, something to do with that. Just to take my mind off it.

The escape was, however, only temporary, and, even when seeking behavioural distraction, the women could see how negative the situation was: 'You sometimes give up. Nothing is fun. Sometimes you phone an acquaintance and that, stuff like that, just acting totally, not know what's happened, so have a quick call, "blaah, blaah, blaah, see you in a minute, how are you", acting normal.'

Women commented, however, that they could rarely completely mentally disengage from their problems, even when they sought to concentrate on other things. Here a woman, overwhelmed by the unexpected aggression, defiance and behavioural problems of her pre-teenage daughter, tried exactly that. The problems would seep through to consciousness, regardless.

> Think. Because we were under so much stress we tried not to think about it all the time… We knew but it was just so stressful at the time… We tried to do positive things with her like swimming, walking, watching movie… Buying a video maybe and trying to think of something else to think about, really. It's not always possible, but we are trying to think that aren't we?

However, the distractions were not always neutral or benign. The distraction itself, where linked with a means not only of mentally disengaging from the stressful situation, but also of enabling the woman to feel better, could lead to dysfunctional activities which created further problems, as was the case with this woman's use of 'retail therapy':

> And every little problem I've had. I mean I've gone so sad that I used to spend, I'm a shopaholic, right. I used to spend rent money and we got in trouble and all that… I thought if I buy [son] things it might make me feel good about him. It doesn't, of course it doesn't work like that, but I thought that. And I got in some quite serious debt problems and all that and we nearly lost the council house we were living in.

Behavioural disengagement

Behavioural disengagement in the form of giving up was in some respects not dissimilar to some elements of mental disengagement. It was designed to disengage the woman from the problem, and hence to enable her not to focus upon it, at least for a time. The situation could be so bad, at the extreme, that disengagement was seen by the women as permanent, because the problem was not worth the effort, or they no longer had the energy to deal with it. One woman, who felt she had a right to beat her children, but felt that to do so would bring her into conflict with the authorities, commented:

> I just give up. You give up in the end, 'cos you know that you like ain't gonna win, no matter what. 'Cos they know that. You can only take so much, you know, crap from them. So, I just go out, I just walk the dog, get out. Take the baby one with me, that's it. Let them get on with it.

Behavioural disengagement could also involve *giving in* to demands, a theme which emerged in various contexts. One woman, demoralised by the violence and abuse heaped on her by her children, disengaged from the 'fight' by seeking the 'quiet life'. When pressed for more money she gave it to them, even though this created more problems because she could not afford to do so:

> Yeah, I've stopped trying. I give up on it. I think it really is a waste of time 'cos they still gonna do it. So, I've just left it… They wanted more money to go to school and I give it to them, then I know that they will be at school. They won't eat their breakfast here, they want it in school, so it's gone from two pounds to £2.75 a day each. Then I'm thinking 'Uh, I've got no money, where's all my money gone?' Then I'm working it out and I'm thinking, well they are having £45 week off me, these three kids.

This urge to disengage could be so great that the women thought about disengaging themselves physically and permanently from the situation by *running away*. This was the case with one woman, following a violent altercation with her son, when she ended up bruised and bleeding. Despite the support of her adult daughter, who castigated him for his behaviour, she nevertheless wanted to get out. She was particularly appalled because she had suffered violence at the hands of his (estranged) father, and her son's behaviour 'brought it all back'.

> I wanted to run, I'd come to the point, I didn't know what it was but I think it was because of what his dad had done, and now I'd got it with this child, who was never been brought up with violence, but this child was starting to sound exactly like his real father. His biological father.

Rather more women saw themselves as '*taking time out*', generally, as with other forms of disengagement, in order to give themselves a break from the stress of their problems by removing themselves from the situation:

> And…I thought 'that's that', I just ended up…getting stressed and I ended up like, going away for a few days to give meself a break away from the house, which was good, I just couldn't stick it… I went up to Cheltenham to have a break from it all, but it hasn't to do, it was a little bit to do with [daughter] and

what she was doing to me, she was being stubborn and gone out of the window.

Some women disengaged from the situation by *taking drugs or alcohol*. With the latter, it was often a means of releasing tensions, taking a break, in which the act of drinking would divert them from their troubles. Drink was also a (classic) means of drowning their sorrows – drinking so much that they were no longer able to think straight (nor, hence, to think about their problems while they were drunk). One woman, in a state of indignation, decided to get drunk, justifying it to herself by reference to her daughter's penchant for inebriation:

> When she left last, I was so angry. I thought, if she can go out and get drunk, so can I (laughing). So, I went to the pub couple of times, had a few drinks, got drunk, not steaming, falling-down, crawling-home drunk, but I did have a drink. Who doesn't, when you've got worries, what do you do? They will go away for ten minutes.

Drugs could be similarly used, and some could be highly addictive. Again, they could be a means of 'forgetting sorrows', but the habit could also then take on a life of its own, the use of drugs in order to forget being added to a psychological and physical dependency which could lead to long-term use. Such was the case with one woman:

> Yeah, I was in, I took drugs and… yeah. I was trying to block things out. Because he was doing it as well I'd done it, but then it got to a habit. And then I couldn't cope if I didn't have them in, I got stressed. And basically trying to learn how to cope, 'cos I've had a lot of things happening to me at the moment. Trying to cope with what, that was the only way I could do it at the time.

Adjusting to the situation

Acceptance

Women could also undertake self-referential coping strategies which were less about denying or avoiding the problems, and more about adjusting to them. One response was for women to accept a situation, which implied that they were going to 'live with it', and could additionally imply that they were reconciled to it, perhaps even changing their attitude. This would happen where, for example, they had in the past been hostile to the child's behaviour, but were now prepared to accept it as legitimate, as when a mother felt that her teenage son or daughter was staying out too late, but then changed her mind. However, while women at times accepted that the situation could not be changed, they were rarely reconciled to it. Their acceptance was generally a hostile truce, or a matter of having no choice or alternative. Acceptance, in other words, was generally forced.

Acceptance, therefore could first involve being *resigned* to the situation (learning to live with it). This was the most frequently cited form of acceptance, a form in which the women stated that 'they could not do anything about it'. This sense of resignation comes through from one woman, whose relationship with her daughter was torrid, and where they periodically had heated and violent arguments. She was accepting the situation:

> Because of the fact that I knew I had to learn to live with it. Because I knew in the end, what else can I do… I mean, it's not gonna happen. But it's the thing that I had to learn to live with it in my head because it happened so many times… There's nothing else I can do about it… That's something that I'm gonna have for the rest of my life… Because she gets so agitated, like if she can't do something or she's got something on her mind. Rather than talk to me she blows it into an argument and then she's gone.

While this was a reflection on the behaviour of the child, such resignation could also relate to the situation. More than one woman, made homeless by her landlord, found that social and other services were prepared to do little, and that housing had to be the focus of her attention. In these circumstances, the woman had no alternative but to accept these constraints, although of course this did not mean that she accepted the problem itself. When, in the case of one woman, social services said they could do nothing, she said, 'I found [this] absolutely appalling.' On being told that she was not 'needy enough', she 'asked her exactly how much need she would be in, if she was in my predicament, em, which obviously met with a flat response as – "well, I'm not, basically" – so you have to get on with it, there's nothing we can do.'

Another approach was a form of *qualified acceptance*, where the women were prepared to accept the situation up to a point – reluctant, and not, by any means, totally – a strategy, often, for keeping the peace. This, again, reflected the theme of resignation and reluctance, but also a determination that this should not totally compromise what they saw as their integrity. This was the case with one woman who felt that her children were always trying to gain a position of power in relation to her, by threatening and arguing with her (they were largely pre-teenagers). She felt that she had the right to beat them severely, and she had been warned about it by social services. The result was a qualified acceptance, but a persistent hostility, as she really wanted the children accommodated.

> *Woman:* You learn to live with what you go through. If you don't, I think yeah, my life is a misery as it is, so I ain't getting a lot of kids like that put me down where he wants to put me... You know, I'm determined he's not gonna put me where he wants me to go...like you are here and you can think how you would make it different. But then you go into that plan and it never comes out. Something always goes wrong in the end. So, you just want to give up, give up completely.

> *Researcher:* Can you give an example of that?

> *Woman:* Putting them all away. Not just one, the lot. Then I know if I do that I've got a fight on me hands on me own. 'Cos one won't go into care at all, not at all.

A similar partial acceptance was evident in the case of one woman, who recognised the need to compromise with her 16-year-old daughter. She did not do so willingly, or because she thought the daughter had a valid point, but because it was the best way of gaining some uneasy truce, and reducing the degree of conflict.

> We compromised, that's what they call it. She goes out but she's got to tell me where she's going. She's got to phone me to let me know she's coming home or she's not coming home. And then I just got to learn to live with it. I got to sit here and worry for six or seven hours and accept it. You don't really accept it, but. You are sitting and waiting for that phone call, all night. Then she doesn't phone, too drunk.

Positive reinterpretation and personal growth

The most positive self-referential coping responses involved reframing the situation or the 'self' in a more optimistic way. This occurred with *positive reinterpretation* (which reframed the situation more positively) or *personal growth* (which reframed the experience more optimistically as contributing to the woman's personal development).

These responses occurred with some frequency. Positive reinterpretation could focus on the events in a situation, or the reframing of the situation itself, or the contribution the situation made to the woman's life. In one case, the woman began to realise that she had focused too strongly on her own position and views, and in so doing had not really taken into account the ways the children understood their situation. She had not listened to them, and was therefore now reframing the problem by bestowing more legitimacy on their views. Hence, while in the past the problem had been their behaviour, it was, while still remaining their behaviour, one also of communication and listening. The result was that she could see that their actions were at times *reactions* to her own failure to hear their position, and this meant that she could look more positively at the problem, and the prospects of resolving it. The outcome of this positive reinterpretation was, as far as she was concerned, a wholly more positive coping strategy: 'We can talk about the problem in a calm and reasonable way – which we try to do.'

Positive reinterpretation could emerge with the optimistic reframing of the situation or the way the situation contributed to the woman's personal development. This was the case with another woman: while recognising that she had been under severe pressure at the time of crisis (being threatened by a former partner, living in cramped conditions, feeling depressed and with two young children whom she found difficult to control), she nevertheless felt that the experience had made a positive contribution to her life. It was no longer simply negative, but something which could be considered to have strengthened her:

> Yeah, I believe that anything you do makes you stronger. It won't get rid of you being naive, 'cos everybody's naive to certain extent all the way through life, 'cos that's the way we are learning things. But yeah, I think what happens is that the more bad things that happen to you even though you shouldn't – the more you are learning, the more you can relate to other people and people's problems, if they've had a harder life themselves. And make you a stronger person. Makes you...sit down and think a little bit more about the situation rather than just go about screaming and shouting.

Such positive reinterpretation would also entail the recognition of some personal growth. Women generally recognised personal growth occurring in two ways: *self-oriented personal growth*, and child-oriented personal growth. Self-oriented growth was displayed by one woman, who felt that her own coping responses were inadequate. She recognised this, even while finding the situation difficult (coping with the unruly behaviour of her young daughter), realising that if she could control herself better, then she would be able to cope with her daughter better, and that her behaviour might improve.

> …temper management, that sort of thing, you know. Dealing with my own emotions. Learning that I'm not getting anywhere…by shouting and screaming, the only person I upset is myself. It doesn't bother her that I'm shouting and screaming, it's good for her, she's getting my attention. And so, learned a lot in, you know…making me a lot stronger and a lot more aware of my own emotions and problems now.

The same was the case with a woman who knew she had to draw on reserves of 'inner strength' to deal with the problem of her homelessness, and, with a choice between getting nowhere and acting, that the latter was the better course. In this she was helped by others. 'So I just pulled myself together, as I have the ability to do from some strength from somewhere, bless me, and, em, thought, no, you know, I've just got to sort this out.'

Child-oriented growth involved the development of better ways of caring for the children, or the mother's ability to assert herself as carer for the child against other people or influences. That was the case when one young woman finally left her partner, enabling her to care for the children in the way she felt to be best. This had other welcome side effects, such as giving up smoking (a more person-oriented focus for growth).

> I thought…this is the last time, I'm not going back, that's it now. I gonna like get on with my life and bring them up how I wanna bring them up, on my own, knowing that I couldn't have done it otherwise… Yeah, when I, when, when I was living with them I was like a chain smoker and I gave up. And like, thinking he's gonna grow up knowing that she really loves him and like, even though like she's doing everything for him, I don't know, I just didn't feel like it was good for him.

In another case, the woman resolved to involve herself more with her daughter, having partly blamed herself for not noticing carefully enough the way her life was going, leading to a situation where the daughter was seriously assaulted by one of her peers. The mother sought to pay more attention.

> Er, I listen to what they're saying and I ask more questions really, and I can be there more for them, not physically, you know, twenty-four hours a day, but, em, for her to know that she can talk to me, and I say, 'Oy, stop!' You know, I have got a problem, and I want to be there to be able to listen, and to listen to what she is saying, and try to understand it from her point of view, whatever.

Snapping

One area which was conspicuously neither about denial and disengagement nor acceptance and adjustment, but was more an emotion-fuelled immediate response to the situation, was 'snapping'. 'Snapping' is a good term, in that it indicates (a) that the mother's willingness to put up with the child has 'snapped' and (b) that her self-control has also snapped. In a sense, therefore, it might be considered less a coping mechanism, than one which indicates a lack of coping. However, it was clearly behaviour-oriented, in that the mother was not trying to persuade or understand the child, but was acting, often directly, on them, demonstrating to the child, perhaps in an extreme way, the unacceptability of their behaviour. At the same time, and more fundamentally, it was about the expression of emotions on the mother's part.

'Snapping' could involve a range of behaviours, but they generally came under the umbrella of verbally or physically aggressive behaviour by the mother. Very frequently, in the nature of such things, they were not premeditated, and came in the heat of the moment. One woman responded to the continuing abuse she had received, alongside her daughter, at the hands of her teenage son:

> ...and you get a load of verbal abuse, but this was my own child doing this to me and it was like, hang on a minute, and I think something inside me just snapped. I actually chased him and as I chased him out of the kitchen door, because he was bullying [daughter] as well, [daughter] has got special needs, she goes to special school, he was calling her, as we were arguing, she said, 'You shouldn't speak to Mum like that,' and he called her a dog, 'Shut up you, you dog, you don't shut your mouth, I punch your face in.' It was all abuse and 'you fat mong', that's how he was calling her. Now I draw the line at – he's not gonna do that to her...and I'm sorry but that wasn't going in my house.

An incident like this could, however, have long-lasting effects. Having 'snapped', the mother was frequently unlikely to alter her perception of the situation or her behaviour towards the child. Another case well illustrates this phenomenon of snapping, here with a 16-year-old with whom there had been constant arguments.

> And, that's one incident…right on bedtime. We are tired, we got to get up for work in the morning so we go to bed reasonably, sort of 11, half past. We'd got to bed, we said 'Right, if you want to watch a bit of telly bit later we don't mind as long as you get up to school in the morning.' And she'd come up to bed and finds the littlest excuse to come in the bedroom and annoy. Stand in the doorway, you know, with the light on.
>
> And this particular night she said her room was cold, she wanted the heater on. I said, 'The heater has been on in there for nearly half an hour, your room is not the chilliest room, just get off to bed.' And right off the top she'd say, 'Well, I'm effing cold, and if I'm cold you are not going to go to sleep, so I stand here until you put the heater on for me.' You know, and that was like stubbornness in her. And this particular is the night I hit her, because I got out and I just said, '[Daughter], I'm tired, go away, get into bed or whatever, keep your clothes on if you're cold, I don't care, just get out,' and she would not move. Then I just leapt, grabbed hold, hit her, pushed her out of the room. She was hysterical, I was hysterical… But you know, there were so many little incidences that built up to that difficulty. You know, 'cos we'd taken an awfully lot from her before I actually physically hit her.

Although this woman clearly recognised both the violence and the highly strung nature of the situation, she showed no regret about actions in circumstances about which she still felt considerable anger.

Summary and conclusion

1. These situations presented women with considerable strain for them personally. Part of their coping repertoire, therefore, was not just about managing the problem, but the emotions associated with the problems. This was emotion-focused coping.

2. There were two main groups of self-focused strategies. *Avoidance strategies* included denial and disengagement. *Adjustment strategies* involved some degree of acceptance of the situation, and positive reinterpretation and growth. A more immediate response, separate from these two, was 'snapping'.

3.   *Denial* could involve different types of response where, in denying some event, women sometimes recognised some dissonance between experiences they were having and recognition of these events.

4.   *Mental disengagement* was where the woman separated herself, in her mind, from the problems she was confronting. *Behavioural disengagement* involved undertaking behaviours which had the same effect. Amongst the behaviours identified were mental escape, mental disengagement, giving up/giving in, time out, and alcohol and drug use.

5.   *Acceptance* involved adjusting to the situation – implying that they were going to live with it. Women may have accepted, but were rarely reconciled to, the situation. Acceptance was generally a hostile truce, or a matter of having no alternative. It included being resigned to the situation, and qualified acceptance.

6.   *Positive reinterpretation and growth* involved reframing the situation or self in a more optimistic way. The situation could be viewed with more optimism, or personal growth could involve reframing matters more optimistically as a contributer to the woman's personal development. This included self-oriented and child-oriented growth.

7.   '*Snapping*' was an emotion-fuelled, immediate response to the situation. It indicated that the woman's self-control had snapped.

CHAPTER 11

Four Case Studies

The direct child care coping strategies of these women show a range of approaches which would be recognisable in families without such severe problems. There were extremes of coping behaviour, particularly, for example, when they descended into violence, and there were times when it is apparent that expectations of the child were rather greater than most would consider reasonable.

One is nevertheless left with the question: why should these problems emerge in this way? The perspectives of the women are apparent in their accounts of responsibility for the problems, which could lie with the women themselves, the environment or the children. They provide an indication of the discourse on child care problems explanation. It is not surprising to find, for example, that among mothers with teenagers, the teenager him- or herself was frequently identified as the problem, and this reflected the age-stage and egocentricity widely attributed to adolescents.

There is, furthermore, a certain degree of 'internal coherence' in the women's accounts: if they saw problems, especially behavioural ones, as resulting from the self-serving, sometimes aggressive behaviour of a teenager, then child-controlling coping strategies might appear defensible. However, as the women's perspectives, they offer only a particular view of the situation, and it may be that behavioural problems attributed (for example) to cussed and self-serving behaviour, result from perceptions of the mother as rejecting or failing to respond to the emotional needs of the child. That is not to say that women who blamed the child for behavioural difficulties were necessarily wrong, but that part of the difficulty could, at times, be a mismatch between the mother's perspectives and the child's needs. The coping strategies themselves may, at times, have contributed to the problems. This, of course, is given only as an example, and we might as easily find mothers whose anxieties made them see bigger problems than in fact existed.

Another issue, furthermore, is the sheer complexity of the individual situations. Although vital to an understanding of these situations, the separate analysis of problems, responsibility and coping strategies necessarily disaggregates the complex relationships between these areas which occur in individual cases. This is only to be understood through the examination of those individual cases. This chapter, therefore, will provide some case examples, seeking to identify different ways in which the dynamics of situations contributed to the emergence and sustaining of problems.

Case 1: overdose

One case involved the parenting of a young woman of 14, who lived with her mother and 16-year-old brother. They were estranged from the natural father, from whom the mother was divorced, and she did not have a current partner. The mother worked as an auxiliary nurse, and the family was not in receipt of state benefits. The referral was made by the daughter, who was described by social services as 'hysterical', asking to be removed from home, apparently because her mother was very restrictive about her going out. The referral was by telephone and there was an ongoing argument between mother and daughter providing the backdrop to the referral.

The mother described a number of elements in the situation. Her primary concern was for the vulnerability of her daughter, as a 14-year-old, particularly to the possibility of becoming pregnant, an image haunting her because of what she saw as her peers' behaviour.

> Like, I mean, if she gets pregnant... I don't want her to ruin her life. I was 25 when I had my first. But she doesn't have to be silly like the rest of her friends because they're all pregnant, all got babies, and they're only 14 or 15. It's no life, they've ruined their life, they can't go out and enjoy themselves. They've never had a job.

The mother also feared that the daughter could be assaulted, and she tried to keep in contact, which the daughter deliberately resisted. She commented that the girl could 'get molested, or bombed off or anything', and that 'She could always get picked up by anybody. I bought her a mobile phone only to keep it on her. She don't take it and she leaves it behind deliberately, and I'm ringing and in the next room I can hear it.' The result was that the mother sought to gain as much control as she could of her daughter's movement, which was, in turn, resisted by the daughter. The result was suspicion and an increasing use of child-controlling strategies. This started with restrictions.

> …she don't go out at all. I know she's only, she likes dancing, I know she's only dancing up there and I've seen the landlady and she says she don't drink up there. She said all she likes to do is dance but she's still only 14, …to be in a pub.

However it escalated further to something that sounded a little like imprisonment:

> I locked her in one day. It was last week, I locked the door so she couldn't get out, 'cos I didn't want her going to this pub. She's only 14. 'Cos the week before I let her go to this friend's engagement, a lot older than her, she went out and didn't get in until half past one, quarter to two, and I was worried. I sat up all night, she came in drunk. I wouldn't let her out the next day.

The woman became increasingly strident and aggressive, arguing that the best solution was violence. Revealingly, this led to a comment from her own mother (i.e. the maternal grandmother), which clearly, if implicitly, admonished her:

> What if I hammered them. I thought that's what they need, a good hammering. Strictness. And now it's all this Childline thing, you can't hit them, never did me no harm, did it?
>
> *Grandmother.* Your Dad wouldn't hit you…
>
> I don't think there's any discipline now even at school, they've got no discipline, they're out of control, they get away with it.

Behind this controlling strategy of the mother was, however, a serious breakdown of relations with her daughter, which the mother did not really acknowledge, and did nothing, in her coping strategies, to address. On the surface, this was a matter of trust, which the daughter felt she had been denied. The mother, in turn, felt that she had done nothing to earn it. The mother placed restrictions on the time her daughter could return home (9.00 p.m.), the result of which was that she could not go 'clubbing', and, according to the mother, said, 'You treat me like a baby, Mum'. The daughter, perhaps unsurprisingly, overstepped these boundaries, the effect of which was that the mother felt she had proof that the daughter was untrustworthy.

> ... she just says 'Trust me'. And I trusted her and she lets me down. She had her chance and she don't go out at all. I know she's only, she likes dancing, I know she's only dancing up there and I've seen the landlady and she says she don't drink up there. She said all she likes to do is dance but she's still only 14, she's not 15 till a couple of weeks, to be in a pub.

Behind this were more, arguably very much more, serious issues. This was a young woman in some emotional turmoil, which was, in some respects, recognised by the mother (who nevertheless did little to address this turmoil, except by seeking to use controlling strategies). This was most evident in self-harm.

> And one day she kept ringing all morning, I said [daughter], don't ring me no more, I don't want to know... And she went and took an overdose. Then the school phoned me up to say she took an overdose and they took her in an ambulance and I really panicked. And I really thought I never ever say no to her again. If she makes calls from school, she can come home from school. But [she's] trying to blackmail me now by staying in, and if I say no, she will say, 'Well, that's it, I'll take an overdose.'

Although alarmed by this, her primary perception was not of emotional distress, but of manipulation by her child. She commented twice, at different points in the interview, that the overdose, and threat of it, was used to blackmail her: 'I thought where she was blackmailing me all the time it got too much and I just give up. I thought, if she's gonna do it, she's gonna do it. And I ain't gonna stop her.'

Yet this was part of an emotional pattern which indicated that the self-harm episode was far more than a matter of manipulation (a convenient term which enabled the mother to justify, if only implicitly, her child-controlling strategies). The mother described this depressed and emotionally insecure teenager as a 'very depressed little girl':

> She just won't come out of herself and do good, she always thinks that she's not doing very well. How can I describe [daughter]? She's in herself all of the time, she'll never come out, she doesn't mix with anybody, she likes one person at school and now they've broke up and she's all on her own again. And then it's back to in herself again, she won't attempt to make friends...

> She's terrible. She's argumentative to her friends and she likes to buy them, she wanted them one-to-one and they didn't want that, they wanted other friends, but [daughter] couldn't get on with that.

Here we have a description a of a girl who lacks confidence to a point where it acts as a drag on her performance, who is insecure in both making and sustaining friendships, who is only comfortable with one-to-one friendships (possibly because she does not have the confidence to share friends), who argues with others, and is even prepared to use bribery ('buying them') to gain favour with her peers. Alongside this, she had an elder brother (16) who was beginning to be in serious trouble for offending behaviour. The mother was dismissive of her son: 'He wanted to go in the army. He don't go to school, nicking things. Goes up the garage with his friends – he'll just be nothing.' Her mother's dismissiveness was not reflected in the daughter, whose concern for her brother was a factor the mother considered was affecting her:

> Because she gets upset over him being picked up by the police all the time and she hears he's in trouble, but she worries about him, but they fight like cats and dogs, but she always worries about him. That's the only problem. I think she worries about him all the time, getting into trouble.

The mother also recounted events which might be expected to have a serious effect on her daughter. One in particular concerned comments the mother had made herself:

> I remember saying to her once, when she got upset, 'I didn't have to have you, I could have had an abortion,' but they told me I should have never said that to her... I don't think she's ever forgiven me for that. She said, 'You didn't want me,' if I didn't want you wouldn't be here now, but that's what she thinks. She's not a happy kid is she?

The daughter did not miss the underlying message of rejection, and comments like this, possibly easily made (for some), are liable to cause permanent damage to the relationship. Whereas the daughter needed unequivocal acceptance from her mother, a message (at the very least) of ambivalence was imparted. This, alongside the worry about her brother's offending behaviour, and the separation of her parents (which was alluded to but not commented on in any detail) provided a convincing backdrop to the behaviour of a girl tormented by self-doubt, unable to make stable relationships (and as a result perhaps still more desperate to go out 'clubbing'), and generally depressed.

In this context communication, both in content and affect, was far less than required to help the daughter. Attempts by the mother to engage her daughter when problems arose, were met with resistance. Throughout her troubles, the daughter was reluctant to engage with her mother.

> She didn't talk to me about and say, 'Mum, I'm really depressed, listen to me.' She didn't say anything like that. And she won't tell me about school, she's totally quiet about the school. I know she didn't like school, she just kept on saying there's nothing wrong, nothing wrong. She just didn't like school. She didn't say it was her friends or anything.

Fortunately for this young woman, she had a grandmother, but in engaging with her grandmother, she demonstrated the poverty of her relationship with her mother. 'She's got to have someone. She has got my mother, she always runs to her nan. She's got a problem, she'll talk to my mother, she won't come and talk to me about it.' This was a case where the mother was a little bewildered by her daughter's behaviour, but felt that much of it was an exaggerated form of teenage angst. Although she veered between concern and anger, it was, she thought, a stage through which her daughter was going.

This young woman was in a desperate state, lacking confidence, friends, the capacity to make relationships, and feeling serious concern for her brother. Her mother describes a young woman in emotional turmoil, yet her main response is to develop child-controlling strategies. Her concern is with keeping her daughter in, yet the girl's drive to go out may, at least in part, be connected with feelings of loneliness, and need for involvement. Feelings of rejection and experience of her parents' estrangement are quite likely to have contributed to the difficulties she has had in sustaining a relationship with her mother. This desperation, combined with her mother's inability to respond, perhaps, at the child-nurturing rather than child-controlling level, have left the young woman in serious emotional turmoil, and quite possibly with her life at risk from self-harm.

Case 2: the over-anxious worried mother

This case involved a young, single mother aged 19. She had one child, a son, aged three. She was not employed, and had no contact with her birth family. She was in receipt of state benefits. She had formerly had a drug habit, particularly taking amphetamines, but for about a year she had taken none. She had previously had a relationship with the father of the child, but she no longer saw him. This did not mean she was socially isolated, as she described herself as having a number of friends. The referral concerned possible sexual abuse of her son, but the information she had was vague, and she agreed (with the social worker) that it was likely that she had misinterpreted the statements of her son (from whom she received the information).

Her central concern was with the emotional wellbeing and behaviour of her son. She catalogued a range of behaviours, without, in general, managing to display much precision. This may have been because this was not the way she would normally expect to provide accounts, but it did make it difficult to pin down the extent of the problem. Her first statement about him betrayed both her concern, and also some awareness that it might be inappropriate. The problem, she said, was:

> Controlling him, because he's a brat (laughing). He is three years old, you know, but he's just, he thinks if he screams long enough then he gets he's own way, which most three-year-olds do think like that. But he's just like ridiculous, every little thing he's got to scream his head off.

The statement indicated that she found him a problem – that he had a problem – yet his behaviour was not that dissimilar to that of other children of the same age. She commented later that 'every three-year-old that I know – well, not everyone – but they scream to get their own way, yeah? but their parents think they've got kids with behavioural problems.'

It was, however, difficult for the interviewer to obtain more detail. When asked if she had any specific examples of his behaviour, the woman said, 'No, not really, it's just everything.' This may, of course, have reflected the routine and overwhelming nature of the problems, but she did not describe, as she herself knew, behaviours that appeared greatly out of the ordinary.

This was evident from another issue which involved the question of bedtime. Like many women, she relied on her health visitor for advice.

> I think the other thing is getting him settled in his bed. He's been sleeping with me, but I'd like to ask how to get him back in his own bed, but I'm gonna see the health visitor this week and ask. If she told me to let him scream his head off in his bed, then I'll do, but I won't do it before I've been told to do it.

Nevertheless, she was very worried about his future. She said she was concerned that he would 'become a bastard', citing his play with another little boy as evidence.

> …he became a bastard, and then they were bastards together, and it was a nightmare, do you know what I mean? They would just deliberately do naughty things.

This theme of focusing on the future led to some apparently odd statements. In particular she was concerned that the behaviour he manifested as a three-year-old would be maintained, extended and worsened as he became older. This concern existed oddly alongside the earlier recognition that some, at least, of his behaviour, was not unusual in three-year-olds.

> Yeah, he's just got to learn a lesson, he's got to realise he's got to stop it, because there's just no way he's gonna get through life screaming his head off all the time, it's just not gonna happen. He's got to realise it… No, no, you know, he's good, but when he gets in his head, don't it, he's on one, it's just unbelievable.

This theme of putting together his three-year-old status with future adulthood was evident elsewhere in her account, when she commented, again rather oddly, that, 'if he wants to be treated like an adult, he has to start acting like one, and if I say, "No, you can't do that", then he has to understand that and respect it.' This suggestion that he might want to be treated as an adult may be appropriate in relation to a teenager, but is rather incongruous with a three-year-old.

Of course, this was a young mother, who gave birth at 16, and had little familial support, and this helps our understanding of her situation. Indeed, the child's behaviour may well have been an exaggerated version of that of many three-year-olds. This mother's behaviour, however, seems to have reflected, on the one hand, a plausible understanding of why there might be exaggerated behaviour, yet at the same time, a degree of anxiety, which might have helped contribute to the problems. This young woman was wracked by feelings of guilt about the effect of drug use on her parenting. She described this period, which lasted a few months:

> That's because of me, because of the amphetamine use and I'd like to say I feel really, really, really guilty for it. It's like I would say I'm a good mother, I've always been a good mother, no doubt about it, yeah, but when I split up with

my partner, me and my next door neighbour were really on to have the amphetamine... We'd give them [their children] all their meals and always clothed and bathed them and looked after them in that respect, but we didn't always give them much attention. We just let them get on with it some of the time. And I feel really guilty, I've cried a lot over this.

It was, of course, likely that this had an effect on her son. At the same time, her own description indicates an attentiveness, even during that period, greater than that of many parents involved with social services. However, the guilt she felt engendered a negativity which, she recognised, impacted on both her perceptions of the situation, and her own mental health status:

And I'm on anti-depressants as well 'cos I'm depressed quite a lot. I see everything in a negative light, I now need to be more positive, I got to. I think everything is crap about me, my home, my life, the way I am. Everything obviously is crap all the time and I got to stop it because I'm not gonna get through this like that.

The implication of this, of course, was that she saw her son's behaviour (and her own), as with other things, in a negative light. Much of her account involved reflections on herself and her feelings. Referring to her star sign, she displayed an expectation of high standards, or improvement in standards, which seems to have contributed to her harsh judgement of herself:

'Cos I'm always constantly, one thing about me, I'm a Virgo right, I'm always constantly on about self-improvement. I mean, that's personal and like motherly and flat and like job and everything in my life. I want to improve all the time, that's all I ever think about but I wouldn't, that's it, I would think [son] is screaming all the time so that was constantly in my head, how I'm gonna deal with him in that state.

With this pressure, at least in part put on herself, she feared for her mental state, commenting that she was scared: 'I will crack up, you've got to have your own life or you will lose the plot.' She was also concerned that her depression would affect her son. Her reflection on her parenting reflected this general anxiety. She was, it appears, very aware of any possible shortcomings. One of them was inconsistency:

I still can't stick to myself, one minute I'll be like, he screaming and I give in and then the next minute I won't give in. So, like I'm still, like keeping that nightmare there. I got to be strong about it all. But I do give in too easy, me.

Another involved the need to adopt an approach of extinction to his tantrums:

> I got to ignore him, but I don't I spend all time trying to talk to him going like, 'Don't do that [son], going like blaah, blaah, blaah'. And then he's not listening to you, but you're listening to him, type of thing, and he knows it. So if you don't just listen to him, it will all stop. So I got to sort it out.

Yet in the next breath she suggested she needed entirely the opposite approach:

> I'm giving him attention, I tell him I love him and I'm always listening to him, and that I'm always here for him and that I'm looking after him. I let no one hurt him or, do you know what I mean, so he can like feel safe again, he's secured, you know what I mean. But I got to build his trust again, 'cos you know, I took it away, I took all his stability away like in a matter of a week... I hate myself, I ruined everything.

The exaggerated concern is clearly present here, in that she considered she caused all this instability, or a good part of it, within one week. Again, however, she was expressing feelings of guilt and self hate, alongside her depression.

She was, however, also aware that her perceptions were slightly absurd, if viewed from the standpoint of an independent onlooker. The social worker had none of the concerns about her son, or her care of him, that she herself displayed, and told the mother that she had lost her confidence. She also emphasised the significance of age and stage, and that her son's behaviour was not, as yet, so out of the ordinary.

> ...the woman...said that he was fine. She said that he was fine, he was a happy kid. But she said like I got to realise that a lot of the things is just a stage of a three-year-old, I got to realise that, you know what I mean. I can't be so paranoid and pick up on every little thing and blame it all on me, because it's not happening, you know what I mean.

She went on to reflect on herself: 'He is a three-year-old boy at the end of the day, and I'm just a paranoid mother.'

Despite this, she felt her son had taken a very dim view of her. She commented that he felt unsettled and insecure, 'he thinks I've been a selfish bitch, which I have'. She felt he would say, if he could, that 'mummy lost the plot for a while, do you know what I mean? He's angry with me... I think he thinks I've been a bitch really'.

The main theme of this young woman's account, then, was her high degree of guilt and self-criticism, and her sense that she had neglected her son. While this may well have had an effect, her feelings and perceptions were themselves really negative and raised her anxieties. She seemed unable to comprehend what she knew to be the case: that her child's behaviour had much to do with his age and stage. The result was that she was constantly on edge about his behaviour, and constantly worried about her own. This was related to tentativeness and inconsistency in her parenting, which itself could well be expected to have an impact on her son. The risks to his behaviour and development, in other words, could be at least as much owing to her anxieties as to any past experiences he might have had.

Case 3: the rejected, violent son

There were a number of cases where there was at least some evidence that teenage daughters were presenting behavioural problems which were related to the parenting, but where the mother had not recognised her own contribution. This was less evident with teenage boys. Although there was a considerable amount of behavioural disorder, often including violent behaviour – sometimes extreme – this was generally seen to be the result of clearly recognised rejection on the part of mother or father, the influence of peer group, or Attention Deficit Hyperactivity Disorder (ADHD). It was less clear how the coping process might have contributed to the problems. In the case of ADHD, however, much depended on the accuracy of the diagnosis. In some cases it was difficult to distinguish between the behaviours described as indicators of ADHD and those which might simply be defined as severe behavioural problems. In these circumstances ADHD could be a convenient term which meant there was no need to look more closely at the parental contribution to the problems.

One woman's account gave good reason for thinking that, at the least, parenting behaviour would have contributed – if not solely – to a deteriorating situation. Her son was 15. He was part of a family with six children who lived with his mother and stepfather. Three of the children were full siblings, and he had a half-brother and -sister who were the children of his mother and stepfather. His natural father lived separately, and had remarried. He lived with two of his full siblings.

The son had been given a diagnosis of ADHD and prescribed Ritalin. However, the medication was ineffective, and there was little in the account which indicated attention deficits or hyperactivity. There was, however, clear evidence of behavioural difficulties. He displayed considerable aggression within the family home. His general attitude around the home was summed up by his mother. Referring to the range of problems he presented, she said:

> It's all of them. It's really difficult. If he can't get what he wants he gets really nasty and starts punching, swearing and he gets really mouthy. Or else he starts getting aggressive and I can't handle it.

She was worried about the effects of his behaviour, as an example, on other, younger, children in the family. One son (aged ten) was described as 'mentally impaired', and was particularly vulnerable to this:

> …he thinks that's the way it's got to be, like, because he's copying what [son's] doing and when I tell him off he'll have tantrums and he'll punch the doors, but he's going to a special school that can help him, but it's not helping him while [son's] doing it. Because [brother] will do exactly the same thing as [son's] doing, but I keep telling [son], at the end of the day what he's doing is gonna rub off on [brother].

His behaviour was, she felt, becoming so extreme that he ran the risk of imprisonment. He had a tendency to violence in response to mild provocation, and she felt there was little time to remedy this:

> Violence. Violence and beating the kids. He can't have what he wants then he'll take it all out on the kids… What I'm afraid of is that he's gonna start doing because he can't get what he wants from the other kids and I don't want that to happen…he's 15, but he's 16 next May, but I need to actually get him on the straight and narrow before he leaves school, and I don't want to see him being put in prison or anything like that.

However, the mother recognised that he was full of anger, and that this lay at the heart of his behaviour. She commented that he was 'out of control, and I just can't handle him'. There was a need 'to sort out his anger and thumping basically, whatever'. While this behaviour could occur outside his family, it was perhaps revealing that it was primarily directed at members of his 'lived with' family. The mother and stepfather (who was also present) gave various examples of the nature and direction of his behaviour. His attitude and language towards his mother was dreadful: 'He's been calling me a cow and a slag, every name under the sun…that's not the way to talk to anybody.' He also showed contempt for his stepfather:

Husband: He'll swear and curse at me, and his vocabulary is bad, he puts his fists through the doors. I've just finished plastering his bedroom, and he pushed his fists in the walls, straight through. That's what you get.

It was, he felt, almost as if he wanted to attack his stepfather by these actions. His behaviour towards his young stepbrother and stepsister (both under five) was, according to his mother, if anything even worse. At any time they tried to place boundaries on his behaviour, he could become very aggressive:

Bloody hell, comes out here, slams the doors, kicks the doors, slams plates and then starts beating on the kids. I say 'You're not doing that'. 'Well they shouldn't be in my way'. 'Well you don't do that'. When I tell him that he starts racing upstairs. He goes upstairs and there's banging. And he's up there banging, playing his music.

The boy's aggression towards his family, particularly his stepfamily, provides some indication of the direction of his anger. There was a strong sense running through the account, of his reacting to experiences of rejection in the past as a result of the separation of his natural parents, and of feeling an 'outsider' in the new familial arrangements, particularly after his half-brother and -sister were born. There was little evidence of affection from him towards them, but good grounds for thinking there was some jealousy.

At the heart of this seems to have been the divorce of his parents, together with his mother's subsequent remarriage, and the birth of younger half-siblings. The situation was not very satisfactory, with each parent being given custody (at that time) of three of their six children. This was a traumatic separation, with considerable acrimony between both parents, which occurred when he was six years old. The original decision about his residence, his mother felt, was wrong:

But we went through a separation like, and then it was a court decision that three went to live with him and three lived with me like. So he had [son], where I should have kept [son], but it's gone the other way round like, he's gone down there.

Although she felt this was an unsatisfactory decision in relation to her son, she did not discuss the possible effects of splitting up the children in this way, particularly the ways they might have felt about it, and there was no evidence that she connected this with his current behaviour. She did, however, note the difference between his behaviour now compared with when he was younger:

'Where he was a polite kid and said "thank you" and "may I have this", and "may I have that", it's just gone all wrong.'

He suffered from a further destabilising situation when he was 'transferred' from residence with his father to residence with his mother:

> He was living with his dad until five years ago and was brought back up here to get him settle down there like, and he's been fine for a while, but it's just gone wrong and he doesn't, he doesn't accept, if he wants it he will do it, no matter who's in his way he will do it.

Having returned to his mother, he did not find that she was his only parent, to be shared with his sibs, but that she was married to someone who was now his stepfather. His stepfather clearly showed that he expected to be able to behave as if he were the boy's natural father, with full parental control, claiming the right to discipline him, and direct his progress in the manner expected of a natural father. There was no evidence, in the woman's account, that the way her son may have seen his stepfather's role had been discussed. He was thus confronted with a situation where his natural father did not want him, but his stepfather claimed 'normal' parental rights, without his being able to influence these 'claimed rights' at all. On top of this, of course, two half-siblings were subsequently born of both parents, while only his mother was his own natural parent in his family home. The scope for jealousy was great, and his behaviour towards stepfather and half-siblings is consistent with this.

The coping strategies used tended to be confrontational or undermining, rather than responsive to his behaviour. Although his rejection by his father was not his mother's fault, her position as messenger may itself have contributed to his sense of rejection.

> I said, 'Look, [son], your dad don't want to know.' Because he wants to go down for weekends or holidays, they [his father and his wife] won't let him have them down there. I've said, 'At the end of the day you've got to realise that your dad don't want you.'

His mother felt she was very much under attack, and that she had to defend herself from him. In doing this, however, she effectively labelled him as 'bad', plausibly contributing to a further sense of rejection. She commented that 'there is no way he is going to bring me down to his character. I'm not gonna go as low as he is. So I'm rising above it to be honest and telling him that he's not going to get to me as much as he thinks he is.' Yet there were times when her response, perhaps understandably, contributed to the downward spiral of relationships and behaviour, as things simply got too much for her. It simply served to fuel his defiance.

> Couple of months ago we had a really, really big argument and I just let loose on him. I mean, I really hit him, and I hit him and hit him and he just got up and he laughed at me, and he said, 'That didn't hurt.' But it hurt me, 'cos I'd never ever hit kids, but he just got me so really angry that day I just blew and my husband pulled me off him… I mean he can stand there and call me a bitch, cow.

They had sought to use many of the milder control strategies identified earlier, such as 'grounding' or depriving him of pocket money, but these, too seemed to have no effect. Indeed, while there were clear efforts to talk to him, without a clearly thought out understanding of the link between rejection, jealousy and aggression they were unable to do this effectively. They were left to respond to him primarily with child-controlling strategies, which simply served to escalate the trouble. In the end they were left with nothing but a strategy of rejection, which, in the apparent preference given to the younger half-siblings, could do little to reverse the deterioration. They made it clear that they could not wait until he left and that they did not expect him to return:

> We said, 'You know, when you move out we'll be doing your bedroom for one of the little kids.' 'Oh no, they're not having that bloody room,' and we said, 'Look, if you're not here then they can have that room.' 'Oh no, I want that when I come back.' 'You're not coming back. Once you've moved out you're out' (laughs). And he wouldn't accept it. 'I can come back whenever I want to.' 'No you can't. When you're 17, 18 and you've got your own place, like, you know, you're not coming back.' 'Oh, what if something goes wrong?' 'Something goes wrong, you've got to sort it. You know, if you make your bed, you lie in it.'

It is easy to sympathise with the position of this mother, whose tolerance had been tested to the limit. We should recognise that this was an aggressive, at times violent, young man, who could have tested the most sensitive and responsive parent. It would also be wrong to assume that his mother did not retain a deep affection for him. Yet at the same time she struggled to understand the pain that this young man may have felt, because it was expressed in such an aggressive manner. His sense of jealousy and rejection, it would appear, was very deep rooted, but was not really recognised by his mother (or stepfather). The result was a coping strategy which, by emphasising the controlling aspects of child care, became increasingly conflictual, as her son seems to have felt more and more alienated. The coping strategy itself served, if anything, to underline his sense of rejection, with severe criticism, violence and an obvious desire to 'get rid of him'.

Case 4: the bewildered mother

On some occasions the women's accounts indicated that the parenting task represented a challenge for which they had insufficient personal resources. This was the case with one mother, about whom the researcher formulated the view that she might suffer mild learning difficulties. For her, it was difficult to understand and interpret her children's behaviour, or to respond to them in any flexible or imaginative way. She was bewildered and very depressed. This woman was married with three children – a girl and two boys – aged between 10 and 13. She had an extended family nearby, which she used for support. Her situation was, however, fraught.

The children were largely beyond her control. They were headstrong, her wishes were largely ignored, and she found she did what they wanted just to keep them happy. However, this situation simply left her enormously frustrated.

> They don't do what I say. They try telling me. If they wanna go out they just open the door and go… And their language is disgusting, but they do it when their dad is not around. When their dad is around they are good. When I've got them on my own they tell me, they tell me what they can have for tea, they tell me how much money they need, so I do it for them just to keep them to shut up. This morning Amelia said, 'I need a pound for school or I'm not going.' So, when she was gone I asked what she was like in school, she a completely different child. So, when it's here they are fighting, they are arguing, they are swearing and I just can't control. I just go upstairs and leave them. 'Cos I said to my husband, I said to him, 'I will kill them.'

They were also aggressive and highly competitive with each other, but she felt powerless to control that: 'they just fight among each other, who's got what, and how much they get. Then one's got more than the other one, then they go fighting for it.' She felt a failure with the children, who, she felt, showed her up in front of other people. The criticism of the children led to suggestions that they should be 'put in a home', comments which the mother took to heart as reflecting on her parenting.

> Or if I've got friends here, they try to show me up... And many times they've said, 'If they were my kids I would have them put away.' And I said no, I wouldn't have them put away. I can't have them took off me. Then they say, 'Well, then you got to learn to live with that and do something about it.' But many times my family has walked in, they've listened and they've spoken to me and they have shouted at them. And then they shut up until they've gone and then they start again.

Another feature was the constant demand for money, which she could ill afford to give, and yet gave to keep them quiet. However, she kept this from her husband, 'and then [husband] is saying, "Where's all the money?" and I'm saying, "the kids, the school". I won't tell him how much, he will put a stop to it.'

Her coping strategy, then, in part, involved 'giving in' to their demands, which, in turn, can be expected to fuel further demanding behaviour. At other times she sought to exert a controlling strategy. However, she was largely ignored: 'I say, "Right, you are grounded," they just go out the door and say, "We are not grounded, you don't tell me".' Her general experience, when she tried to exercise control, was total lack of it:

> I try to keep them in and they just go out of the door again, like [son] came up to me and I said, 'You are grounded' from the night before, he said, 'No, I'm effing ain't.' And out he goes, he wouldn't even change his uniform. And I'm calling him and calling him and there's no answer from him. Then he comes strolling in at seven o'clock.

The number of children presented a problem in itself. While she might be able to cope with one – indeed, she commented that they could be very compliant on their own – the three of them together seemed to bring out the worst in them. When this happened, she tried to deal with them individually, but in the process she would give the impression to the other children, of giving one preferential treatment:

> It's all arguing amongst each other. To solve the problem I say, 'Wait until these two have gone out and I give it to you.' But then when I've given it to her, she's tell them that I give it to her. Then they'll cause a big riot in here. They go stumping up and down the stairs, throw all the cushions across the floor, that's gone down more than once (pointing to the table).

Whatever she tried, she seemed unable to exert control, partly, no doubt, because of the inconsistency she showed, on some occasions giving in to demands, and on others resisting them. The children seem to have learned that they stood a better chance of getting their own way if they behaved in an ever increasingly poor manner. As a result she increasingly resorted to a violent response, describing, like some other mothers, the need to 'hammer' her children.

> And I won't give in to them. They start, well they do start a riot in here... Yes, I do hit my kids. I [think I have] nothing to hide as I going to, I'm honest, yes, I do hit them... I try to control them...but they just fight amongst each other.

Of course, the violent response also provides a model of violent behaviour for the children.

At the heart of the problems, however, was one particular child, her daughter, aged ten (the youngest of the three). She was described as aggressive and attention-seeking, and the most disruptive of the three. The mother's understanding of the child, and her response to her, was very revealing. Her daughter had multiple problems:

> [Daughter] will start in front of him, she will play me and him against each other and we two end up having a row. He's going to smack and I say 'Don't hit her'. Then she just laughs behind his back. She is the worst one I've got because she wets her bed every night. I mean she's got no bed because...because she's peed it so much.

There was little sympathy or understanding voiced for the daughter, merely an implicit reprimand for her eneuresis (alongside her manipulative behaviour). This became more explicit later, when the mother commented that 'she only sleeps in the boxroom and it is really smelly. I said I'm not letting people in my house and smelling this'. There was little appreciation of this girl's vulnerability, even though she demonstrated it in a number of ways. She showed herself to be highly insecure. If her mother tried to go out '[daughter] is blocking the door and screams, shouts... I don't have the right to go out'. Likewise, she had problems sleeping on her own, which were, however, interpreted as wilful behaviour:

> And she won't go to sleep until about 12 'cos she's staying up in her window, watching. Or she's got to go to my bed to sleep first. I let her go to my bed first, wait till she's asleep and carry her into her room.

This, however, was a disturbed and distressed little girl. The mother recognised that earlier abuse had probably had an impact, but she lacked an understanding of the child's needs arising from this. Despite this recognition (and without true realisation of the implications) the mother felt that she was being treated in a way she did not deserve:

> …she was, the fact that she was sexually abused when she was five years old, and I think that's what has turned her really nasty. I've said it to her many times, 'You are not my little girl I used to have.' 'Don't effing blame me, blame him.' The man that interfered with her.

The bedwetting, aggressiveness, disobedience, and signs of insecurity are all consistent with this abuse, but added to it was the bewildered inability of the mother to respond in a way that gave the child the nurturing she needed. Indeed, the damaging effect of this combination was already, at the age of ten, emerging in terms of an eating disorder:

> …food all the time. [She] eats from the time [she] come in to the time they go to bed. And people are calling 'fatty' and they don't like it…she is bigger built than me… And I told her she is, I said, 'You are fat.' She said, 'You wanna look at yourself then.' I said, '[Daughter], I'm a size 10, you are going into 12 and you are only a ten-year-old little girl and you are fat', and she didn't like it (laughing). [She's] got to stop, they are called names and [she] don't like it.

The consequences of eating this way were criticism from her mother and goading by peers. This girl was rebellious, but living in an emotionally impoverished world, in which her behaviours increasingly encouraged rejecting behaviour by others. This was a very sad, negative situation.

Her mother seemed unaware of the extent to which her (and others') behaviour might be damaging her daughter, bewildered by the challenges set before her, and had a sense of failure as a parent. She was very depressed, and simply did not know what to do. Her understanding of the issue as one of control rather than nurturance led her in completely the wrong direction, and bereft of solutions. Her family and others were generally more successful in getting control of the children, which fuelled her sense of failure. Her controlling actions could become quite extreme. She feared serious physical violence, 'because in a minute I'm going to end up really damaging one of them by belting them and belting them'. On other occasions she felt that threatening suicide was effective:

> Many times I've threatened to take an overdose because I just can't control them. You know, they say to me, 'Yeah, you are thick, you can't read, you can't spell, we got a thick mum'.

Her personal hurt was very deep, as was her depression. This was a very sad situation, which was likely to continue and worsen. She thought a great deal about death, and wished herself to die. This was expressed in terms of her dead mother:

> Yeah, I prayed for my mum to come and get me. That's how much I've got, because I just don't want to be with them. Because the way they are. My husband says, 'Oh, you are praying for your mother to come and get you.' I just can't, I say 'yeah'. He says, 'What do you mean?' I say I just don't like living in the street.

Conclusion

These case studies are instructive, containing as they do both common and divergent themes. The key for our understanding is their capacity to bring together themes which we have earlier considered separately. In all four cases there was a problem in the way the mothers 'framed' the situation. On the basis of their own accounts, their framing of problems could be partial, lacking awareness of some of the implications of what they were saying; or their response, even when they showed greater awareness of the situation, suggested they had not appreciated, or were unable to appreciate, the implications for parenting. As a result it seems likely that the direct coping actions of the mother (and, where present, the partner) actually contributed to the problem. Even when the children were designated as the problem, there were times when the mothers seem to have had a 'blind spot' in relation to understanding their own part in the process.

In one case – of an anxious mother – this framing seems to have involved an exaggerated negativity about her son's behaviour, combined with severe guilt about past 'neglect' on her part, which together made her both very concerned about her son's future, and desperate to 'put things right'. She saw his tantrums as the result of her neglect, and veered between feeling the need to be fully responsive to the child and operating a policy of extinction. Her inconsistency, fuelled by her guilt and depression, cannot have helped create a basis for stabilising her son's behaviour, so that a large part of the problem, as the social worker observed, seems to have been her own anxieties.

The other three cases were similar in placing a crucial emphasis on the pre-dominance of child-controlling coping strategies, where there was strong evidence that a greater emphasis on child-responsive strategies would have been appropriate. In one case – Case 3, the rejected, violent son – it may be that matters had gone too far. There was little sign that the mother had at any stage understood the emergence of his aggressive behaviour as an indication of distress, yet there were good reasons for this: divorce, sibling separation, de-construction and reformulating of the family, being faced with an entirely new, reconstructed family, with 'rival' half-siblings. The mother understood that he was angry, but seems not to have connected this with a strategy which involved recognition of the likely cause of the anger, or a mode of parenting which was sympathetic towards her son in the repeated trauma he had suffered.

The emphasis on a child-controlling strategy, alongside a high level of distress, was also evident in both Case 1 and Case 4. In Case 1, there was clear recognition of distress – the mother commented that her daughter was depressed – yet the mother nevertheless operated a child-controlling strategy. Of course, we may sympathise with fears about pregnancy, and the daughter's age for going out, but this, when viewed holistically, was part of a pattern which involved distress and difficulty and tentativeness in her peer relationships. The mother's emphasis on control had alienated her daughter sufficiently to make it difficult to adopt child-responsive coping strategies. At the same time, actions displaying distress were seen as manipulative.

Case 4 was, if anything, even more desperately sad. This is a family about whom there could be severe concerns for the future. The mother was clearly totally out of her depth in attempting to cope with her children. Her responses again emphasised controlling strategies, which, partly because they were incon-sistent, did not work. Her daughter, sexually abused, anxious, and showing her extreme distress somatically, was defined as a problem, to be managed, like the others, by child-controlling strategies. The mother, meanwhile, suffered herself, with self-esteem shattered by her manifest failure in parenting, a wish to die and 'join her mother', and in a state of clinical depression. There was little sense that this situation would improve, and the future looked bleak, particularly for the mother and daughter.

In all these cases, there seem to have been disjunctions between the needs of the child and coping strategies, apparently indicating that the coping strategies were themselves contributing to the emergence of the problems. These were not the only cases where such disjunctions could be identified, but they do serve as examples of the ways in which parents, without necessarily intending so to do, can contribute directly to the emergence and exacerbation of child problems, through their coping strategies.

PART IV

Using Social Support

CHAPTER 12

Informal Support

Social support is usually discussed as if it is provided ('the provision of social support'). For example, the literature on family support in relation to child care focuses exactly on its provision. However, the principle that has been at the heart of this research is that the mother is an active agent, and support is, at least potentially, part of her coping repertoire, i.e. she can solicit support in order to cope better with problems. Of course, this, in turn, depends upon the availability of support, and from the point of view of coping strategy, emerge two dimensions of support: the nature and availability of support, and the way in which women wish to use it.

There is a range of ways in which support can be offered or utilised. Seventy per cent of women, for example, felt they needed quite a bit of advice, and over half felt they would have benefited from a lot more advice than they received. Likewise, only a quarter of women felt they needed no help with children, while over half felt they needed quite a bit of help. Under half, however (43/102), felt that the help they received with children was adequate. Even more women felt they needed quite a bit of support with their private feelings, yet only 46 (of 102) considered this help to be adequate. Indeed, 39 women felt they needed a lot more opportunities to talk about their private feelings, than they actually had.

No, or little, support

It is quite apparent from these data that women frequently struggled to obtain the kind of support they felt they needed. This is apparent from women's own accounts. Some women were at a loss to describe anyone to whom they could turn for help, and this meant a high degree of reliance on themselves. Women commented that they had no one to turn to when they needed advice or emotional support, and that this, in particular, made it difficult to attain a kind of psychological robustness when facing the problems of child care. Even if they had a partner, they could feel they had no help. One woman commented that, despite having a partner, 'I have to cope with it all on my own'. Not just the children, but the decorating, the gardening and the cleaning: 'I does it all meself.'

Other types of support could equally be unavailable for women, who sometimes felt isolated or lonely. One woman with two children, aged two and six, had experienced a series of losses: her mother had died of Huntington's disease, her mother-in-law had died of cancer, and her partner (not the father of her children) had recently left her. She felt desperate, with no one to whom she could turn. She tried the children's natural father, but he was not interested, and after a brief period of help they were returned to their mother:

> It was, you know, it was hard, it was hard, even though [partner] was with me. But when he left I just thought, 'Oh my god, I've got nothing.' To deal with three, you know, three deaths basically, so the children went with their father I think it was about a week, and then the second week he was bringing them back to me you know, they were still coming here and I couldn't say anything… You know, I'm a very strong person but I'm just losing it with the kids.

Women also identified an absence of substantial areas of support, without being entirely bereft of support. This could leave them feeling, to all intents and purposes, pretty well as isolated and pressured as those who had no support at all. This was the case for one woman whose 13-year-old daughter was engaging in self-harming behaviour. She felt the isolation of her family. She felt that there was no one to provide advice or emotional support, to which her partner (who was present) ironically said, 'Thanks'. She commented, 'I've already said I mean outside the house'.

One aspect of social network that is particularly significant is conflict. This is double-edged. On the one hand, it is a source of stress itself, while on the other, it involves the absence of one or more potential sources of support. Women regularly identified conflict with neighbours, people who were formerly friends, and, particularly, family. They did not always talk about this as a potential support loss, however. Often, in this area of stress and support loss, a double element of conflict arose if the mother and her (usually) former partner, in particular the father of the child, were estranged (as was generally the case). One woman had a teenage daughter who had run away from home, and was, from the mother's point of view, almost impossible to manage at home. She described herself at a complete loss, but was unable to call on the support of her mother, at first because the two of them had fallen out, and then because her mother fell out with her daughter.

> I fell out with Mum and I haven't been speaking to my mum for about three years, and I phoned my brother, he said he heard that mum was blah, blah, blah. Basically I traced her, and phoned her at work, and my mum phoned me back, and I just because my mum absolutely adores [daughter, she] can do no wrong in my mum's eyes, you know, it's my fault. Anyway she comes, she moved [here] within three weeks, and she's actually [got a] cushy job, but my mum then kept [daughter] then for me for a weekend. You should have seen her, she brought [daughter] back, she had enough of her basically, and [daughter] stole booze off my mum and put it in a little vinegar bottle, and I got a phone call Sunday afternoon, '[daughter] is out of her head,' and of course my mum is like 'Oh my God, no,' you know? And I'm like 'Well, live with it, now you, now you know what I'm living with,' you know?

Another woman spoke similarly about her estranged husband. She was desperate for him to provide support, but the circumstances, and acrimony, made that impossible. 'It was, you know, hard enough though [husband] was with me. When he left I just thought, oh God, I've got nothing. The children went with their father, I think it was about a weekend, the second week he was bringing them back to me…and I couldn't say anything.'

There were a variety of reasons why women would not call upon support, even when, in principle, it might be available to them. Many women felt the crushing burden of trying to cope with their children's behaviour, yet they did not want to burden others. One woman relied on her mother, and when she died 'I closed off, so that I couldn't see anyone. I'm just trying to deal with every day, and I don't wanna be a burden to anybody.' Another woman, who had just moved into the area, had a 13-year-old girl, with whom she constantly argued, involved 'with boys', and 'excuse my French but apparently they were having a good shagging session'. However, despite this, she did not feel she could burden others.

> I'm on my own all the time, there's nobody to help me, to talk to. And what friends do come here, we talk about other things than the children. I don't really wanna talk about the children at this stage. I mean, I don't wanna know about my friend's problems with her child, and I don't wanna know and she don't wanna know my problems that I've got with my child... I don't want to know my relatives at all. All my relatives basically can go to hell.

Some women were concerned about using the help of others because they were 'not on the same wavelength'. Where they disagreed profoundly about child care issues, women tended to feel that they could not use others' help, because they would not be supportive. For example, one mother, estranged from her husband, had very little support in relation to her seven-year-old son, who had very unpredictable and aggressive behaviour. She nevertheless felt reluctant to use him for respite 'because I don't like them going down there because of what's going on, and the things he (father) says'. Another woman found that even discussing her children with her mother could add to the trauma because of the lackof agreement in child rearing practice.

> No, because, in her days she believes, well we wouldn't answer like my [daughter] does, we wouldn't dare. I mean if my mum said something, she meant it. She thinks we are far too soft with her and that's why. She's got a way with what she says but...what she says more or less goes...

A number of women simply did not trust their children to behave in an appropriate way with others, and so effectively refused to call on support that otherwise would be there. Respite became impossible because they took such a dim view of their own children! One woman stated this very well, in relation to her 15-year-old son, whom she described as having frequent tantrums:

> I'm always afraid to go out and meet people in case he does throw a wobbly. You know, like I said, it's bad enough living next door to the neighbours and he's throwing a wobbly. When he's through the wobbly then I come in and say, 'Come in now'. ...So no, I haven't got any friends, you know.

Another woman, with a difficult, pregnant teenager, stated similarly that 'I couldn't drop her off with a friend and leave her 'cos she wouldn't stay, 'cos she would scream the whole time'. In other cases, the mother feared that looking after the children could have a serious effect on the supporter. This was the case with the physically frail mother of one women who had a six-year-old son. She felt that her mother could not cope, but I was very apprehensive about him going to my nan, because she's 70, she's a pensioner and I don't want to stress my nan, she's got a bad heart, and it's something that would upset me more, to think that I was putting my stresses on her, that it would be helpful to me.

Routine support and integration

The frequency with which some women identified a lack of, or severe limits to, available support, or opportunity to use that support, clearly had a significant impact on their coping strategy. At the opposite end of the spectrum were women who felt sufficiently enmeshed with friends to call upon support extensively, in a variety of ways and in relation to a range of problems.

Some people regarded routine support as not being support at all. It was taken for granted to such a degree that something quite special was required for the woman to regard herself as supported. For example, one woman whose parents looked after the children, who was helped in a variety of ways when she was ill, and who was 'picked up and taken places' when she was not mobile, nevertheless said that she had little support and no one for respite with the children. She seems to have considered support to be rendered only when a response was made to a serious crisis. Others were really effusive about the help they received, generally from mothers or long-time friends. One woman with two ten-year-old boys who had reacted badly to the separation of their parents commented on the way her mother helped in a variety of ways:

> She listens…or she just comes shopping with me because these days I have to take the two children. So she's there you know, she has one and I have the other you know, she helps me in that way. Or if I have to go anywhere for appointments or anything she comes with me, so that I have got somebody there to help with the children… And listens, they all listen, they are all very good at listening, you know.

For many women it was the responsiveness of their supporters that was most significant. In this, they were distinguishing between routine support and crisis support in some cases. They were also indicating that they did not need support all the time, and responsiveness meant that supporters were there when needed but not 'in their face' at other times. Women pointed to the importance of both friends and family in this respect (although families could at times be intrusive and domineering, part of the problem rather than the solution). One woman commented:

> With my family mostly it's just the support, you know, 'We are here if you need us for anything'. They've obviously helped us a great deal financially, providing things for their future relation, whatever it's gonna be. Er, emotional as well, they would offer, you know, especially my family, my mum, my sister. Er, and it's just a general feeling of a whole, you know, everybody's helping and you don't feel so isolated on your own, you know. It's a family thing, you know.

As important as anything here was the sense of integration, of 'everybody helping' and 'not being isolated', which was with her at all times. Such support could provide a powerful base for the psychological robustness which could see a woman through difficult times. This sense of integration was evident in the account of another woman. She had what she considered was a psychotic episode (with a history of mental illness), and social services had not responded in the way she had hoped. The response of her friend was crucial, and she said, 'She was just there for me. I went and stayed with her for a week...and that week when I was really desperate she helped me out.' She also commented that 'if it wasn't for her I would probably be dead'. This togetherness was generated in the context of the women's own expectations and beliefs. Where they were religious, for example, praying together was of immense importance. It demonstrated care and concern. One woman commented that 'they just talked to me and prayed for me and things like that, you know. Every time I talk to [friend] she makes me feel better'.

The scale of the support was evident with some women, for whom help was available from friends or family in relation to any problem, with all kinds of support, and at any time. It was a kind of total commitment, which provided an immense sense of security. One woman, in the grips of depression, who felt she could no longer cope with her son or her life, was able to turn to one very significant friend, who provided consistent help when needed. Where it worked, such support was reciprocal. One particularly productive mother with five children valued the support of another, equally productive, mother. Each was prepared to support the other, and the reciprocity helped cement the relationship, together with the common understanding which emerged from both raising large families and having similar life experiences.

Yes she has, you know, because she has five. Her five and my five have grown up together since babies and we actually met in the family centre through social services ten years ago, so we have both grown up together, both learnt the problems with kids together, she's going through worse than what I'm going through. ...Sometimes I help her out by having a couple of her little ones, and she'll have a couple of mine, so we are always swapping kids, basically to give each other a break. Because she is on her own, not by choice or anything, but it's the way things have happened. Her old man used to knock her around and my old man basically buggered off with one of my friends, last July. Never mind, it's the way things go.

Help for the mother

For women who were under pressure, lacked confidence, or whose confidence was lowered by the impact of child care problems, encouragement and acceptance were often a key element of social support. These could have a crucial effect on making them feel less like a 'bad person', or on their belief that they might resolve or live with the problems. Acceptance and encouragement could provide the kind of support for self-esteem which would keep them going in difficult situations. These were very much emotion-focused forms of coping, and women sought the reassurance which came from encouragement, as part of their coping strategy. This could be achieved by actively seeking such support at the time of crisis. It could be done more generally by seeking the kinds of friends who were likely 'to stand by you' and encourage you, so that, at the point of crisis, they would expect the friends of the family to be there for them. Acceptance and encouragement could give the woman a sense of validation, both as a person, and in terms of the action she was taking, and were crucial psychological elements of coping which were actively sought by many women.

Many women emphasised the importance of acceptance, suggesting that in fraught circumstances there was some sort of psychological relief in the knowledge that someone important to you was with you, and did not criticise you for your actions. Feeling accepted, women said, enabled them to feel confident about using support more widely. Hence it became a prerequisite for some women to take up a wide variety of forms of support. This was the case with one woman, who stated that she simply 'couldn't cope with her son any more'. Her catastrophic mood collapse into depression accompanied serious attitude and behaviour problems on the part of her 11-year-old son, which reached the point where she 'just wanted to kill him'. For her it was important both that she could say anything to her friend without criticism, and that being helped by her friend in a variety of ways could give her confidence:

> The main [help] comes from [friend] really. She's been immense support, you know, she's always there and I can say anything to her and she never criticises what I say – you know, she always tries to, she's had [son] out there, staying there for me you know, she's been fantastic. She is the main one, given me most help and making sure that I'm alright you know, and so there's a difference isn't there. I mean [friend] is a friend, …Definitely [friend] is the most important person, definitely.

Encouragement was an important element of this acceptance. It was a 'keep going, you are doing the right thing' sort of support, which the women valued greatly. It could kick in most effectively at the very point of crisis where women were, there and then, having to deal with some kind of outburst or aggression. The immediate pre-teen and early teen period could be particularly difficult with girls, and faced with just such a problem, one woman commented about her friend that 'she does [provide encouragement], she's saying, "Come on now, she's coming on to 12, can't you remember what it was like coming on to 12?" She's always there to talk to'. This was accompanied by more general support as, at the point of crisis, her friend gave her both a 'bolt hole' (her house) to go to when things became too fraught, and that advice that her older daughter, who was 18, could look after her younger sister. More generally, women could be given some kind of personal validation by friends or family. One young mother, struggling with two children under three years old, received reassurance that she was a good mother:

> I think it was nice when my mum said that she thought that I was a good mum, it was good to hear that. I don't know that ever I do, they don't say I'm doing it wrong, or if I do it wrong they help me to do it right, so they encourage me with everything.

Some women were only able to accept support if it involved basic *agreement* with them about their behaviour, their interpretation of the situation, or coping strategy. Acceptance of support was conditional upon this basic agreement, and women sought friends who were uncritical and in agreement on fundamentals. It was a kind of validation through agreement. In one case, of a woman with two ten-year-olds, this again involved the issue of 'being a good mother' (a major issue for many of these mothers):

> All of them do that, you know. They all say, 'No, you're not a bad mother, no, you haven't brought them up wrong, you know, it's just what they are going through, because of what's happened, you know.' So they do encourage me quite a lot, you know.

In practical terms, this did not involve just validation through verbal agreement with the woman when she expressed her feelings, but action in relation to the children. Women described how supporters could give support for their authority as parents: 'He...make the point that you know, you can't keep doing that.' One woman described in detail the importance of agreeing with the mother, but, crucially, her supporters also backed her up by doing things her way. Their support was consistent with her actions:

> They all, they all help in a way that, aam, if she's told about something, they all stick to my way of doing it, they all back me up as far as she's concerned, if she's not allowed to do something here. When my mum has got her she's not allowed to do it there – same one if she's with my brother. They all know the set rules that I've got and they all keep to that.

The importance of general agreement with (and support for) actions, as a pre-requisite for a supportive relationship was evident in its absence. Taking a very different perspective, for some of these women, did not add to their potential repertoire of coping actions, but was a nuisance which distanced them from the potential supporter. Here is one woman talking about the extent to which she was prepared to take up her mother's advice:

> Not advice as such, they do say, 'Oh you should do this and you should do that' you know, but to me that's not advice but just putting another obstacle in the way you know. I mean, take my mum for instance, 'Why don't you give them a good hammering and get it over with' you know, but you know, she was brought up that way so you know, very different...so to me it's not advice, you know. I just let it go in one ear and out of the other and I go 'yeah'.

This, of course, could sound positive because the woman was resisting advice to 'hammer' her children. However, it could equally occur the opposite way: where a woman was advised to hit her children less, she could dismiss this because she believed that corporal punishment was a central part of parenting. Advice would be ignored, and social distance even created, where it did not agree with the woman's preconceptions, as with one woman who rejected her whole family in this respect and said, 'The only decent advice I get is from the police.'

The opportunity to express feelings, and be listened to, was one way in which women could feel valued and validated. Being valued was implicit in being listened to: often the expression of feelings was strong and fraught, so that the friend or family member who listened was showing commitment to the woman. However, listening and not saying anything meant also not disagreeing. The woman was able to tell her own story without contradiction. One woman put this point clearly, pointing to the fact that others were not sitting in judgement on her:

> Yeah, …the support is there she doesn't always give advice but she will listen, and half the battle is just having someone to listen, someone that you can rant and rave and talk and it's nonjudgmental. She just listens and you know… Someone I can just talk to and she'll just take it all in you know, not criticise, not judge, she just listen and that's really, I really need someone that will do that.

Another woman found that her mother, in refusing to make suggestions or have a view, was, for her, enabling. Her mother's view was that she couldn't have a view: 'My mum has very much got the attitude that all children are different and she doesn't really know [child] like that, 'cos she only sees her four times a year.'

The common factor in listening without giving advice, and the offering of advice is that both broadly allowed the woman to retain her own perspective, or framework, for understanding what was going on. Useful advice was generally advice which might draw out a new possible action, while nevertheless agreeing with the fundamental views of the mother. Where the view contradicted the woman's overall framework for understanding, it was liable to be rejected or seen as undermining her position.

Of course, this was as much about emotional support as advice. Listening to the woman allowed her to express her feelings, and provided her with a sense of validation which could be emotionally supportive. Women felt that the availability of others provided them with emotional support. Talking of this, one woman said: 'I get that from my my father and [?] …If I need support I will phone them up on the phone, they are my family.' The availability of family and friends on a '24/7' basis was highly valued in this context. Speaking of a friend, one woman said:

Yeah, yeah, she's been there, 'cos we had a row couple of weeks ago and she was here till four o'clock in the morning 'cos I was felt I was going mad and I cried my eyes out kind of thing, so yeah, she's good like that so.

Women could use respite for emotional support, besides the practical issue of having support care for the children. One woman spoke about the capacity to get away (with the kids) specifically as a form of emotional support:

If I'm feeling a bit low I can go and stay with my sister, like in the weekend, and sort of get out of this environment. And get the kids away from town and get out and do things, so basically butt myself up really, you know. She's there, I can talk to her all the time you know, she rings me up all the time see if I'm OK, she's always there for me really.

Child care and practical support

Child care support was the other major area of support provided by women's social network. This was mentioned more frequently than any other form of support, which is not surprising, in view of the nature of the problems. The support was generally presented as practical, and overwhelmingly about respite from the day-to-day grind and pressure of parenting. Woman after woman said practically the same thing – that the pressure of caring grows, and letting others look after the children provides a metaphorical safety valve allowing the women a breathing space through which they can recharge their batteries.

Some women emphasised the crisis element of respite. Women talked of the build-up of stress through tantrums, misbehaviour and arguments, and even violence. The frustrations of having to face the school, or the police, or some other formal service again because of concerns about their child at times meant that they just wanted to be rid of their child for a while. (With older children, such as late teenagers, some wanted to be rid of their child for good.) One woman commented that it was rare that matters reached a point where this was necessary, but, when provided, respite was a considerable relief.

If I need it, yeah. It's very, very rare [son] goes anywhere else. Occasionally he'll go down and stay at [friend's] and [friend's]…they've got kids and that down there that are [son's] age. But mainly, well, [son] is in the house and he doesn't really go anywhere, just the odd night. He's been [friend's] two or three times and he's been at [friend's] three times but that's that.

Child care respite for many women, was woven into their coping routine. Of course, not all women had networks with others who were prepared to provide respite, but where this was the case, there was frequently a routine element about it. This did not mean that such support could not be used in crisis, but that crisis support was part of a more general and routine respite offered by their network. At times this respite was, although routine, nevertheless *conditional*, suggesting that some kind of moral judgement was going on. Others were not available for just any purpose, but only in relation to situations that they felt merited respite. One woman with young children did receive this kind of support from her mother and sister, but distinguished times when she went to college, or was interviewed for a job, from times when she would just like to go out to the pub. Respite was forthcoming for 'serious' career purposes, but not for recreation. The result, as she commented, was 'I tend to, you know, if I'm gonna have a drink I have it indoors with my friends'. This could be short-sighted, especially where women had few friends, since, as we have seen, they could feel isolated, and without adult company. Respite to aid socialising could be as important as respite for other purposes.

Routine child care support manifested itself in a number of fairly predictable ways. Children were picked up from school by friends when the mother was unable to do it herself; babysitting was frequently identified by women as a means for them to socialise more. Children went to their friends' houses for 'sleepovers', often including the evening and next morning. All these would be helpful when there were no particular problems with child care. Where situations were fraught, as was the case with most of these families, routine support became of fundamental importance to the women, struggling to cope. These women are typical. One is talking about the open-ended respon-siveness of a friend:

> [friend] was very, very helpful with the children because I work night shifts and [friend] will have the children overnight and takes them to school, so she didn't hesitate, she said 'yes'. Any problems I had in between, [friend] would look after children, she's fantastic with them so.

Another talked about the way in which her partner and her friends were available for practical child care support:

> Aam, if she's getting too much [partner] takes her out... [partner] does as much to [daughter] as I do, aam. If she's too much he'll take her out, they go

out for the day, amuse her. They as well, because it's such a, such a drag when they are with you constantly, they take them away and they have fun with them. So they sort of keep them happy rather than putting them away and punishing them, they take them away and so they take her out and they'll take her to the park or the football or the cricket or wherever he's going and makes sure that she has a good time... And that's how, that's how they help basically and they, they look after when I wanna go anywhere... They help me in all aspects with all the children.

In other cases holidays could be the focus for a break from caring for the children, and also potentially enjoyable for the children, although this was not always the case.

She'll have them on the holidays i.e. six weeks holidays, she'll have them for a week, but because it's in the middle of nowhere neither one of them likes to go up there although they love their nanny a lot. They don't like to go up because it's...it's not a city, it's a country you can always find noise but you can't find peace and quiet.

While these were routine – indeed, particularly because they were routine, these breaks became a key part of the way the women planned the care of their children. Support was not simply something which happened to them, but was something they sought, or arranged. It was part of their active coping with the situation.

Summary and conclusion

Informal support was an important part of many women's coping strategy, but was not always available to all women, or in the same kinds of ways. As an aspect of coping strategy there were two key elements: whether there was support available in the first place (did the woman have any friends or helpers?), since if there was nothing or little available, the woman did not have the option of actively using support – she could not use what was not there. Where support was available, the woman could choose to use it, or not, depending on whether she wished to. Here they could have support as an option in an active coping strategy.

Informal support as an aspect of coping could be emotion-focused or problem-focused. Where it was emotion-focused, it enabled the women to cope better with the emotional consequences of dealing with child care problems, by, for example, providing emotional support. Where it was problem-focused, it could help deal with the problem itself, as, for example, when an individual reinforced the statements and authority of the mother when talking to the children.

1.   Some women were *at a loss to describe anyone available* to them for support. Absence of such support deprived them of the possibility of using support as part of a coping strategy, and could make it more difficult to develop a psychological robustness which could take them through their problems.

2.   Some networks were conflicted, and *conflict* could be a double-edged sword. The conflict could itself be a source of stress, and it could also deprive the woman of a possible unit of support. Two frequent sources of conflict were the mother and [ex] partner.

3.   Women also decided not to call upon support that was, in principle, available. Some women *did not wish to burden others* (with a quid pro quo that they were not bothered themselves). Some women felt that others were *not on the same 'wavelength'*. When there was basic disagreement about child care philosophy or action, women felt that they could not call upon others because it would not feel supportive. Some women felt they could not call upon potential support because they did not trust the child to behave well enough when with others.

4.   Routine support, and reciprocity (where each supported the other) could give a sense of *social integration*. For some women it was the responsiveness of supporters which was important: they were there all the time, but they reacted with support when needed. The sense of integration was important, providing a sense of security, of people being there for you if needed them.

5.   The scale of routine or integrated support could be considerable. People could be available at any time. When *reciprocal*, the relationship enabled the woman to feel she was contributing to others, rather than just 'taking' herself. This could help maintain self-esteem, by ensuring that support was not one-sided.

6.   *Encouragement and acceptance* were key elements of social support
      when the mother was low in confidence. These were
      emotion-focused coping strategies. Acceptance and encouragement
      gave psychological relief in fraught circumstances, and the latter
      could be most helpful at times of crisis.

7.   Some women could only accept *support based on a high level of
      agreement* about the key aspects of the situation or the woman's
      behaviour. Where the women valued listening, but not giving
      opinions, as was the case with some of them, this prevented a
      challenge to her position emerging from the helping process.

8.   *Practical child care support,* such as looking after the children, was
      often of particular help at the point of crisis. However, it could also
      be routine, and this very routinised element meant that the helpers
      were in place to provide support if and when it was needed.

CHAPTER 13

Seeking Help from Social Services

Approaching social services, when the women directly referred themselves or agreed to being referred, arose because of their secondary appraisal of the situation. Their primary appraisal focused on the problem itself, and the threat posed by the stressor(s). Their secondary appraisal focused around the issue of controllability. Secondary appraisal involved examining and using resources or potential resources which could, in the view of the women, enable her to gain control of the situation and hence reduce the threat posed.

Where social services were approached, it was because the women hoped that they could exert some control over the situation. At the theoretical level this involved linking the form of coping (problem-focused or emotion-focused) with the resources through which stressors could be controlled. Behind this lay some notion of what social services could do. This could be broadly divided into four categories, along two axes. On the one hand, they sought actions which were either parent-focused or child-focused, that is, the action they sought was primarily directed at either one or the other. On the other hand, they sought approaches that were either problem-focused (concentrating on the problem itself) or emotion-focused (concentrating on the emotional consequences of the problem). These, as we shall see, were not altogether discrete categories – the emotion-focused coping strategies, for example, could entail problem ameliora-tion or resolution – but they did represent the main dimensions of help-seeking behaviour.

Problem-focused coping strategies

Approaches to social services were most frequently utilised as problem-solving coping strategies, where the mothers sought to engage social services in the process of problem resolution or amelioration. However, there were times when women had no clear expectation of what social services could do for them. Referrals were made because they felt social services might be able to 'do something', or because they thought this was the kind of issue on which social workers were engaged, without any clear indication of what was expected.

Vague requests for 'help'

In these cases, the woman tended to state the problem and the effect that it was having on her. This occurred with one woman with three children aged under five, who had particular problems with her three-year-old. Her stressor was not simply problem-focused (the behaviour of her son), but also emotion-focused (her reaction to this). She feared losing control:

> Just things he was getting up to, not being able to control him…he seems to have a nasty streak in him, like he's alright a lot of the time, then all of a sudden he does sly hits or whatever, just things out of the ordinary outside, hitting on the two younger children, in particular me and my friend, because her daughter has done something… I'm suffering from depression, like I said before, I'm worried about what I might do, even though I've done something once and it's a real pressure on me, that's why I try and get help.

This general idea that they 'needed help' was echoed in the expectations of other women. One example of this was related by a woman in a family containing four children, where the oldest, a ten-year-old boy, presented behaviour problems.

> Because I've got a lot of problems with my eldest son's behaviour problems, and mainly it is a lot of running away but taking money and things like that… He never does what he's told to do, he's very aggressive, very, he doesn't understand if I don't know what it is… Main problem is I tried to find some help.

Where there was a clearer idea of a social service role, women were able to articulate their expectations more clearly. For some women, social services were there to back them up by threat or boundary-setting in relation to their views of appropriate child care or child behaviour. In this respect, social workers were expected to act to 'police the family', not on behalf of the state, but on behalf of the mother. This, of course, indicated a strong sense of self-righteousness in the woman, which was most evident in relation to the perceived behavioural excesses of their own children.

One woman described her teenage daughter as 'running wild'. She had hit her daughter, according to the referral quite severely, and social services contacted her following a referral from the school, where, according to the mother, 'she told the school I beat her savagely'. However, she had contacted social services independently at the same time because of her problems with her daughter, which she considered to be squarely the daughter's responsibility: 'It was basically down to my daughter being a teenager.' Having blamed the daughter (despite her own violent outburst) she expected social services to reinforce her position by telling her daughter that she (the mother) was right. If that failed, she even felt that she had a right to accommodation services from the local authority (all to back up her position).

> I expected them to tell [daughter] that she can't do what she's doing, that she has to live at home and she has to do it by the law. Which are, you are not allowed to drink, you live under your mother's roof and you do as your mother tells you. Naive maybe, but that's what I expected. That's what it was like when I was her age. If she didn't like those, she couldn't decide where she wanted to live, she'd have to go in care and then she'd realise that maybe she hasn't got it quite so bad.

This theme of presenting a threat designed to support the mother's position was reiterated by a number of mothers. One, for example, said (again after beating her children) that she expected that 'at least they would have come out and speak to the kids, and tell them what could happen if they didn't behave'. Interestingly, this policing and threatening role was often identified by mothers who had reached the point where even hitting their children failed to control their behaviour, so social services were an external way of threatening the children, and 'upping the ante' still further.

Others saw the use of social services in this way as a 'reality check'. In these cases, the women felt that the poor behaviour arose, at least in part, because the children failed to appreciate the positive aspects in their family life. The looked to social services to show the children that the 'grass was not [necessarily] greener' elsewhere. This was the substance of one woman's expectations:

> I expected, what we wanted was for them to show [son] that the grass weren't greener on the other side, you know what I mean. I mean he has everything here, you know like, he's always had everything, whatever he's wanted, he's got, you know and, you know Christmas and birthdays… He don't wash the pots, he don't tidy up and I wanted them to just take him…this thing you know, like maybe a week or two weeks you know, like just to show him.

A third respect in which the women sought to use social services to exert control was in relation to those in or outside the family who were harming the child[ren]. The women sought to set boundaries, or to gain some retribution for past behaviour. This was the case with one family where the mother and father disagreed over child care, and she regarded him as over-controlling, bordering on violent. Social services were contacted to emphasise the need to set boundaries to his behaviour:

> Just general concerns about what was going on with him, going over the top with [son]… Generally it was a way of making sure that it, I don't know (laughs)… A protection really, just to make sure that things didn't get out control and that [partner] was aware that, you know he's got to learn that some things are acceptable and some aren't.

In another case, the woman's daughter alleged sexual assault by other children at her school. She expected social services to deal with these children, set boundaries, and exact retribution if necessary. In the event she was bitterly disappointed. She blamed the school and social services for delaying interviewing the children:

> I expected them to go in and deal with the problem, so to come to the, like the actual behaviour and assault…[to get it] out of these children, because the other girl and my daughter they said exactly what happened. But when they went and talked to the children they just accepted what they said… You know, you've got a gang of six children, they're bound to make a good story to cover themselves because they've had a week to decide what they're going to say.

Advice on parenting and children

A further group of women sought advice from social services, either about where they stood or what they should do. This involved a diverse group of problems, unified by the idea that some expertise existed in social services, and that expertise should be used, not directly with the child, but to enable the woman to act in a more informed manner. The gaining of control, therefore, was to be achieved through the accretion of information.

This was the case with one woman, who was thrown out of her home by her (depressed) partner. She was frantic, because her partner would neither let her back into the house nor allow the two children, aged two and six months, to leave. She had contacted the police for advice, but they said (inaccurately) that nothing could be done because she and her partner shared parental responsibility. (This was not the case, as they were not married.) The social worker was able to advise her that the police were wrong, and that she should contact a solicitor to regain the children:

> I was kicked out by my boyfriend and he wouldn't give me my children, so I went to them [social services] for a bit of advice to see where I stood and I can't remember who I spoke to now, but I had to go to a solicitor and get order over my kids and everything. Then they would help me if I needed their help. But it all turned out OK, I got my children and they're back in the office and he had to leave, that's the only reason I got in contact with them, to see where I stood.

Another example involved advice about where the woman stood in terms of how she could respond to her teenage son's aggressive behaviour. This was a theme of many women's accounts, although they were generally less likely to seek advice than to demand 'back-up' for their position from social services. In this case, her son was not attending school, misbehaving when he was there, taking drugs, and was aggressive and difficult at home. She sought to know what she could do if this continued.

> I just wanted to know where I stood, where he was putting knives at me, which is assault, and he said if he tries it again don't hesitate to phone the police, which he didn't try again so I did not need to contact them. And he ran away…for a weekend and he told me if he's not found within 48 hours to phone them if I needed to. But my family assured me he would be home and he came home on Sunday.

Counselling

Women also sought counselling from social workers. This was not generally alluded to directly, but had a different quality from advice. Where advice was primarily about experts dispensing information, the focus for counselling was talk. Beyond this the women were not very clear in their expectations, but behind this was the notion that matters might be improved, or understood better, by talking about them with an outsider.

One way in which talk could be important was where women faced a real dilemma, and ambivalence about alternatives. One woman was the subject of an unwanted pregnancy, and feared that she would be unable to cope with a second child. Furthermore, those who might have supported her through this were highly critical: 'When I was pregnant…I had trouble with the family, they went mad on me being pregnant with my son [as well].' Faced with the force of this opposition, and on the advice of her midwife, she wanted to place the child for adoption. But even as she did so, she had doubts. She expressed this clearly:

> Well y'know, they got really, I think they [the family] were maybe shocked more than anything and their shock was to shout about it. It was only after the first child, I wasn't ready on him and definitely not ready for [daughter], I didn't know what to do and the midwife put me onto social services for adoption on [daughter], and [without that] I would never know what to do.

The woman was clearly seeking some way through her uncertainty and ambivalence. She commented that 'I didn't know how to cope with it, and [social worker] was there to help'.

Talk could be important where real communication had broken down. Families beset by parent–child conflict often found that their capacity to talk through the problems was diminished, or non-existent. Deprived of lines of communication, women turned to social services to encourage talk, even if it was only with the child. One woman described her son's behaviour, stealing from home and school and becoming increasingly aggressive:

> And that's when we did get involved was when, mainly when he had his aggression mainly got worse at school. It is a case of if he got into a fight, and sometimes I don't agree with it, but apparently he got into a fight and a dinner lady had gone behind him to grab him… But mainly yeah, it's a case of I was hoping that someone could try and talk to him, bring him out of his shell…because he just don't open up to us at all.

Other women did not focus solely on themselves or the child, but saw talking as a means for bringing together various parties in a constructive direction.

> My 12-year-old son, he's a handful, a real real handful and I, they're having problems with him at school, I'm having problems with him home here, and I contacted social services to see if they could offer some sort of help, to speak

to somebody, because I truly believe he has got a problem. [I expected them] to come and see me, to come and speak to me… And speak to [son] and speak to the school, and that's what I thought was going to happen.

Assistance with accommodation

Women also focused on a range of issues relating to their accommodation. Social services were seen to have influence in the allocation of accommodation. In some cases it was believed that the accommodation could be directly provided by them. One woman, homeless, unable to stay in bed and breakfast during the day, was dragging five children round town, with nowhere to go (within her social-security based) means. She wanted social services to provide her children with 'somewhere to stay'.

> …but I expected them to say, sort of, you know, two days a week or just on a part-time, you know, 'we can arrange for the children to stay somewhere and do something', that would have a positive effect for them, rather than being dragged around [town], you know, with no particular aim and a parent with no money.

Most others sought to use social services' influence rather than direct action to ameliorate their accommodation problems. One family, having recently moved into the area, were 'trying to get some help from them to push the council to get us a house', while a woman who wished to move out of the area because her daughter was being bullied, commented that 'I hoped they would help me, you know, and put in a word that, towards a council to house us'. Another family commented on the direct dangers to their infant child of remaining in the same accommodation, and hence their wish for social services support for rehousing.

Emotion-focused coping strategies

Underlying many of the referrals made by these women was a strong need for validation. While some saw themselves as the 'culprits', having parenting problems, more saw the responsibility lying with the children, and sometimes the environment. For many of the women the validation required was that they were (broadly) in the right, and we have seen this in referrals where the women saw social services' role to be that of supporting them in conflict with their children. However, there was a broader sense of validation than this: that they somehow were worthy of being taken seriously, and given respect. Whether or not they felt that the problems were their responsibility, they were aware of themselves in crisis, and a response to their sense of need would show that social services regarded them with respect, and at least considered them to have some value. This sense of 'seeking and expecting validation' was clear from one woman, whose comments showed the link between this sense of self-respect and service expectations:

> I expected them, firstly, to take me seriously. I expected them to empathise with the situation I was in, to recognise that it was seriously distressing for myself and the children, and then to offer me some financial support and some child care or, you know… Em, I just wanted them to see the seriousness of my situation and say, yeah, we'll help you how we can.

For her, being taken seriously entailed empathic recognition of the seriousness of the situation, and a preparedness to act appropriately. This was similarly expressed by another woman, who described her negative reaction to refusal of service as 'shutting the door in my face'.

> I got a phone call back saying they wouldn't take her and I could contact somebody to talk my problems over about her. But you know, I've heard that hundreds of times, so basically they sort of, like I felt like he was shutting the door on my face to that. So and that was it and I haven't heard nothing from them since.

The unsurprising core of many women's emotion-focused coping actions was stress relief. In some cases, this was a crisis response, where the child began acting quite differently from previously. Faced with these unexpected behaviours, and with pressures with which they found it difficult to cope, the women sought relief from the stress through social services intervention. The help sought was not, in these cases, designed to resolve the problems, but rather to ameliorate them, to make it easier for the mother (and partner if there was one) to manage the stresses of the child's behaviours. This mother expressed it in terms of 'fighting for ourselves' but also in terms of their worry and anxiety about their daughter. For them, 'space' was essential.

> I think at the time, even though we love her, I think maybe somewhere she could go just for the night, because the behaviour was so bad and we were fighting for ourselves. And when actually I was phoning them, she threw a glitter bottle through the glass panel and I was underneath. And she was

kicking furniture and being violent. I just felt at the time, maybe we could have, could have had a bit somewhere for us to calm down, even for a night. Not to calm down but to have some space really. We were very worried and very anxious about [daughter].

Many women felt the relentlessness of their problems, particularly where these were long-term and there was no obvious end to them. This was the case for mothers of children diagnosed with ADHD. While Ritalin might provide relief through medication, this was not always the case, and their powerlessness to resolve the problem rested, at least in part, in a sense that this was beyond counselling, advice or some more practical solution. The help in these cases (whether or not involving ADHD) was focused on the mother, by relieving her stress levels.

...if you watch Coronation Street...at the moment they've got [something] about fostering and they were saying to them you know, you might have a child for one night while...you have family problems and that's OK, so I'm thinking right, perhaps that's somewhere we can go, social services, to see their scheme or other local, how do you call it, where someone who just has [son] every month, just to give us a break and him a break, just so we can, say, just basically have a night where we are not having someone coming down the stairs 12 times a night.

The stress relief here was designed to enable them to care more effectively over the longer term. Women felt this particularly acutely if they had sole responsibility for their children. Indeed, some thought that social services were primarily there for single mothers:

Well with all the problems I've gone through in the last four years, you know bringing up a kid on your own is like, is a big responsibility, you need time to yourself, which you don't get... I was just like not handling the life very, you know what I mean.

Other women felt the same need for stress relief, but emphasised also the dangers of not getting such relief. Women described the pressures they were under, and their fear about their own reactions to these pressures. Having a break was not only a stress reduction strategy, but a means of ensuring child safety: 'It kind of got to the stage where a fortnight or three weeks ago I'd had enough you know, I wanted her away from me because I was afraid of my own actions at the time'.

A closely associated coping strategy was one that involved seeking security and support. Women here were seeking a situation where they no longer felt isolated in caring for their children. Social services, through their involvement, would enable the women by giving them a sense of a 'trouble shared'. The importance of involvement here, therefore, was not just relief from continuous care, but the *psychological* effect of no longer feeling solely responsible. One woman expressed this in terms of social services providing a 'safety net':

> I was looking for support and I was looking for a safety net for myself. …I tried to explain to them that this had been going on for a quite a while and I got to the point where I can't cope. And to say to somebody on the phone, a stranger, 'I can't cope', that's out of my character, 'cos I've always tried to deal with the problem, whatever. But I wanted somebody to be there for me and it all boils down to…the child. I, I don't know, I just think I rang them for support, yeah, I did ring them for support and as a safety net.

Sometimes professional expertise was important. The sense of security here was the security that came from knowing that an expert was 'on the case'. One woman expressed this in terms of the use of what she saw as fostering 'day care':

> …maybe it might be time for them to try and put you like, to foster people or someone who's trained to deal with people like [son]… I've never had training, I've just like, had to trying to work out what he wants and what he needs. But I always see people with foster children with behaviour problems, they've always seen it and might have a different approach.

The final area of emotion-focused coping applied less to the parent than the child. This was *insight-oriented* coping, and had in common with some security- and support-seeking coping strategies the pursuit of expert intervention. In these cases the women sought to get help so that the children could be enabled to understand their own feelings and actions rather better. Invariably, the women saw themselves as having tried and failed. They considered that emotional dimensions lay behind the direct problems they had identified, and they wished these to be the focus for intervention. This was expressed clearly by one woman whose son had stabbed her in the leg with a six-inch nail, and had also attacked his sister.

> A couple of days before he laid into her on the bed, laid into her something chronic, really hit her, and I said to him, 'I'm not putting up with this behaviour', and that's when I phoned up social services. And said, 'Look, [son] needs

some help' and 'Has he gone 16?' He was just 16 want it? '[Son] needs to talk to somebody.' ...He was having all these violent mood swings and you know, and I said, 'And I can't understand it'.

Others expressed their concerns in a similar way: 'So, yeah, I asked them for help and I asked them like, you know, just take him away for a couple of days like. Put him somewhere where someone might be able to understand him.' All these women had in common their failure to resolve the issue themselves, but, in addition, the inability to engage at the emotional level with the children. The result was that the emotional dimensions behind the manifest problems needed addressing. This was expressed by another woman:

> He can sit there and tell them how he's feeling but he won't tell me. If I ask him what's wrong with him, he'll say, 'Nothing to do with you, like... He's got to the stage like he doesn't want to talk to me about anything and feels like he's got a few problems, but he's not, he's causing other problems. I was hoping that they're gonna send out somebody that can talk to him and deal with it that way.

Unsolicited referrals: expecting the worst

Controlling the definition of the situation

Although the overwhelming majority of women accepted that they had significant child or parenting problems, not all sought control by referring themselves, or getting others to refer them. Where unsolicited referrals were made by others, this was generally unwelcome, and involved child protection or inadequate parenting accusations. The women's agenda, under these circumstances, was quite different from when they themselves solicited help. The problem over which they primarily sought control was here not child care, but the intervention of social services. In particular the 'definition of the situation' was of concern. At the point of referral, it was not they who were the definers, but the referrers. In view of the child protection content, the definition was generally hostile to the woman herself, and contained very negative allegations about her parenting and children: she was being defined as 'a bad mother'.

There was a difference, at the theoretical level, between unsolicited (indirect) referrals, and those that were solicited (direct) referrals. Direct referrals from women themselves were about secondary appraisal, the main characteristic of which was the issue of controllability – that is, how they could get control of the problem of the stressor. While secondary appraisal focused on resources, personal or otherwise (in this case, soliciting support from social services), the main feature of situations created by unsolicited referrals was a *primary appraisal* of *threat* – that some undesirable event, most frequently identified as their children being 'taken away', was about to occur. From the theoretical point of view, the unsolicited referral itself had the same status as the child or parenting problem in solicited referrals: the referral (and its consequences) was the *problem*.

Some women appeared 'matter of fact' about referrals. They displayed either a confidence in their parenting, and the capacity of social services to recognise its (adequate or good) quality, or an absence of concern or awareness of the potential gravity of the situation. One woman was not fazed by her referral, commenting that children are bound to get knocks when they are at play:

> Yeah, they had an anonymous call saying that I was beating one of the kids up. And they had marks on their legs and they said I was hitting them with a stick, so they had to investigate… But…it was proved wrong all the time. The kids will get knocked, you know, bruises and whatever.

Women's expectations, however, were generally negative, and their immediate responses predominantly emotion-focused. All the women became in some way (understandably) defensive. For many, the immediate response was fear of the powers of social services if the allegations were accepted by social workers. The primary, and immediate, concern was that the children would be 'taken away' (because that was what 'social workers did'). Alongside this, however, was the woman's realisation that she was being defined as a 'bad mother', with its implication of immorality and incompetence. Shock, fear and demoralisation were the immediate response to the mere knowledge that social workers were intending to make an unsolicited assessment of her parenting. One woman expressed these feelings clearly:

> Shock. Basically. I thought, God, you know, I've been down here on my own for, what was it, six, seven months, eight months? and now I've got welfare on my back. I thought, well that's it, lose the kids. Obviously, I mean, that in my day when welfare were called in it meant either that you were bad or you were doing something wrong and the children were taken away. I mean, I didn't realise that they could act as sort of, like mediators and things like that. Yes I was, shock – and horror.

Other women expressed in a similar way the primary threat they felt in the face of unsolicited referrals. 'I was petrified' said one, 'that they were going to take my son away...and I didn't know about it until after I got back [from holiday].'

Faced with this situation, women generally felt the need to act urgently. Their desire to gain some kind of control involved finding out the exact nature of the allegations, the way social services were viewing them, and what they intended to do. However, while their impulse to act was strong, this was not always matched by social services, whose response could at times be slow, bureaucratic and frankly insensitive, almost to the point of abuse, when looked at from the standpoint of the mothers. One woman commented, 'They sent a letter in the post to say they were coming over, and I was worried sick for three days.'

> ...there was an anonymous call from the neighbours in the street saying my children were being left on a regular basis, right, on a Sunday. Now I had a letter saying...that 'we've, it's very important we've got to have a meeting with you now about your family situation,' from the social workers. Now I got worried, I rung them and it was, say, teatime maybe five o'clock, and I said, you know, 'Right, what's this all about?' Got through to the office and then they said that, you know, 'Oh it's the one person who is dealing with you, she's not in and we can't give you any information what it's really about.' Now I said, 'I'm really worried, you know, I'm upset and I would like some answers like.' They said, 'No, I'm sorry we can't,' and I said 'Is there a boss there?' 'No, no, no we can't, I will put an important letter on the girl's desk in the morning that's dealing with you and just saying "this is Mrs 'X'" a minute,' and she will get back to you first thing in the morning nine o'clock.'

Of course, the fact that social services were not acting immediately was an indication that they did not regard the situation as urgently serious. The women themselves, however, did not know this, and officious letters, together with bureaucratic and delayed communication, only served to feed their terror. The period up to (as far as they were concerned) vindication, was, for many women, purgatory.

Fear, trepidation and indignation represented the primary appraisal of threat from social services. Alongside this was anger, aimed either at social services, or at the referrer. Interestingly, this was expressed by some women who were nevertheless generally positive about social workers' helpfulness, as well as by those who were not. Where social services were bureaucratic, insensitive and slow, such anger was understandable, but the anger was generally directed less at the social workers' response, than at the fact of their involvement. One woman commented that 'I was angry, I was so angry I was crying. I was in a hell of a state. I actually still got the letter'. Another woman expressed her indignation by suggesting that social services spent their time 'badgering' competent mothers like her, at the expense of those children who really needed help:

> I don't like social services full stop, never have done. But they have got good points, I mean, I know they're not there just to pick on people, but it seems rather badgering families like mine. Look at all them poor little babies, you know, that are being sexually abused and all they've got, well, where are they when they need help? I mean, there's my three kids, I mean, fit and healthy, all good kids really, and all they can do is knock at your door and say, 'Well, do you need some help, are you coping?' You know, I think they should be doing something else.

Anger was also directed at the referrer. One woman who had been the subject of five anonymous referrals commented that she 'was angry basically that somebody thought that my kids were getting mistreated. I was angry, very angry'. Another woman – who considered social workers to be helpful – nevertheless related the emotional response which could be directed towards the social worker, before expressing her anger at the 'real' culprit, the person who made the referral:

> This lady [social worker] could see right through…it was from the neighbour next door and she said that I was abusing [son] and, I mean, not just mentally but physically, he was being neglected. I got very upset. I shouted at the lady when she came, but I think that is a lot of parents' reaction when the social services are in the scene… I was very angry. My husband was very angry. He went and knocked the door and he asked the husband very nicely, 'Did you call social services?' And he admitted to my husband that he called social services. And I was very, very angry.

Social services, as many social workers are aware, are at times used by individuals who want to 'get at' some families or parents, and make child care referrals, knowing the pain this will cause (malicious referrals). Some of those referrals by neighbours fell into that category. Social services may also be contacted in custody disputes, with the aim of making one parent appear to be unfit to care for the child[ren]. One woman described exactly this kind of situation, and believed that social workers had become 'dupes' of her former husband. She erroneously believed that it was their involvement, even though they quickly found the accusations to be unfounded, which enabled him to take proceedings.

> They got in contact with me because my ex-partner actually rang them up and put me across as an unfit mother, thought I was drugs and all that, and they come out and questioned me…and he actually grassed me up to social services for that. A bloke from social services come out seen me and he said he'd closed the case, but when social services got involved he's actually taking me for custody now, and there's nothing social services can do about it.

Of course, it should be remembered that while initially these were child care or child protection referrals, the women were successful, pretty quickly, in refuting, to the satisfaction of social services, the accusations made. The assessments by social services were quick, and did not go near a child protection conference. Nevertheless, the simple fact of social services involvement entailed strong primary appraisals of threat, with associated emotions.

Summary and conclusion

1. Where women approached social services, or agreed to be referred (together being 'voluntary referrals'), this arose because of their *secondary appraisal of the resources that were available*, through social services, to help them cope with problems. When approached in this way, coping theory indicates that referrals would be seen as a means of exerting or increasing the women's control.

2. Approaches to social services were most frequently used as *problem-solving coping strategies* which involved a number of different elements, including vague requests for help, backing for the mother by means of threats or boundary-setting (policing the family on behalf of the mother), advice on parenting and children, counselling, and assistance with accommodation.

3. *Emotion-focused coping strategies* associated with voluntary referral to social services included the need for validation, seeking security and support, stress relief, and insight-oriented coping.

4.   Unsolicited referrals were less about controlling the situation than controlling the *definition* of the situation. Where unsolicited referrals were made by others, this was generally unwelcome, involving allegations of inadequate parenting or abuse. Here the women sought to get the situation redefined as one where they were adequate, or preferably good, parents.

5.   The main feature of these situations is that *contact with social services involved a primary appraisal of threat,* rather than a secondary appraisal of controllability, which occurred with voluntary referrals. The threat came from the definition, and from the possible actions of social services. Fear, trepidation and indignation represented the primary appraisal of threat from social services.

CHAPTER 14

Client Discourses of Judgements on Social Services

Taking control in adverse situations is, according to coping theory, at the heart of coping. This has helped us to understand why social services were approached by these women in adversity, and the nature of their expectations. However, it is also the case that women made judgements about social services subsequent to their involvement, despite, at times, this being very limited. As with expectations, the issue of control is critical to our understanding of their judgements, just as threat is critical to understanding their appraisal of stressors.

What did control mean for these women? Were they only happy if, following social services involvement, the problem, as far as they were concerned, was brought under control? Or was some lesser achievement sufficient to gain their approval? Indeed, how would greater control manifest itself for these women?

These questions point to a need to provide an understanding of the meanings through which these women made judgements. In much of the social work literature, we are confronted with client views as a means to 'evaluate' practice. At the worst, subjective notions of satisfaction or helpfulness are used to make positive or negative comments on the value of social work. The Barclay Report, as long ago as the 1980s, commented that social workers would be surprised at the number of their clients who were satisfied with their intervention.

However, social work is not like, say, counselling or medicine. The essence (in general) of the client–counsellor, patient–doctor relationship is twofold: it is voluntary, and it is non-stigmatising. The frequently involuntary (and, even more frequently, potentially involuntary) nature of the social worker–client relationship in child care, together with the stigmatising nature of involvement with social services, is bound to have an impact on perspectives. Parents, and particularly mothers, feel a sense of blame and shame merely through coming in contact with child care social services (Sheppard 2001). At the same time, we have seen how desperate these women were when seeking social service help. Their need to take control was a major factor in the contact made. There was, then, a complex set of factors around which an understanding of client judgements needs to be reached.

We are not here seeking to present positive and negative views of social work, and then go on to describe what it was that the women saw as being positive or negative. While these views undoubtedly can have something to say about, for example, the ways social workers behaved towards them, their judgements could have as much to do with the women (as clients) as with the social workers themselves. It is apparent with depressed mothers in contact with child care social services, that at times, their aggression and antagonism towards social workers have more to do with their own sense of guilt and low self-esteem, which seems to lead to projection, than with the actions of social workers themselves (Sheppard 2001). We are engaged, we believe, in the much more productive process of seeking to understand the judgements made – technically, the discourses through which these judgements manifested themselves – and so we shall seek, in this chapter, to identify the themes around which judgements, whether positive or negative, were made.

The chapter focuses on the link between the women's sense of control and their views of social services involvement. Of course, women may well have been influenced by the manner in which a service was provided. We are aware from the literature that polite, sensitive and attentive responses are associated with positive views about social work. These are evident, from time to time, in the accounts provided here (and are relevant for the sense of validation outlined in the chapter on expectations). However, the link between control, or potential control, and judgement is evident in a number of discourses.

The 'right to service' discourse

The 'right to service' discourse revolved around the idea that the particular circumstances in which these women found themselves meant that they ought to be given access to a service, or to be treated in some particular way. This was based on an idea of justice: that if those responding were to be fair to them, to treat them equally with others, they would respond in a particular kind of way (whatever the woman felt to be appropriate). The basis for these judgements were notions of desert or, more frequently, need.

Desert

Women could consider themselves as deserving some response from social services, or, at least, not deserving *not* to have them involved. This broadly reflected a clear perception, on the one hand, of social workers as responders to people's problems, and on the other, as controllers of people's behaviour. In the former category were those who saw that there were aspects of themselves, as a person which meant that they deserved a positive response from social services. One woman, who felt her children's behaviour was stretching her beyond her limit, but who seemed unconcerned about the effects of her own, sometimes harsh, disciplining ('the kids will get knocked down, you know, bruises and whatever'), was absolutely clear about this notion of desert:

> I was literally screaming at them to help me… But I am phoning them this, like I am phoning them today, and I'm gonna say if they don't help me, then they can come and get them, because I ain't taking any more. I deserve a life and I intend to get one, with or without my kids. I deserve a life and I'll get what I deserve, what I don't get, 'cos I'm the doormat. They don't wanna to do it, they may won't do it, but there's two of them up there and they are adamant they are not going to school. Who gets in trouble? Me.

Another woman showed a similar notion of deserving services, but on the basis of having earned them. In this case, she earned them by recognising that she ought to act early, before matters got out of hand. She was being a 'good parent'. Rather than have a breakdown in her parenting, it was better to have help:

> …and I've three children to bring up, I don't want to be a wreck, this is why I tried to get hold of social services, because I want to get that sorted, before, y'know, I have a breakdown or anything… Now he's behaving because I told him yesterday that I've got social services coming round, and he's going to be, y'know, he's got a heart of gold deep down, and then he just does things that upset, y'know, bring me down.

Her judgement of social services was predicated on the idea that she deserved help, that she had acted responsibly, but that they did not respond. Indeed, they did not give her the time of day: 'There didn't seem to be anything in between being able to cope at home and getting the assistance of social services, there's no in between because you get a door shut in your face there.'

Other women felt that they did not deserve to be involved with social services, because they had done nothing that warranted it. This reflected the controlling, stigmatising side of social services, where social workers were responding to referrals about poor parenting or for reasons of child protection. One woman – who was quite positive about social services involvement – felt that she was being unfairly (and maliciously) targeted, that others were much worse, and that she did not deserve social services attention:

> She said, 'It has been allocated that you've been leaving your children on a regular basis,' you know, like on a Sunday. So I said, 'Well that is not true, you know it's not true. My older boy is 13 anyway,' I said, and I do go out in the day, but I've got a big family, my mum has them most of the day, they come back, say five, they left here approx. could be one to two hours,' I said, and that is it basically. I got really like sort of mad as well in between, I said, because I said, 'Why am I being penalised? There is worse mothers out there, blah blah blah'.

Her sense that she was being penalised was reinforced by advice from her solicitor that, with her 13-year-old at home, she had left her children legally supervised.

Desert was used in relation not just to the appropriateness of social services intervention, but also to the *process* of such intervention. Where child protection was involved, some social workers sought to visit without prior appointment, so that mothers could not prepare the child's presentation. This attempt to obtain a real picture left a woman, where nothing was found, feeling that she did not deserve such treatment. She was a good mother:

> I was flabbergasted because he done me a visit where he didn't tell me he was coming, he just turned up. So and I just told him about [daughter] and he was on about behaviour and that was it, that's the last I heard, and then I had that letter and then he took her to the GP. Now I actually got my health visitor out the next day and got her to check her over, I actually just got a letter off the school and the school nurse has just checked [daughter] over and she's come back satisfactory. But I shouldn't be doing it, I think 'Oh my kids are all right,

but why should I prove that they're in good health and all that?' I've gone through their wardrobes and think they have got nice clothes.

One woman, who declared herself 'petrified' that her children would be removed following a second (as it transpired, unwarranted) child protection referral, commented on social workers' judgement:

> I understand why they do it because children do get abused, but on two occasions that I've dealt with them they've overreacted. They just said they were satisfied with the explanation… I wasn't abusing him.

Need

Need was also a justice-related notion. In this case, women felt they had a right to a service because their problems were such that they fell below a particular standard of parenting or child behaviour. The standard was general, and their particular case, implicitly, fell under this general standard for need. The women could refer to their need in terms of their condition or *problems*. In one case, the woman used the term quite explicitly, yet found, to her disgust (and bemusement) that she fell below the level of sufficient 'need' to receive a service:

> They actually said they would send a social worker out to the B & B to assess my needs, and one never turned up. Em, when they didn't turn up, after a couple of weeks I contacted them again, and that's when I was told that it was, em, they couldn't do anything for me, it was too late anyway, it was too far into the summer holidays for them to sort anything like that out… And I spoke to another lady, on my mobile because I didn't have a phone… Someone finally told me that we were really not in a serious enough condition and that we didn't warrant any help, and they didn't give me any.

Some women were, therefore, aware about levels of need which could trigger receipt of services, although their reference point did not necessarily coincide with that of social services.

Other women referred to need, and also gave specific ideas of what their needs were. In these cases, their notion of need concerned not so much problem identification as *services required*. As in the previous case, there was an implicit notion of a level that should trigger receipt of services, a level below which the women perceived themselves to have fallen.

I didn't find they gave me much support because when I first moved down I had nothing, I mean I had nothing. I needed money for carpets, and social security wouldn't help me out and I had to go round social services because I needed help to move up to here. I rang them, I've left a message and they never got back to me, but when someone grasses me up they're on my doorstep in a flash. But when I wanted help they weren't there for me, so I can actually say that 'they weren't there for me'.

Two of the more frequently identified practical needs were for accommodation and respite from the children, both of which have been mentioned in the previous chapter. One woman's need for a new house was supported by social services when she was out on a waiting list which could be up to five years: 'So I got in touch with social services to see if they could help out with it. Which they did, but not very much'. Others judged social services in terms of their response to perceived need for a break. One woman just wanted them 'to come and take her for a couple of days, that was all I was asking, just a break. I need a break'. Another woman was disgruntled by the lack of response to her need for financial support for a part-time nursery place: 'I phoned them up again, and said they would get back to ya, and there's nothing again. So I have just left it now, I ain't bothering.'

'Response of service' discourse

The ways women viewed social services could be affected by their perception of role and function, as well as resources available. They had a 'response of service' discourse: the nature of the response was to be judged in terms of how they understood social services' role and responsibilities, or even what they thought they should be (regardless of what they actually were). However, unlike health or education, social services tends not to be a universal service, so there are no clear, informed, widely held expectations of what they will do. This meant that women frequently made abstracted judgements, not really knowing clearly what might be expected, or made judgements based on experiences of other services, or indeed, on previous experiences of social services, which contextualised their judgements.

Contextualised expectations and judgements

Women made judgements about social workers in the light of experiences they had had of other services, or of previous experiences of social services. These contexts enabled them to make judgements against other real world situations, rather than holding abstracted expectations. In view of the fact that the interventions examined here were relatively brief, without longer-term social services responses, it is perhaps not surprising that they should use past experiences of social services, where they had them, as a yardstick against which to judge these occasions.

Social services could be regarded in a positive light (regarding them as helpful, or being satisfied with their response) despite the fact that, according to the women's accounts, they had done little, or nothing of any substance. One woman made precisely this kind of comment, tending to generalise about the helpfulness of social services, rather than isolating *this* particular referral.

> *Researcher*: So do you feel that they helped you at all?
>
> *Woman*: Well, they give me advice, but then the advice they give me the step I already took, so I don't know.
>
> *Researcher*: If you had to rate their helpfulness, would you say that they are very helpful, helpful, neither/nor, or unhelpful, or very unhelpful?
>
> *Woman*: Well, they are helpful I think, if a person who doesn't know at all, I think they're quite helpful, but 'cos I've been there, I think you know, I knew. For the first time I think they were very helpful, when I got in contact with them the first time.

Her reference point was a previous referral where she received some 'time out' from her children. Despite the fact that her situation was similarly poor this time, and she did not get anything more than advice, she retained a positive view.

The reverse could happen. Women could have experienced what they regarded as little help in the past and they would judge current action against past inaction. This could lead to a rather positive view, despite limitations to the current action, as previous inaction had lowered expectations. That was the case with the following woman, who regarded social services to have been helpful:

> Then she come here and said like, that's when we made up little plans of disciplining, try and like, removing certain things... Well, basically she took him

out twice and talked to him and find out what he was, why he was all bottling it all up. But then of course it was only the two... I mean of course, when he was younger they completely did not do anything. When I really needed them when it started, nobody come out, they didn't seem to want know, which of course was not very helpful.

In other cases, it was the experience of *other* services which provided a context for making judgements about social services. A number of women approached social services when one of the emerging issues was the adequacy of their housing or environment. Housing stock was a rationed resource, and gave them the experience of having difficult access to these resources. Here social services had the opportunity to appear 'on their side' by writing in support. The idea here was to enable the women to have higher priority (and hence a greater opportunity to gain control of their situation). Even such relatively little help could lead to a positive view:

> Helpful of them to write a letter on our behalf... They got in touch with our area manager who basically said, you know, they need to be moved to the ground floor premises... Social services help as much as they can, but the council have got so many loopholes you've got to get through to get the move, you might as well go and join the circus... Basically, the way the council [housing department] works is disgusting, it is terrible, I mean you know, for us both to get three beds into the size rooms that we've got, we're looking at buying a set of bunk beds, the sort with a double bed underneath. ...But it shouldn't have to be like that. We shouldn't have to cram the children in the room.

In other cases, the women's views were coloured by an understanding of the role and limitations of social services. This woman did not get what she wanted – which was respite care, so that she could have a breather from her behaviourally problematic son – but understood this in terms of the pressure on services created by more serious cases:

> So, yeah, I asked them for help and I asked them like, you know, just take him away for a couple of days like. Put him somewhere where someone might be able to understand him. And, aaaa, that was a case of 'Hmm, OK, well there is a number, if he's naughty again or he runs away again, give us a ring'. 'Ok, so that's gonna do me a lot of good!' ...I suppose they are helpful, because if I'd phoned them up and asked anything, they'd probably would have tried to do it, at the end of the day. But I suppose they've got lots of kids to sort out with

more serious problems than [son] obviously. He's not been sexually abused or anything like that.

Another woman proclaimed herself satisfied with social services intervention, despite being the subject of a referral suggesting she had been neglectful of her children. This was based on the notion that social services 'had to do their job'.

> I don't think anybody do like social workers, do they? Do they, though?
> …But I know they got to do their job and I don't, I can't, do you know what
> I'm saying, I can't knock them, because it's true. Because you could have a
> poor little girl, you know, a child in distress, and they don't take any notice.

Abstracted judgements

Others made judgements about social services without apparently contextualising matters. Their judgements were made essentially on the basis of whether or not social services carried out what was expected of them, or at least the extent to which they did this. While there was a tendency for those who contextualised their judgements to be positive, those who made abstracted judgements were less positive.

One woman was referred to mediation in order to resolve a violent conflict with her teenage son. This was not something with which she felt motivated to engage, and she could not get over the fact that this was not what she was looking for:

> I don't feel I got… I felt from them that they were just, oh, I don't know how
> to put this… I just feel that it was like 'Oh, let's quiet her down, go to her
> house, this woman sounds upset, we got to be there for her'. But I don't think
> they were there for me. Within weeks of all this happening they actually sent
> me a letter and I was a bit disgusted actually, it was 'We are closing the file
> down, but if you need us any time, you've got our number, contact us'.

This was also the case with another woman, with a son with ADHD. What she wanted was not clear, but what she got was clearly not what she wanted:

> Er, we phoned a few of the numbers they gave us and there were people in
> exactly in the same situation, banging their heads against the brick wall,
> saying 'Where can we go for help?' And that's how far we got with those
> helpline numbers. And locally there aren't any support groups… I contacted a
> few of them. Basically they were parents in the same situation as us, you know,

you get support from other parents and that, but as I said, that wasn't what we were looking for, so.

One woman, with problems dealing with three young children, particularly her three-year-old boy, who could be quite aggressive, expected direct social work intervention. She was instead offered parenting classes, which the social worker felt was appropriate to her particular problems. For her, however, this was being 'fobbed off'. This theme of having really quite specific expectations, without particular knowledge of the services, was apparent in another woman's account of what she expected of social services to do while she was waiting to move house:

> Well, I would have expected them to get back to me, and I expected them to give me the backing for the last weeks before we moved, to either keep them home or making some arrangement for a taxi service. But nothing, nothing at all.

Problem control discourse

Women, unsurprisingly perhaps, also made judgements based on the extent to which social services involvement helped them gain control, or gave them the prospect of gaining control of their problems. Of course, social services were only involved for brief periods, so they were unlikely, as clients, to achieve a great deal in terms of the more intractable problems. However, where they did not achieve a great deal, this tended to be framed in terms of a 'rights to service' discourse: they might not have achieved much control, but that was because their rights or the social services response did not enable this to happen.

In some cases, women framed their view in terms of the degree of *actual* control (rather than potential control) that had been achieved. This was generally framed in a positive manner, and could be identified in terms of clear material gains or changes. One woman, who felt her husband was harsh, verging on violent, in his discipline of her children, saw changes in him arising directly from the brief involvement of social services. Commenting on the extent to which social services had helped her, she said:

> Yeah (laughs). Yeah they did… It was me making the decision to do some-thing and then seek out what was available. What help was available… I think [partner] recognised that he had to go and get some more help…he needs somebody really to sort of challenge him a bit more and try to get to the roots

of some of the, you know, where his behaviour is from... But he is generally handling better, things better, things are calmer... Because of his ability to get a bit wound up...but it did sort of put a catalyst on the, him going to get some more help, really.

Acting as a catalyst for change, rather than being directly responsible for that change, seems to have been a major way in which social services helped this woman gain greater control. This was evident also in the account of one of the women who was seeking re-housing, and where the social worker simply contacted the environmental health department in support of her:

> She come in and seen me and she met my [son] and my [son] and she said, 'About the damp over there,' I said, 'Yeah, I'm not going to decorate it,' I said, 'I don't see why I should 'cos the whole house is damp. I've got water coming through the roof, blah blah,' all this lot, she said, 'Let's see what we can do,' she said, 'a nice little house for you would be good.' So she got the council round, so they done an assessment on the house and thousands and thousands of pounds' worth of stuff that needs doing, so the council approached my landlord and now he's evicted me. Which is good for me because I get a house.

Similarly, social workers were, in the brief time they were involved, occasionally able to bring a more positive outlook to negotiations with schools arising from non-attendance at school, or behavioural difficulties. One woman commented, after her son had been excluded, that 'since I've been to social services and had a meeting with the school...he has been alright since', having successfully re-entered school. Another, who felt her child took no notice of her, welcomed the intervention of the courts to ensure school attendance, which she attributed to social services intervention (even though they had little part to play).

Another way control was achieved was not so much the result of changing the situation, as of enabling the woman to change her perspective of that situation, and thus gain a greater sense of control. Social workers, in effect, helped the women have a greater sense of control through reframing. One woman made this clear when she said that social workers had allowed her to review her action, and in the process reinterpret both the comments of her child (which were inflammatory) and the basis on which they were made – through understanding the child's perspective better.

> They were good because they were able to speak to the children, and, em, ob-
> viously when I spoke to them, em, because I've seen it in a different light, I
> mean obviously I didn't realise it when he came right up to my face and called
> me a bitch, and I slapped him... When it's the first time that your child has
> actually to your face called you a bitch, I think it was more shock than
> anything, plus, to me, coming from [son], you know, the quiet one in the
> family... He'd had a very, very bad day at school. He'd been hit a couple of
> times by one of the children and he'd been coming home and taking it out on
> me, and his reaction was to call me a bitch. And of course my reaction was a
> slap.

With a changed interpretation of the situation came a changed sense of its threat
and a greater sense of control. This was similarly the case with the woman who
had felt she had to have her daughter adopted because of the pressures put on
her by her family. She felt, however, that the social worker had enabled her to
make choices, and realise that she could make decisions for herself:

> Yeah, y'know, I can't fault them in one way... They helped me with
> [daughter] mainly, why I went through social services in the first place, he was,
> he made me feel like I always had the choices to make. My auntie and uncle
> and my family always made decisions for me, so, y'know, he gave me the
> choice to make by myself. They always said, 'you can't do this' and 'you can't
> do that', he said to me, 'Whatever you decide, it's down to you.' He made me
> feel quite, that I was able to do things myself, so.

The result was that she was able to take back control of this immensely
important issue, and decision, for herself.

In other cases the women felt that social services had created a greater
potential for control. In these cases, nothing material had happened (nor a
reframing), but they felt they were in a better position to gain their objectives,
and hence control, as a result of social services involvement. In some cases,
knowing their legal rights, particularly in relation to parenting, when in conflict
with partners or former partners, was very important. In the following case, the
woman was able to establish that she, and she only, had parental responsibility,
and social services were instrumental in enabling this:

> Without them I didn't know where I stood... I think, if I remember correctly,
> he said about phoning a solicitor because they needed to tell me where I stood
> and...to let them know what my solicitor said, so that they can help me if I
> needed them, that was it... All good changes happened 'cos I went all the

right way about doing it, and after everything had settled down I remember the bloke [from social services] phoned me up to ask me if everything has been sorted...to ask if I need any more help or anything, but that's been it since then.

Other cases showed how advice could operate to enable women to gain greater potential control. This most frequently related to the responsibilities of child care. In one case, the woman was helped by advice on how to respond to difficult behaviour – whether depriving the child of privileges, or by ignoring the behaviour. In another case the woman, having been subject to an unwanted child protection referral, was impressed by the advice she received on ways of avoiding such referral in the future. This came following her exoneration. She commented on the low-key way the advice was given:

> And then...she did like, chat to me after, 'Can you make aware if you do go out sometimes, like up the shop, blah blah blah, can you make sure...when people go to your door...can you warn the children that you know not to let anybody in, and if it's like show their card, if it's somebody come like that.' And I said, 'Well, yeah, that's true, you know, because I mean, it could be anybody,' she said, 'There's a lot of bogus people around,' so I said, 'Yeah, yeah...' So she did help me in ways, yeah.

Threat and the convergence–divergence discourse

Women were frequently concerned, as we have seen, that their situations be taken seriously. In part, this meant that they received the services they felt they needed or deserved. However, in other circumstances, the extent to which they *agreed or disagreed* with social workers was fundamental in the extent to which the women felt they were able to exert, or regain, control of the situation. This was most evident with child protection referrals, where the level of threat generated was not so much about the apparent problem with parenting or children, as about the actual involvement of social services, and the fears arising from this, particularly that the children might be 'taken away'.

The degree of concern generated by this issue has been identified in the previous chapter, and it could be so great that the sense of threat that it caused coloured all subsequent judgements. With child protection this meant that the negative perceptions and emotions overwhelmed any subsequent convergence of view between social worker and client. Even – as in all these cases – where the situations were quickly found not to be serious enough to merit anything more than a brief assessment, women could retain a negative perspective, and a fear of losing control.

This was the case for one woman, for whom the experience of a brief assessment (rather than investigation) was the pervasive memory, rather than the fact that social services took matters no further:

> ...they phoned me up...and I thought he said, 'I'm coming to see you with a view to taking your children off you.' I said, 'Oh are you?' So when they came you know, I told him what I thought, I wasn't rude or anything like that but I just said, 'Look, you know this is the case this is happened. And you know, and I do have six other children and you know,' I said to him, 'you took a complete overreaction on [daughter's] part, and you know, and that's it.' And they wanted me to go to [child/adolescent psychiatric unit] and blah blah blah.

Her anger (and concern) were evident, even though she recognised that she had probably made a mistake in thinking that the social worker had said that he was 'taking your children off you' (an unlikely statement in view of the fact that no assessment had actually been made). So her judgements about social work, strongly linked to a sense of (lack of) control, were negatively coloured by this experience.

Another woman expressed the effects of these assessments when she commented that, despite having found nothing against her, 'they seem to have made my life worse than better now'. Having been accused of mistreating her children, even the supportive and reassuring approach of the social worker was insufficient to remove this sense of threat:

> And the bloke said, he looked at me and he knew, but he came in and talked to me and he was just very nice. He said, 'I can tell by you, you're a nice woman, and I can't see you doing that sort of thing.'

When women were not overwhelmed by this feeling of threat and dread, the subsequent assessment could have a significant impact on the relationship between their sense of control and judgements about social services. It is perhaps unsurprising that the most pervasive impact was achieved through a process – which could be quite quick – of exoneration. *Exoneration* involved a convergence of view between the woman and the social worker, in particular that she was not maltreating the children, but also (frequently) that the referral was inappropriate, or even malicious. Exoneration generally meant that, despite the trauma of social services involvement, the woman was positive, on the whole, about social services.

The significance of the assessment is evident from the vividness with which women recalled this process. One woman detailed, for example, how the social worker checked things through, but also emphasised the normality of her behaviour in disciplining her son. Indeed, she gained great satisfaction and self-justification from the criticism the social worker made of the referrer.

> They came round and well, checked out [son], made sure he was ok. They were concerned about [son], saying I was doing things to [son] that I wasn't doing. When they saw [son] was ok, they well, just cancelled the complaint. It was next door here. I had an argument with this old couple next door and then, they heard me shouting at [son]. I don't care who you are, you must be the best carer in the world, you still shout at the child. They heard me shouting and then they called the social services. And as I said, they came in and said there's nothing wrong with [son] at all, nothing. And they, social got them into trouble, writing them a letter saying, 'If you do it again, make nuisance telephone calls,' then they are gonna be taken to court.

Another woman showed an almost euphoric sense of satisfaction with the social worker who was instrumental in her exoneration. Indeed, even the son who remained a concern, was, as far as she was concerned, not being blamed on her, but had, because of his age, to take responsibility for himself:

> ...on this case for instance, my social worker, she's been absolutely brilliant and she sent a letter the other day and said, 'Look I feel like I can closed the case, your kids all wonderful kids.' She's met them all, she said, 'The only concern we've got is for [son].' She said I haven't got a problem with the other two. So I know they're fit, healthy, they're looked after, are clothed well, but [son] is not going school, so he's got a year left so everyone's like washing their hands of him now. Once he reached like, 15, they're like, 'Well, he's only got a year so we'll just, don't worry about him, he'll sort himself out'...they're not interested.

Women felt the exoneration most keenly where they were not simply cleared, but where the referrer making the allegations was criticised. This served to reinforce their own innocence, and the sense that they had been the victim of malicious, over-zealous or misguided concern. They could join the social worker in being dismissive of the referrer. The social worker spoke to this woman:

'I didn't really want to mention this,' she said, 'but I'll mention it to see how pathetic it is,' she said, that 'your children was playing out in the street' – we're talking in the day time unaccompanied by adults – she said, 'and I thought that was so silly.' She said, 'Even then I didn't make a comment on that, I mean they're allowed to ain't they, they're not babies,' so she said, 'I thought that was a bit over the top.' I went, 'Well, thank you'.

Convergence of view did not always lead to positive views about social services. Social workers could retain some reservations about parenting while nevertheless recognising that the situation did not represent a child protection risk. In one case, the woman was referred for beating her children. The case was not viewed as one of child protection, and the social worker gave the woman 'permission' to use corporal punishment. Despite this she could only consider this a small amount of help:

The only thing they did help me with, they told me if she was really naughty – she tells me that I can't smack her, and they said I can. 'Cos she tells me, 'You are not allowed to smack me at all.' I said, 'It's very rare I do smack you, but they say if I have to, then I'm allowed to.' But not go whack, whack, whack, which I wouldn't do anyway, but they said if she pushed me, they said... she shouldn't push me too far. So I have to turn around and tell her off.

Conclusion and summary

1. Coping theory would suggest that women made judgements about social services based on their perceptions of control resulting from social services' help. However, those judgements depended on what that meant to them in the context – as well as reflecting their perceptions and assumptions about social services.

2. Women formed their judgements through a number of perspectives or discourses. One was a '*right to service*' discourse, revolving around the notion that, in their particular circumstances, they ought to be given access to a service, or treated in a particular way. It involved notions of equality of treatment.

3. Some women based their perceptions on desert – they *deserved* to receive a service, or conversely, not to be bothered. Women based their notions of desert on factors like personal qualities, 'earning' a service, or being too good for consideration.

4. Others based their perspective on *need*, another justice-related notion. Women felt they had a right to a service because their problems were such that they fell below a particular standard of parenting or child behaviour – a general standard of need. This could be based on problems manifested or services received.

5. The *'response of service'* discourse entailed women's perceptions of the role and function of social services as well as resources available. Whatever the reality of the situation, women's perceptions of role and function could affect perceptions of the actions of social services.

6. *Contextualised judgements* on role and function were those based on experiences of other services, or previous experiences of social services. These enabled some real-world, comparison-based judgements.

7. *Abstracted judgements* were made apparently without contextualising matters, and essentially on the basis of whether social services carried out what was expected of them, or the extent to which this happened.

8. The *'problem control'* discourse related to the extent to which social services involvement enabled women to take control, or gave them the prospect of gaining control of their problems. This could involve changes in actual control achieved, social services as catalysts for change, a greater sense of control through reframing, or the potential for increasing control.

9. In the *convergence–divergence* discourse, the extent to which the professional and the woman agreed or disagreed was fundamental in the extent to which women felt they were able to exert control. This was most evident with child protection referrals, where, for example, convergence between woman and social worker in a positive view of her parenting reduced threat and enabled her to gain control.

CHAPTER 15

Referral for Support to Outside Agencies

A key element in the development of family support services is the availability and use of agencies and professionals in situations where social services are not involved. Local authorities are expected to develop (as we have seen) a range of support services for families in need, and these, in principle, should be available when social workers are not themselves able to provide support following referral (exactly the position for women in this study). Thus, it is not necessarily the case that inability to provide a 'caseload service' to families referred means no support from any local agencies. Women were directed to other possible sources of support for themselves, their child(ren), or the family as a whole.

From the mother's point of view, the use of support provides a strategy for coping, since in principle this can help reduce the threat of the child care problem, and help them gain control of the situation. This support focuses upon the actions and decision-making of the mothers themselves. From the perspective of social services, it would be about agency responses to *need*, while from the women's point of view it would be about the effort to gain some control, and hence to *cope*. However, there are, in the first instance, two elements of decision-making: that of social services to refer on, or advise the woman what services to seek; and that of the mother on whether she should take them up. The key issue here is: to what extent does the agency's assessment of what the woman (and her family) *need* fit with the woman's view of what will help her to *cope* better?

This primarily concerns the mother's response to referral and her use of agencies, to which we will now turn.

Women who were not referred on

Women were not always referred on, or even given suggestions as to the kinds of agencies which might help them. This could be because there were no available appropriate agencies, because the woman herself did not want to be referred on, or because the problems had been dealt with as far as possible in the short time she was involved with social services.

No referral – no problem!

Women, it should be remembered, did not necessarily expect to be referred on. Most frequently, particularly where they referred themselves, they were looking for some form of direct service. Some women, therefore, were happy with this situation because *they had received a service from social services, or had got from them what they expected.* In one case a woman with three children had been subject to domestic violence from her now estranged husband. One of her children was badly affected by contact with his father (the estranged husband had a contact order), and she said that after seeing his father 'he comes back to me, I have three or four days of constant abuse, and it's like my husband's voice talking through my son'. She needed advice on her legal situation, and social services were able to provide this.

> *Researcher:* Did they do what you expected them to do?

> *Woman:* Yes, I think so really, yeah. I mean that's my only involvement with social services really… Just gave me advice…that's the only contact I ever really had with the, just gave me advice on what to do. 'Cos I was concerned that my husband wouldn't let me to speak to my son…and as it happened I managed to speak to him later on that night, but they were quite helpful when I spoke to them, you know.

Obtaining a service which fitted with their prior expectations gave the women both a positive view of social services, and the feeling that there was no need for referral to another agency. There were various ways in which this could occur. As in the last example, this could involve legal advice, brief counselling, providing suggestions about child care, information, or (as in the next case) provision of financial or resource help. Here, a woman referred by her health visitor needed help with nursery fees because her two-year-old slept very little and alternated, during the day, between periods of being very lethargic, and lengthy spells of whining and crying. The woman needed some kind of escape from this, and the lack of suggestions about other possible helping agencies was of no concern to her:

> I can't do housework because she's whinging around me, I mean she hangs on to my ankles when I'm walking across the floor, you know, 'cos she just wants me. She doesn't play on her own, you got to play with her. ...I went to see them and spoke to [social worker] the lady up there, and she said she'd speak to her manager and got back to me, and she said they'd pay £5 a week for three months and that was it... Er, I thought it was great getting £5 towards it...because I'm on income support, I don't really get a lot of money and I do struggle each week, and the only way for me to get a break is for her to go to nursery.

Some women expressed a feeling of threat about being involved with social services. The child protection function clearly has such a pervasive impact on public perceptions that some of these women, who did not refer themselves, became anxious at the mere involvement of social services. One example involved a mother about whom concerns were expressed in relation to alleged emotional abuse of her 15-year-old son, who had learning difficulties. Her own view of her son was that he had 'behavioural problems' and that he was more 'like a ten-year-old', who had 'thrown a wobbly' and then run away. As far as she was concerned, the intervention was not really appropriate, and hence not much use. However, the quality of the service was not the issue on this occasion. Her main concern was to sever all involvement with social services or social service-related agencies, which meant that not being referred on was something of a relief:

> *Researcher:* Did they suggest any other agencies?
>
> *Woman:* No, no... Well, I just came home from work really, and the phone went and it was the social worker, and she just said it was the social services and checked my name, you know. And she said 'I've got some concerns in regards to your son,' and I thought 'alright' so...I was really taken aback you know, I mean I got really upset, and why had she done that you know, so. But it was like shock then really, more than anything, you know.

Even where referrals were not made specifically for child protection, as we have noted earlier, involvement with social services could itself be seen as the problem with which the woman had to cope, and removal of that threat would remove her anxiety. This could extend not simply to social services involvement, but even to their part in referring the woman to some other agency. In one case a midwife contacted social services about a pregnant 14-year-old. The mother had a strong feeling of relief that involvement was brief.

> No, no, it was a very brief, just sort of quickly said, 'We see that things seem to be OK. Your family being very supportive, we don't need to contact you further, if you need to contact us please do so,' and that was, yeah, they hadn't offered any other support, but then I suppose they thought we didn't need it at the time... And I think I felt a bit threatened because there is that element of they could sort of intervene too greatly you know... So it was a bit of a relief when...they said that they wouldn't be involved in the near future.

No referral – not happy

Women did not generally approach social services to be referred on, although they might be seeking information or advice about where help could be obtained. However, lack of referral to an appropriate agency could prevent their obtaining the kind of service for which they were looking, if this was not to be obtained from social services. When social services did not help, this could leave the woman *feeling undervalued and unimportant.* One woman who was receiving psychiatric care, diagnosed with a psychosis, was concerned that she was 'doing serious damage to [her son's] mind'. She wanted help directly, or to be sent somewhere where help could be found. They did not, she commented, even give her any phone numbers where she might get help:

> I didn't get anything positive from it, what I needed was all around them, as an emergency, because I really was getting in quite a state at the time I made the phone call. And wanted them to come out straight away, it was an emergency, I wanted to get him out of the house straight away because I really was ill...and I don't hear from them for about a week. They were told it was an emergency and they didn't help, and it took them about a week to reason with.

Referral on might not have helped because this woman was clearly in a crisis. The search for respite from their children was a continuous theme of many women's approach to social services (although some women accepted other help, such as brief advice or information, when given). This occurred across age groups. Clearly, in view of the brevity of social services involvement, respite was not generally forthcoming. Where this was the case, referral on was less the issue than the fact that the woman *did not receive any respite* (unless the respite was itself seen as referral on). This was the case with a woman with a teenage daughter who, she considered, constantly challenged her authority, lied, stole and cheated:

> I expected them to arrange proper respite care and I said I need at least two weeks, preferably a month and what I got... It had no effect, no help at all... I needed a proper break for at least for two weeks.

At times the refusal to give attention to the women's concerns, even to the point of not referring them for appropriate help to other agencies, was veiled, the women felt, in excuses:

> I think at that time [I was] very dissatisfied because they keep saying that they were going through reorganisation, not good enough. Service still has to go on. In which office they work from and which area that person refer to, because we were on the boundary and they were changing it, is not a good enough reason for not doing anything.

Some women took action in the absence of any action by social services – 'if they won't take action, then I will'. If they did this, it was generally when they had some knowledge of what was on offer from another agency. Such knowledge would normally require previous experience, as was the case with one woman who was experiencing increasingly difficult behaviour from both her children, who were approaching their teenage years. She had previously been involved with the local child psychiatric unit.

The lack of action by social services was the precursor to her self-referral to the child psychiatric unit. She felt this particularly keenly because social services had reneged on a promise to provide some direct help:

> ...they went off and did their assessment. Er, they come back again and more or less they just couldn't see a problem... I mean I sat down and talked to them and I said I need help, and then of course I never heard from them again, you know. They were gonna do this for me, they were gonna try things, like different things for me to help me, and they never got back, I never seen them since, I thought, 'Oh fine, you know, if that's the case, you know. Then you're not ready to help me, then you just stay away, I don't wanna know.'

Women who were referred on

Of particular interest, both theoretically and in terms of policy and practice, and in circumstances where we wish to link the strategy for coping with the response to need, is the response of women where they were referred to another agency.

Some women were positive about being referred to other agencies, even when they had expected social services to intervene directly. Such women characteristically felt that there had been a response appropriate to their perceived need (one of the key criteria for judging social services as well as referral on) and also that the referral had led to a speedy response, or one appropriate to their own timetable. In addition the agency would be seen in a positive light, because the woman felt that it had helped in some way. Where this combination of appropriateness, timeliness and helpfulness existed, women were happy with referral on. One woman in her early twenties approached social services because of a delay in sorting out her claim for income support, which meant that she had received no money for over three months since leaving her last job. She was, she said, 'at her wits' end', and was referred to a counselling centre for young people.

> Yes, I went to the… Centre …they were…as helpful as they could be, it was more counselling really that they gave me, because at that point I was extremely low. I had a couple of sessions with them, which sort of boosted my confidence a little bit. Because I…felt like I had failed, like I'd just got myself into a big pit of desperation. …But I suppose they did pick me back up again and gave me a kick to say 'this is not the case, you have just hit a low for a little while and you can get back up there', because I was very depressed about it, but yeah, they were all quite helpful to me.

Interestingly, such brief counselling was certainly within the remit of social services, even within the realm of initial referral and assessment, yet she did not feel that social services had been remiss in suggesting another agency for help. Of course, her own actions were important in this, since she responded quickly to this suggestion, and was very quickly able to obtain help from the agency to which she was referred. This was far from the norm, however.

Another case illustrated the importance of appropriateness, but as part of a process of developing understanding of what was needed. The woman's 13-year-old son had become increasingly violent and had tried to stab someone. She feared that he might try to kill someone, and was told by the doctor that she should seek social services help. However, the social worker persuaded her that this was really a medical (psychiatric) matter, and in the subsequent 'tug of war' over who was to take responsibility, it was the GP who eventually gave way, much to the satisfaction of the mother, who had become convinced that social services were right.

> They just talked to me, they said to get the GP involved. So I rang the GP and he said no, so I wrote the doctor a letter and he said, 'It's a social services matter,' I phoned the social services and they said, 'no, it's not, it's a matter of medical help, he needs medical help not social services help.' And then they phoned up my GP and said, 'Look you got to, he needs medical help you know, you need to help [son].' So that's it, they helped a lot because they managed to, you know, get the GP to actually listen you know. It looks like we might get through this time with a bit of luck.

In other cases women were positive about referral on because this meant social services were no longer to be involved. This was part of 'getting social services out of their hair', and generally featured when they had been referred by someone else because of a child protection issue or some perceived inadequacy in parenting. It was pretty well universally the case, when women did not refer themselves, and there was some question over their parenting, that they feared the powers of social services, and were desperate to extricate themselves from involvement. Referral on was one means of achieving this.

Such was the case with one woman, referred by her health visitor, who was concerned about her over-robust approach to disciplining. She actually made positive comments about social services, despite her fears: 'They helped me to put them into play schemes, play schemes she's in. That's where she goes twice a week… Brilliant, get there like.' While the manifest benefits of this referral are clear, in view of the pressures she felt caring for her children, her enthusiasm was as much about 'moving on' and away from the clutches of social services, relatively unscathed. When she found social services involved –

> I started panicking. I'd had them in, once before they come round, I told them to get out of the house like, not the one that was round, the other one, I told her I don't want her in my house anymore. All because…they went round to my sister-in-law and she had no guard on the stairs and he fell down the stairs and they came round to look. That's couple of years now.

Negative views of referral on

Negative views about referral on predominated by far over positive views. Indeed, wherever there was an absence of one of the three criteria for positive views – appropriateness, timeliness and helpfulness – women generally regarded referral on in a negative light, often as an avoidance of responsibility by social services. It is worth reminding ourselves that women did not generally approach social services for information about other agencies that might help them. Where they referred themselves to social services, they most frequently wanted direct help, often in the form of material help or respite, and so they could quickly view referral on in a dim light.

For many women, referral on missed the point. A mother of a 14-year-old was very concerned about the promiscuous behaviour she feared was being manifested by her daughter. They had recently moved into the area, and she felt this had destabilised the girl, and that she was getting in with a 'bad crowd'. With increasing arguments, she felt that her daughter was not listening to her, and hoped she would give a better response to social services:

> And all I wanted them to do was to come out talk to [daughter] explain the dangers to her because she wasn't listening to me, she won't listen to her father, she won't listen to anybody in the member of the family at all. All I wanted was somebody, an outsider to talk to her, explain the situation, the dangers, but they wouldn't even do that for me.

She was contemptuous of the 'signposting' response (providing her with telephone numbers which she might phone to obtain help). Signposting meant that social services were not actually helping, and the booklet with which she was provided was no better than the one she already had.

> They gave me a couple of phone numbers and then sent me out a little booklet on sexual awareness. Which [daughter] already got a book on sexual aware-ness from Girl Guides 'cos she's going Girl Guides. And they sent them this booklet that tells them the facts of life, …she's got all that, so she's fully aware of it all. But they wouldn't help me.

In other cases, the brevity of social services response was itself the problem: women at times felt that they had so little contact that they could not form an informed opinion. This being so, how could they know about the appropriate-ness of any agency to which they referred on? One woman described her daughter as 'weird', and was afraid that she might have mental health problems.

The mother was also frequently aggressive, had tantrums and also seemed depressed. She seemed to have hoped for social services to provide some respite care and was disappointed when it was not forthcoming. This was not helped by the failure of the young woman to talk to the social worker on her own. However, the key to the mother's dissatisfaction with referral was that it was, as far as she was concerned, based on ignorance:

> They talked to me and put me in the right direction like, but what I expected them to do was to be more supportive. It wasn't, they came out and had a word with [daughter] but that was it. I really expected them to see us for a little bit longer, rather than just one visit. I mean, how do you know somebody after one visit, you don't, I really think they should have got back in touch with me. They said I can any time but it shouldn't be left down to me, it should have made sure that I was happy.

NOT TAKING UP REFERRAL TO A SUGGESTED AGENCY

In these cases where the referral on was felt to be inappropriate, some women simply did not take up social workers' suggestions. While the idea of referral on might, for the agency, represent directing service users to the appropriate services for their particular need, some women saw this as 'passing the buck'. For them referral on for appropriate help was a fiction, they had little reason to believe that this new agency would do anything, and they showed their contempt by refusing to take up the suggestion. In one such case, the mother wanted help to enable her son to remain at a school despite having moved from its catchment area. Social services was part of a network of agencies, none of whom were prepared, as far as she was concerned, to take responsibility.

> *Woman:* Oh, they passed me round every service in bloody building, do you know what I mean, and none of them could help, so I just got on with it.
>
> *Researcher:* Which agencies did they suggest that you go and see?
>
> *Woman:* Er, administration I think, a couple of other places in there, occupational welfare officer and things like that. Only at the end of the day they weren't the people I needed to be talking to. Like when I phoned the council, the woman in the council said, 'Oh no, you need to get on to social services.'

Behind all this she detected something of a fraud. They were not interested in the right service to respond to need, but rather with finding a way to save money: 'and all they ever go on about is "our budget is this, and we are stretched here and we are stretched there".'

Another persistent and, on the face of it, surprising complaint was the frequent tendency of social services to refer back, or 'signpost' agencies which had already been used, and which, as far as the woman was concerned, had already failed. This appears to have been either a failure of imagination on the part of the practitioners, or a failure of resources on the part of local agencies. In one case, the local child psychiatric unit was the one and only suggestion given to the mother.

> *Woman*: Not really, no, that was it. This time that was basically it, you know, it was 'well, [child psychiatric unit] is the only answer' and it had already failed as far as I was concerned. So what's the point of going back you know… they never tackled [son's] behaviour really, which was the main reason for us going there, especially the second time we went there.
>
> *Researcher*: Have you contacted them again?
>
> *Woman*: No, I haven't, I haven't, it's just on hold and as I said, they haven't contacted me either, so. They just put it on hold and not bother to contact us at all.

Other women expressed similar frustrations with referral back to 'failed agencies'. One woman sought help for her young boy, who was showing behavioural difficulties, becoming aggressive and deliberately breaking objects at home. She felt that the support group to which she was referred was really a sham, where no real behavioural or therapeutic work was undertaken. Rather it was a recreational club, as far as she was concerned.

> *Woman*: Yeah, but I've been here before with my other little boy when I was a lot younger actually…it's a long time ago now and they sort of showed different things you can do with them, so whatever she suggested we'd actually already tried, so it didn't really help, so.
>
> *Researcher*: When you were in contact with the support group before, did you find that helpful?
>
> *Woman*: No, they, mostly they sat down and drank coffee, that was about it really, so it wasn't really support.

Sometimes it was not the parent but the child, or particularly the young person, who refused to take up a service which they had found wanting in the past.

When that happened, even if the mother felt it might be helpful (in this case she was far from convinced), the behaviour of the young person would undermine attempts to make use of the service. The mother recalled:

I phoned social services – I explained the circumstances, then they said, they turned around and said they didn't think it was a social service matter, take her into this [Youth Advice Service] place. So I said, 'Fair enough, I'll do that.' …and then she had a phone call to say she had an appointment two weeks ago on Saturday at half past one…she said, 'I'm not going.' I said, 'Well, I can't force, you but it's only polite you phone them and cancel your appointment with them, because you know there might be somebody urgently needing to see them.'

On some occasions women had no faith in the agency or professions to which they were referred. This had similarities with agencies which, as far as they were concerned, had already failed, but their scepticism was based, not on previous client status, but on knowledge derived form elsewhere. This could be through, for example, information from friends or acquaintances, reputation, or acquaintance gained in some way directly. Such opinions were not necessarily informed or accurate – reputations or informally gained knowledge could mislead. However, they clearly had an impact on some women. This was the case with one woman referred to a child support team using behavioural methods. Asked why she had not taken up the referral, she commented:

Woman: Because I work in a school, er, I had, I've had dealings with the behavioural support team through the children I worked with. Some of the things they do I don't agree with, you know.

Researcher: What are they?

Woman: Er, ignoring, ignoring the child when he's having a tantrum or swearing or you know, going absolutely mental, just ignore it. Well, that's not right for me. No, I can put my son in the kitchen if he's having a tantrum and I can stand in the doorway and he'll wreck everything in there you know, and I'll stand and I'll watch and when he's sat down on the floor I'll say, 'Right, have you finished now? Yes, right, now you clean up all this because you were the one that had the tantrum and you were the one that made the mess.' Well according to the behavioural support team no, you clean up the mess, because he's done it and that's the way of showing his anger. …Well, I don't suppose that anyone is gonna find a way that works properly you know, but I just don't agree with some of the things that they suggest. So I didn't contact them.

PARENTS WHO WAIT

A major problem of referral on, or signposting, to other agencies was that the referrer had no control over a range of factors determining when, and indeed whether, a person received a service. The first obvious problem was that they could refuse to take the family on as clients. When signposting occurred, social services might not even be aware of this refusal. The same was the case where there was any delay, because of the fleeting nature of social work involvement. At times, other professionals were gatekeepers to services, as was the case where social workers felt referral to a child psychiatric unit was needed, and the GP was required for a referral to occur. Even where a service might be available, then women were often confronted with a wait. This was the last thing many of them needed. They generally approached social services in a crisis, they were seeking direct help, and they would then be referred on and have to wait for some indeterminate period. They were, at times, however unintentionally, 'left to stew'. Even where they managed, eventually, to gain access to the referred agency, they were left with the prospect of relaying yet again personal, often distressing information.

Some women, although unenthusiastic about referral on and waiting, were, as far as they were concerned, realistic enough to know this was necessary where resources were limited. One woman who was referred to the behavioural team, and to the child psychiatric unit, through her GP, was sanguine, despite the fact that she was (in relation to the child psychiatric unit) 'on the waiting list and would be on it for about eight months'. She had better news from the behaviour support team, where there was 'only' a four-week wait. Her stoicism, in view of the acceptance by all agencies of her need for help, was admirable:

> I think I probably expected a few more suggestions, probably what I could do to sort of control him a little bit more. But I suppose that's what they've done, they couldn't do anything so they sent me to somebody who possibly can, so yes, they did what I expected.

Despite this, it is difficult to see how an eight-month wait qualifies as a response to a family in need. Other mothers were less than impressed by the delays involved in referral. In the following case, the woman was not simply waiting, but aware also that the wait might anyway be in vain, and she might receive no service at the end of it. Her concern was about her 13-year-old daughter, who was aggressive, defiant, and staying out more than her mother would have liked:

> We got to go to the doctors and get a referral. The social worker wasn't 100 per cent sure whether or not we could just ring up and go have, you know, one or refer ourselves, but it was more certain that we have to go to our own GP. I don't really know how long it will take to get you know, a day to come through.

However, this woman felt a high degree of urgency: 'I was so worried about her running off or whatever. I was so scared that she could be raped or even worse found dead, and you know we needed somebody like a lifeline.' Unsurprisingly, the woman was unhappy with this state of affairs:

> ...although he was kind enough to say [child psychiatry unit] it just wasn't, for me it just wasn't enough. When you're distraught and upset and every-thing gone and you've got, you know, he says, 'Oh, she's at risk,' you know, what do you class as a risk? ...but I expected help immediately, not to wait for weeks and weeks for referrals.

Some women, having summoned the courage to refer themselves to social services, felt a rush of negative emotions when no help was forthcoming. Having gained some sense of hope through referring themselves, their hope was dashed as much by the delay entailed in referral as by the failure of social services themselves to provide help. It could, as in the case of this woman, leave them with a profound sense of isolation in the face of threatening problems. She was also doubtful of the likely helpfulness of the referral. She was concerned about her teenage daughter, who alternated between being withdrawn and being aggressive, who threatened to run away from home, and whose behaviour she described as 'weird':

> They wrote back to me and said that I longer no needed social services *and I thought, 'Oh, my God I'm on me own now'* [author's italics]. But she did get me in touch with [daughter's] doctor again, psychiatrist, so we'll be going to see him again as a family soon. To find out what action is needed... We try that road if it don't go too well, then I have to sit down and I'll talk to her and how she's making everybody's life hard, you know.

Another woman expressed similar feelings of despair when she was looking for professional help with her younger family. She was seeking counselling help for herself: 'And I said, "I think I might be having a nervous breakdown," and that was two months ago and I've been waiting since then, and I've been here feeling like (crying) I feel awful.'

Left in distress and even despair, women could have to start the process again of taking the initiative themselves. One woman commented on the efforts she was making to get support elsewhere: 'I [have] been trying, I've been trying so much like, and of course they have got a waiting list for up to six months so it's a case of hit and miss if I can get hold of them, and if I can get one in, then I can get one in, but you know.'

In another case, the woman became so desperate that she telephoned the Samaritans, finding them far more helpful than social services.

> Yeah, and I phoned the Samaritans... I found them by just talking to them, and this woman on the other end helped me more than social services did... I'm not a bad mother and that I've had problems with kids, who hasn't? ...They were willing to listen to me and at the end of talking to them for about half an hour I felt peace with myself, sort of thing. I felt like I can cope for another day, sort of thing.

Distress, however, could lead to demoralisation, rather than taking the initiative. Often social services, as we have seen, simply gave women the names and telephone numbers of relevant agencies, expecting them to contact those agencies themselves. For a variety of reasons, this could be an inadequate approach to helping these women, if they wanted them to take up the service. Simply providing them with names and telephone numbers, together with brief explanations (at times not even that), frequently did not give women a clear enough idea of what was on offer. Without this they may have been reluctant to contact the agencies themselves. Others, vulnerable because of the emotional turmoil they were experiencing, and their apparent failure (at least in part) as parents, may have found it difficult to motivate themselves to contact other agencies themselves. Still others could feel that providing a telephone number was simply a way of 'dressing up' doing nothing. This was the case for a mother with housing problems. Commenting on what social services did, she said:

> Nothing, they just gave me a couple of numbers if I wanted to phone them up to see if they could help me. And they just said to get out, and that only to take one of the kids out, but I mean I can't do that 'cos when he is at work I have to

take them both out, so that didn't really help. They were just trying to find ways of helping me but not actually dealing with the problem, just trying to make it easier for me, it hasn't worked.

Women could find that the suggestions for help were not a great deal of use because they took little account of the wider family circumstances and responsibilities. This was in part the result of the brevity of contact, as was the case with one woman, the mother of young children:

It's called family support group and I can go there. I've got to phone her 'cos you can do art therapy or something like that and I sort of dished it at first, I thought, 'Oh no, I don't wanna go,' but I'm going to phone it at some point when I get some break from the kids. When they are around me I can't focus on anything, I lose the plot completely, all I'm doing is every minute being there for them. Anything that's going on in my life I got to sort out, I can't get there 'cos they are constantly on my head.

Summary and comments

A focus on maternal coping requires us to consider the extent to which social service actions helped reduce threat and bring the problem or stressor under control. It is clear that women's responses to referral on, or the absence of referral on were largely understandable in terms of these issues of threat and control. Mostly, the threat or problem for the woman was one of child behaviour or parenting. However, where mothers were concerned about the very involvement of social services, their attitude was determined not so much by the service provided, or the opportunity of being referred on, as by the desire to get away from social services at the first opportunity.

Apart from this, if they were not referred on, they were content if they felt such referral was unnecessary because they had already received a service, or because their expectations were met by the social service response. In both these cases, there was generally a sense of reduced threat and greater control, because of their experience of social services. They were unhappy about not being referred on if they felt undervalued or unimportant (so that their concerns and feelings of threat were not given the serious consideration that they felt they deserved), or had not received the service they expected, whether directly from social services, or through referral to an appropriate agency. In the absence of appropriate action, the women at times initiated further action themselves, approaching other agencies or professionals from whom they could perhaps receive help in emotional-focused or problem-focused coping.

If they were referred on, there were three key elements which determined whether they viewed it positively or negatively. These were appropriateness, timeliness and helpfulness. These again fit clearly with the reduction of threat and creation of greater control. Appropriateness means that the agency to which they were referred was seen as the right one to deal with the problem or the emotions generated in dealing with it (for example, counselling). Timeliness is important: what would the point be of a referral on when no service was available for some time, and where the woman and her family were in crisis? Helpfulness is obviously significant, since from the woman's perspective this meant that threat was being alleviated.

Negative views of referral on emphasised the importance of these aspects. Where social services were seen as 'passing the buck' by referring back to agencies already seen to have failed, or referring on to agencies in which the woman had little confidence, then they were generally seen as not aiding the women's attempts to gain control, nor taking their attempts seriously enough. Furthermore, the problem of waiting, and waiting to repeat often painful and personal information, did little to help women with problem- or emotion-focused coping.

Evidently while referral on was not generally an initial part of the women's coping strategy, their response to it can be understood in terms of the extent to which it contributed to their coping. Some of the key problems, of having to wait, of tentativeness through insufficient knowledge or understanding of the agency, suggest that women at times felt that they were left up in the air by social services; and that, even though social services could not take these cases on to caseload, because of thresholds, resources and work pressures, a more involved approach to obtaining help from other agencies (for example, by accompanying the women to those agencies) would have considerably helped the women in their attempts to cope.

PART V

Epilogue

CHAPTER 16

Women's Appraisal of their Coping

The analysis so far has shown that the situations which these women confronted (without our denying the women were frequently part of the process by which they arose) were often harrowing. The process of coping was, in turn, frequently quite turbulent. They often sought a variety of strategies, at times with quite limited success, and the emotional toll on them could be considerable. Indeed, they confronted stress as a result of the problem, and stress in the manner in which they tried to deal with it.

Women's judgement of their coping involved appraising their management strategies. Presented straightforwardly in terms of a rating, the women indicated that they felt they had generally been successful. Of 101 who responded to this question, 81 rated themselves as having coped quite well, or well. The rest rated themselves as not having coped well, and of these, 9 rated themselves as having coped quite badly, or badly. This seems to indicate a wide degree of satisfaction with their coping. However, these data conceal much more uncertainty about their coping, revealed by women in their interviews, and they also do not disclose the way in which women made their judgements.

According to coping theory, at the heart of all this would be the women's attempts to gain control of the situations. Control could mean getting their children to behave in ways they wanted, or gaining services which altered the levels of pressure on them arising from the children or environment. It could also involve gaining control of their own emotions (emotion-focused coping). In either case, we might expect control to be considered by the women in terms of outcome: that is, whether or not they had got the situation under control, or whether their feelings or perceptions of the situation gave them a greater sense of control. Had the situation improved as a result of their coping efforts? However, this would not involve a focus on the *processes* by which they reached whatever point they had by the time they were interviewed. Women tended to focus less on outcomes, and more on process – what they did when they were trying to cope with the situation. This chapter will seek to examine the ways in which women sought to judge how well they had coped with the problems.

Process and outcome judgements

Outcome-oriented judgements

Outcome-oriented judgements are ways of viewing the success or failure of their coping efforts in terms of what happened as a result. Did the child improve his behaviour? or the woman cope better with herself? Or were they able to obtain resources, making coping easier? This general notion of success is evident from one woman whose teenage son had behaviour problems, and particular difficulties in mainstream school. Asked how she had coped, she said:

> Brilliantly, brilliantly well. We have come through this as a family and I think that we are stronger for it. Of course children play you up and…you have these arguments, but I think we have come through it brilliantly. …A lot of positive things have come out of the negative thing… The one thing about it is, the three of us will always be together, and we are dealing with it, and we have all come through it.

In other cases, the positive outcome evaluation drew upon the reassurance of others. As one woman commented, 'I mean, I've been told that I can cope with it, but I dealt with it very well 'cos I've done all the right things. But when you're sort of in there you don't believe that. At the time you think, "God, there's so much wrong with her, I don't think I've done enough."'

Even where positive, outcome evaluations could involve critical appraisal of a 'could do better' sort. One woman, again with a behaviourally disruptive teenager, reflected that matters might have been resolved more quickly:

> Perhaps again I'm too soft, perhaps if I'd been a bit more firm and said, 'Look, I want somebody to come out to the house and I want them now,' maybe, but that's me all over you know. But…that's the way I am. Perhaps if I'd been firmer and sort of said, 'I want somebody now, I need to sort this problem

out'…perhaps things would have happened, but I'm not that way, sorry (laughing).

Others focused on coping outcomes in terms of what *they* did (or did not do). One theme was the perhaps undemanding one of not actually hurting the child, although some of these women did feel under constant pressure. Not to hurt the child was a positive outcome, as with one woman who said of social services that 'they know I can cope, 'cos I would never hurt my children, you know', even though they could have provided more support. Another, on the same theme, avoided hurt by avoiding the child. She coped, she said,

> …reasonably well. Sometimes I say to him, 'Look, go away, stay away from me,' and I don't deal with it, I, I've had enough. 'It's been a long day and you've been on at me all day, go and sit in the bedroom or just stay away,' but other times we will deal with it, we'll sit him down and we'll try and ask him why he's doing what he's been doing, and usually we just get 'I don't know', but we do try. We've done everything right? I don't know. Maybe somebody else would have done things different.

For others, more negative, outcomes were still important. For some, the biggest challenge to continue coping in difficult circumstances, as one woman commented, 'because you don't know which way he's going to swing… I worry because I'm scared that he's gonna go out and do something stupid'. Sometimes these were outcomes for themselves (the mothers). Mere survival could be success.

> Well, we are still alive. …I mean, we've only coped by ignoring what happened before and trying to start afresh… I mean, we haven't told her not to do anything…but she hasn't liked it. And you just give in, just for peace and quiet basically.

Other women felt that they had not really created any change, viewing this negatively. One woman with a 13-year-old daughter felt that her daughter had all the power, because she could simply refuse to do what was wanted:

> Because, it's well, I try as hard as I can and…I just feel that I've tried everything to no avail…the only thing I feel now that if the police come it's to scare her. I mean, I have asked them loads of times, 'Can you scare, can you show my daughter photos of a girl that's been raped?' …You know, because the police, the need they kids to be disciplined.

Another woman likewise complained that she was unable to set and maintain boundaries, feeling that she was fighting a lonely battle against modern youth culture:

> There are loads of different ways children can upset you or wind you up. …there isn't any discipline compared to when I was a child…It is quite difficult to discipline children these days, even though you try your best, but your best isn't good enough. No matter, it's a constant battle with parents and children to do anything nowadays for them, I think it is.

Process-oriented judgements

For many women, the problems had not been resolved. Indeed, for some women, the problems were likely to remain with them for the foreseeable future. Here judgement was made on coping in terms of *continuity*. This was particularly the case where problems of physical or learning disability were present, or autism and ADHD. In this case, some women judged coping as a long-term process, involving continuous, day-to-day actions.

One woman commented on how, because there was no escape, as a mother of a boy with ADHD, you just had to get on with your life, especially when unable to access potential sources of help. She was coping 'quite well', waiting for the next incident to happen:

> Er, because at the end of the day you have to, you're the only person that, you know, you're the mum at the end of the day and after all this time I think you just learn to cope and you just get on with it, er…you just carry on and cope with things and wait for the next incident to happen.

Coping, for some women, became a routine process, as a result of learning more about how to manage their child. Such was the case with one woman, helped by a health visitor. She understood that coping involved learning to let her child 'get on with it'.

> No, yeah, I think I can cope with [son] a lot better now because I've learned to let him get on with it in a way, and ignore it in a lot of ways, because he was only getting me upset, which wasn't doing me any good and we were just bouncing off each other then…ignoring his behaviour…and just saying 'all right, calm down when you're ready', you know. And try not to make…a big deal of it because at the end of the day…it just gets me stressed, him stressed, and everyone just ends up losing.

This sense of coping continuity could be seen more negatively. One woman with a four-year-old daughter presenting her with challenging behaviour, on the one hand felt there was some kind of 'genetic inheritance' (she's like her father), while on the other she was optimistic about change. However, she expected the problems to continue alongside her coping efforts, which she did not feel were very effective:

> I don't know that I have coped with it. I think I just get on with it and just deal with it as it arrives. I don't think whether I can cope with it very well at all. Ask me that tomorrow, I'm going to work… I can get away. I think I need to as well, I think [daughter] as much needs a break from home, a break from me.

A process of *change* (rather than continuity) marked the process orientation of some women. As with continuity judgements, the change could be positive or negative – coming to terms with the way to deal with child problems, or finding it increasingly difficult. One case, of a woman who had to deal with the behavioural problems of her pre-adolescent boys following the marital breakup, and felt a considerable degree of guilt, summed up the 'step by step' process involved:

> …and like I say, it's, some things are getting better, we just got to take it step by step, it's not gonna take a week, it's gonna take months you know, for them to… I can't say back to normal because I don't think it ever will be, er. If I can sort their behaviour, they never used to be like it, if I can sort that out, then you know… Some days I have a good day, some days I have a bad day, depends in what mood they come home or get up in the morning you know, so.

Another described the move from shock to resigned support – the inevitable accompaniment to caring for the child of your 14-year-old daughter:

> I think initially it was quite sort of devastating, the news. We got over the initial shock and I think we are, you know, we are dealing with it very well as a whole. Finding out that your 14-year-old daughter is pregnant is a one hell of a shock, accepting it is extremely difficult as well… I must admit my initial reaction was a bit hasty to do with… I mean my initial reaction was 'Excuse me, you stupid child,' you know… I don't know, it's just reaction to 'What, she's 14, she's pregnant, she's having a baby' initially, putting it bluntly, 'if anything can be done about it, it will be. She's too young to have a child, she's got her own, she's still a child herself'.

Problems, long-term as they were, could be getting on top of the woman, if everything she tried seemed not to work out. In one case a young mother expressed her desperate tiredness as she considered the prospect of having to care for her two-year-old daughter, who slept very little and fitfully. She needed, she felt, to wait for her daughter to grow out of it, but this was likely to take until she went to school. Asked how she was coping, she said:

> Not very well. I think you cope because you have to, don't you... I mean, ev- erything the health visitor suggested I have tried. I have really, really tried, but I do think it is a case of her growing out of it and me having that to put up with it till she does. I think when she starts at school it will be a lot better but that's a year and half away...even nursery because she's such a happy child when she comes home.

Self- and other-oriented judgements

Women used a number of, in particular, self-oriented ways of judging the efficacy of their coping. These looked less at processes or outcomes of coping, than at facets of the woman herself. In many respects, they represented women's judgements about themselves, and their qualities as an individual.

Performance and personal character

Here, women made an explicit reference to their qualities as an individual, often in circumstances where there was a sense of being 'under fire'. A fairly prosaic statement of this position was made by the mother of a young boy, drawing attention to the fact that, most of the time, she sought to deal with matters herself, trying to calm things down when situations became tense:

> Er, I think that I've coped very well... And nine times out of ten I deal with the situation that's got to be dealt with and then I try to make it fun after that, because that will bring them back round to being calm you know, before they go to bed.

The 'character' issue was at the heart of perceptions of self. Women described themselves as having 'just got on with it', dealing with matters themselves, although they might feel a sense of grievance that they had to manage matters on their own ('I'm really annoyed, I am'). One woman who saw herself as stoical in adversity commented, 'At the end of the day I'm on my own. If I look at it like you just got to do it and get on and do, you know. No one's gonna come and help… I'm not a refugee or a bleeding smack head… I'm really annoyed I am.' Another, the mother of a teenage son, faced, as far as she was concerned, with unhelpful agencies, had to call upon her own resources and character.

> I think I've come through the worst and it's me as a person and my friends, and that's through me fighting like what [son] like pulling out of school. At school it has been very frustrating, like I said, I went to the headmaster, I told him you know, what was going on like i.e. the drugs and things like that. Basically it was all turn a blind eye you know, and I think, right, well, if they are not prepared to listen to me then I shall go elsewhere, and I do then to do that. It's through me. But I am a person to myself, if there's something that I really want in life I will go for it. You know, something that I really need bad, I may have to wait a little while for it but usually I get what I want in the end.

Other women emphasised the character issue within the general process and time-span involved in coping. These women saw themselves as having negotiated at times considerable difficulties, and in doing so showed great fortitude and development of strength. Women talked of 'coming out the other side': 'All in all, now that I've sort of come out on the other side I think I've coped really well, very well.' Others saw the process as one of gaining strength themselves, although it could be two steps forward and one step back. As one woman said: 'How I'm coping on me own? I've become stronger. Depends what sort of day we've had, if we've had a good day then it's 100 out of 100 but on a really bad day it's 10 out of 100 you know.' One woman placed her difficulties with her six-year-old son in the context of serious problems with income support, including no income for three months, alongside minimal support from others:

> OK, I feel like I'm back on my feet now and that I have sorted myself out, but… I was at a point where I couldn't see the wood for the trees, all I could see was disaster around me, and I didn't quite know how to get myself out of that. But yes, I feel good now and I feel a lot better. I'm hoping I'm going to start going back to work again next month, which I think will help me and boost my confidence a little bit… Just do a little job that I can do in [son's] school hours so I can still spend the time with him.

Others were far more negative about themselves, and this coincided with a generally negative view of their coping. Coping badly was accompanied by personal criticism and self-blame. A common theme in these women's accounts was that of failing to respond appropriately, of being aggressive where they should have been more controlled, of not understanding properly the predicament of the children. This clearly contrasted with the more 'gung-ho' assertion of personal strength seeing them through difficulties identified by other women. For one group, coping provided confirmation of personal strength. For this group it provided the context for angst-ridden personal appraisal. Self-criticism of this sort was very apparent in one mother of a young child whose behaviour, and particularly tantrums, she found challenging. The self-criticism was clearly linked with a sense of coping failure:

> Because I lose my patience very, very quickly with her. I shout, I rant, I rave instead of being firm, my firm is anger. My firm is frustration because I need to sleep and she needs to sleep and I don't cope with it very well… She just, she needs it more than I do, I think. But I can cope with being tired providing she's in a good mood, if she's not in a good mood, God help me and her you know.

This self-criticism was evident in another mother, this time of a 15-year-old, who felt she had little control of her son's loud and aggressive behaviour, which often embarrassed her in front of others. She was waiting until he was 16, in six months time, and then, as far as she was concerned, he could leave. Her efforts had not worked, and as with the previous woman this could overflow into anger. Her comments on herself as a mother were negative:

> I mean, like I said, I'm not a brilliant mum, I'm not gonna say that I'm a perfect mother. Sometimes I got to the stage where I hit him and I'm not gonna say any other and I told the social worker the same, but you just hope to God he doesn't push you that far where you're gonna so something that is gonna get out of hand.

Another mother, receiving support from mental health services, blamed herself for the long period during which her adolescent daughter had gone to live with her father, as a direct response to her inability to cope. For her, this was also evidence that she was a poor mother:

> …don't think I have coped with it very well at all. I mean, she's been living with her father…because I wasn't coping. I wasn't being a very good mother, not as good as I should have been… She went to live with her father when she was nine. That was the best thing I've done as a mother, was to let her go.

These mothers had the sense that they were just not good enough,. This may have been a long held perception of self, but it certainly came out of their assessment of their coping. As one woman said, 'If I had coped well I wouldn't have broke down a few times when [son] had gone to bed... If I'd cope really well, then it wouldn't have happened.'

Personal growth

Personal growth through coping was another theme in judgements on coping. Amongst these women, the main element was the sense that they had learned from their experience, moved on, and this was reflected in the manner of their coping, particularly when compared with their coping at the outset. It meant admitting to themselves some of the limits there had been at the beginning. This is exemplified by a woman who had a young son, but felt the impact of depression on her capacity to cope, and of her young son's behaviour on her depression. Breaking out of this involved recognising the limits to her action, while trying to deal with the depression. It involved finding new ways of tackling problems. While she felt very much that how she managed situations varied according to both her own mood and her son's, she commented, in relation to her coping:

> In the beginning terribly, in the last few weeks a lot better, because I've felt better myself. There's definitely connection between how I'm feeling and how I'm coping with [son]. It's got a lot better, things have improved... I'm finding different ways of tackling his behaviour, different ways of dealing with it, you know. Like I said, it sounds crazy but laughing at him, it calms him you know. It's just something that happened purely by accident, I just lost it one day and I sat here roaring with laughter and he sort of calmed down and I hang on, not normal you know. But he seemed to just melt and calm down.

The issue of support, or advice, was crucial to women who were able to move on towards more competent coping. One woman commented on her pre-adolescent son's behaviour difficulties, particularly his temper, and the problems with which this presented her with in a large family. Having obtained support from the local child psychiatric services, she felt there was an important psychological edge – she 'felt supported' and this meant that she 'managed to get on with it'. So 'I tend to go off and clean the cooker or something, to like get my anger out so I don't have to, you know, take it out on them'. Another woman expressed similar sentiments, focusing on her capacity to act rationally in difficult situations in a way previously not possible:

> I find it easier now to sit down and talk to him not shouting at him, not go chasing after him and you know, like 'argh', all this lot, sit down, talk it over, resolve the problem and that's it, you know. They feel better for it as well so I don't get too worked out then, too aggressive, so.

At times the biggest step was admitting to yourself that you needed help. For some women, their role as mother, and pride in that role, made this, at first, difficult. Their self-esteem could be tied up with their capacity to care for their children without much help from others, and admitting the need for such help was hard. But in the long term it could be positive:

> I mean, I took the big first step by admitting that I needed outside help, which I've never done before and my daughter's 23. I mean, nobody ever helped me with her you know. ...And as weeks go along I can see slight changes you know, so yeah, I think it might be working.

For many women, the help was not just emotional or child care support, but the advice they could obtain from experts, such as health visitors, which could change the way they operated. One woman with a two-year-old daughter felt much calmer, and generally positive:

> Before if she was having a tantrum I just started screaming and shouting at her. Now I'm much calmer with her. Still got my hair left and it's not going grey... My health visitor, giving me advice on what to do if she has a tantrum, and how to not get her to have a tantrum, which has helped a lot... You know, when she's having a tantrum just leave her to it, she only doing it for attention and that... And if you know that she's going to have a tantrum don't put her in a situation where she will have it, don't go near the sweets (laughing).

Coping and mood

Another self-referential element of coping judgements was one which placed considerable emphasis on mood. Interestingly, where mood was invoked, it tended to involve a negative assessment of coping. For some women, they defined coping itself as the problem, so for them the biggest problem was 'just coping' – that is, knowing how to respond to the child care issues and develop some sense of control over the situation. The predictability of trouble, within the context of child behaviour which was sometimes unpredictable, was at the root of this sense of despair, which could associate itself with coping. As one woman said, 'You don't know which way he's gonna swing, you know I've been there, er, I worry because I'm scared that he's gonna out and do something stupid…tried to take his life so that proves to you that he was depressed you know.'

The close, intertwined relationship between mood and coping judgements is evident in one woman's statement, a woman who had a ten-year-old son with behavioural difficulties and phobic anxiety problems. Hers was a problem of depression, which prevented her even recognising the problem:

> I must admit, I think I could have coped with it better really, seen the signs before, but I didn't… I had problems drinking and things like that. Now I realise it was depression that I had. I would know the signs before they get really bad this time. No, I don't think I coped that well really.

Others described complicated situations in which the mood affected family dynamics, which then impacted on child care. One woman, for example, whose children had a wide age gap between them, found that her younger son became difficult with his older teenage sister when the mother herself was depressed. The older sister took over the mother role, not appreciated by her brother – while the mother withdrew from direct caring. Her son was confused – he did not know if he had two mothers – while her daughter was on the wrong end of his anger. While she said she did not know where she would be without her daughter, she had very high expectations of her: 'When I've been really bad I haven't been able to cope with it at all, and she has taken over and run things and put on with it.'

This depressed mood was a widespread feature of women in this study. It could be transient, but repetitive, and the serious difficulty occurred at the point where mood was low. This could lead to general judgements that they had not coped well, which in turn was associated with a sense of isolation. When the buck stopped with the mother, this could exacerbate her low mood:

> …when you're having a bad day everything seems worse anyway, and because you feel you've got nowhere to turn, you know. It's like 'how am I gonna get out of this, how to solve the problem? How to help him solve his problems? What's gonna become of him? What's gonna happen?' And then that makes me obviously feel worse but [I] make the most of it and see what happens, you know.

Other women described much more aggressive moods, a rage which severely damaged the quality of their coping. The rage was often associated with a sense of despair or depression. This could itself arise from various sources: a long-term rage at their own treatment as a child, the absence of others who could take responsibility for caring for the children (not just support, but co-responsibility), or the behaviour of the children themselves. The rage would inhibit coping capacity by making it difficult to relate in proportionate ways to the children. Some women felt that the rage placed their children at risk, especially where they blamed the children for their behaviour. Women described extreme responses ('I'd like to kill her, the way she is'), especially in relation to their teenage children. In other cases it was other factors which caused their rage. One example was a woman who felt that her estranged husband should take greater co-responsibility for the children:

> I could feel all this rage inside me even though I didn't want to feel raged, nobody wants to feel angry. I thought, I don't really need this emotion I got to just get on, but it's I'm only a human being and they are the emotions that I have. And phoning their father I just got 'sorry, I'm busy' ...and I was starting to go downhill and it was just like 'where are you? You are so ignorant and so uncaring and so selfish'.

These feelings were more likely when others were not perceived to be there for support, but some felt unable to use support. Some said that it was their responsibility to care for the child and 'I wanted to solve the problem myself'. The connection between being a 'good and capable mother' and self-esteem is evident for these women, but at its worst it could lead to a breakdown of capacity to care, because of the mother's own breakdown. It was then a case of needing to be cared for themselves. As one woman commented of her friend, 'She played a major part in all this. If it wasn't for her, I'd probably be dead.'

Self-referential coping

Self-referential coping judgements occurred where the mother appeared to have a particularly limited perception of what she could have done. 'What she could have done' was generally, with these mothers, what she actually *did*. They generally rated their coping as being very good as a whole, although they could just as easily state serious shortfalls in the quality of their parenting. This apparent contradiction, involving criticising their parenting while nevertheless rating it highly, becomes understandable where they felt that no one else could have done better, nor even, if they were wise, would have done anything different. Theirs was the best way, even if things did not turn out too well.

One woman, the mother of a ten-year-old boy with behaviour problems, rated herself as having coped very well, but then, rather oddly, went on to say, and in relation to her coping:

> Not very well because it hasn't stopped has it, he's still doing it, but I don't feel that I've never tried to cope because I did, I tried everything, you know. And I've done it, shouting at him, I don't know, I've not coped well at all 'cos the problems are still there, you know. Within myself I haven't coped well because it's stressed me right out, you know.

This contradiction is more understandable because she then states that she could not think of doing anything differently because of the complexity and severity of the situation: 'No, no, there's not just that one problem, every time there's a problem I have to find a different way of dealing with it, so I don't know'.

Others emphasised the context as a means for understanding how well they had coped. If they felt themselves to have been isolated, let down, or to have been treated badly themselves when they were children, this could provide a context for limited achievements, which nevertheless they would consider very good levels of coping. For some of these women, then, it would be about their internal robustness, or the tenuousness of their robustness. There were times when women recognised, for example, that their own past abusive experiences had affected their overall ability to parent. In view of this, they would consider any kind of coping to be good 'in the circumstances'. Limits to their psychological strength or robustness were an important dimension, as with this woman who had an 11-year-old child with both learning and behavioural difficulties. She rated herself as having coped 'very well'. Trying her best equalled coping well:

> I try; now I try. With going to rehab and everything else. I do try, my mum and dad... I was having a bad time with my partner, my dad passed away when [daughter] was six days old, my mum passed away a month and a half later so my emotions were all over the place, but I try. So yes, I do try, sometimes I do blow up and I feel guilty, quite a bit actually, I try to do my best. I have me niece staying with me, she... I try to do my best with her as well... So with the things I have had to cope with, yes, I do think I have coped very very well,

even though I do have drinking problems at one point, and people say I have a drinking problem now.

Other women had a profound sense of the limitations on what they could achieve. In one case of a mother with a young teenage daughter, the mother and father had separated, which had a great impact on the daughter, resulting in self-harming behaviour. The mother's response was that she had tried to 'sit down and talk', but that, as her mother, she could only get so far. Her daughter was far more likely, the mother thought, to confide in friends, and she just had to accept this: 'We're [parents] on the borderline aren't we?' Given these limitations, she felt they had coped very well.

Some were quite self-righteous and not self-critical in their judgements of their coping. One woman was most impressed with her own performance, bringing up two children (aged two and thirteen) as a single parent, commenting that there was 'not really' anything she could have done differently, and that 'with what I've been through for the last ten or eight years, I think I've done marvellous'. Another woman felt that part of her coping was not showing others that she was not coping. She had two teenagers truanting from school, about whose prospects she was worried, but in relation to whom, according to her, the school was unable to suggest anything constructive. She coped well by not showing others that she was not coping well:

> I am coping with the problem fairly well. Deep down inside I'm not, but I can't show that to the kids, you know what I mean? I'm not coping, if it comes down to it, in the end, I'll teach them myself, if it comes to it, but I don't want that. I'm at college, I don't want to give up my hobbies, my Tai Chi, but at the moment I haven't been for a few weeks, because of [son].

Coping as the capacity and opportunity to use support

An obvious contributor to coping is support from family or friends. However, this underestimates the extent to which such support was integrated with the way they defined their coping. Using social support in the right kind of way, where it helped the situation, was seen by the women as good coping. One woman felt she coped well with the behavioural problems of her son. This was very much in partnership with her partner, in that she was able to call on him for assistance when she felt less able to cope properly – leading to a more stable set of experiences for her son, and a more steady response from herself, as she did not feel overwhelmed by the demands on her. Good coping equalled good use of support. Another woman spoke of exactly that kind of dovetailing between her and her mother in relation to her young son:

> Er, she's there if I'm down, er, she'll have [son] for me, she'll have him if I want to go off for the day, er, everything, cooking for me, having [son]. More often than not I'm thinking, 'Oh, God, I can't cope with him,' and she'll come round and calms and sits down with him, so really anything I need, she's there.

The use of support depended on its availability, but also on the capacity of women to use it. One woman found great difficulty in bonding with her daughter, and felt unable to make use of support because she recognised that the problem was 'inside her head': 'There's not a lot anybody can do, if it's not there, it's not natural. I just have to live with it.'

Most frequently, when support was connected with judgement of coping, the absence or limitations of support were linked with negative appraisals of coping. One woman, who felt she had coped badly, stated this clearly, angrily pointing to the absence of help where in principle it could have been provided:

> No, no I have to cope with it all on my own, [partner] doesn't help like that. He doesn't even do anything round the house, I does it all myself, I does the decorating, I does the gardening, cleaning, I do it and then I'm expected to deal with the kids on my own as well, so there's basically nobody... I don't go out. Mind you, I couldn't pay for anyone and no one would look after them, 'cos they are so hyperactive you see, and they just fight. I don't leave them with anybody.

Other women confirmed this connection between support and appraisals of coping, using terms like 'it's a struggle to describe the difficulties of caring for children without support'. One woman commented, in relation to her son with challenging behaviour, that 'I admit I've struggled, and it hurts and it rips me apart sometimes'. Some mothers with young children felt the physical pressure of caring for the child when they became particularly challenging. One woman with a two-year-old had no support, and wider financial difficulties conveyed the sense of exhaustion in having to manage on her own:

> And this one, me being exhausted and not having a mum or a sister or anyone that I can call and say that I really am having a bad day and can you just take the kids off to the park. Or it's just there, I think it's just feeling now that

there's no one there. If you feel that there's someone there you kind of get on with it and know that you're settled, you know, and it's OK, and I don't want us to go back to social services because they are making me to feel scared. I'm at this point now that I feel very scared.

Summary and conclusion

1. According to coping theory, at the heart of women's judgement of their coping is the attempt to *gain control* of the situation. Control could theoretically focus on problems, or the women's emotions. However, we are again confronted with the issue of meaning, in terms of the factors women used to judge control.

2. *Outcome-orientated judgements* were ways of viewing the success or failure of their coping efforts in terms of the results of their coping. This could involve critical appraisal, and a focus on the women's efforts. They could be positive or negative.

3. *Process-oriented judgements* occurred where the problem had not been resolved and was perceived as likely to be with them for the foreseeable future. Judgements could be made in terms of continuity – where coping in adversity was viewed as a routine process. It could be seen in terms of an ongoing process.

4. There was a range of *self- and other-oriented judgements*. Some involved appraisal of the mother's personal 'character' – of how she had personally performed under fire. The character issue could be seen as positive or negative, although it was more frequently the former. Those with little support often felt they had shown considerable 'character', no matter how things turned out.

5. *Personal growth* was another theme in women's judgements of coping (as well, as we have seen, as part of the coping process). This was about learning from their experience, and to the extent that the woman achieved this, she viewed it positively.

6.   Other judgements placed emphasis on the woman's *mood*, and tended to involve negative assessments of coping. Many women defined coping itself as the problem – how to respond to the challenge of child care. Where women were depressed – and this was not infrequent – they were often very critical of themselves.

7.   *Self-referential judgements* involved women making such judgements through the narrow focus of their own perspectives. What they 'could have done' was generally, with these mothers, what they actually did. They generally rated their coping as good – not surprising in view of this narrow focus.

8.   Some of the women judged coping in terms of the *capacity and opportunity to use support*. It was about using support in the right way. The absence of help, including use or availability of support, could be associated with negative judgements on coping.

CHAPTER 17

Conclusions: Prevention and Coping in Child and Family Care

While the central theme of this book has been women's coping strategies in relation to problems and threats they experienced in child care, this has obvious links with prevention. This occurs in two fundamental ways. First, the women take actions which are both aspects of their coping strategy and also, in another sense, designed to enable them to 'cope'. Second, it brings them directly into contact with the agencies whose purpose is, in part or in whole, to have a preventive effect on child care problems. In the first scenario women seek to act, themselves or through their informal network, on their child and parenting issues, without the help of formal agencies. In the second, their actions involve eliciting the help of these formal agencies, or bring them into contact with these agencies (through, for example, referrals for abusive behaviour). Coping, in other words (and in principle), can be carried out, either without direct involvement of preventive services, or alongside those services.

Of course, in some respects it is difficult to see how the universalist services of primary prevention, such as libraries, playgrounds, parks and so on, are not an aspect of coping strategies, and it is certainly true that these women used these services. However, it is also true to say that they were generally side issues when the women were confronting the direct, difficult and specific problems of child care and parenting, which are the focus of this study. To all intents and purposes, if they were not purposefully seeking to engage preventive services in relation to those problems (or were referred by others for that purpose), then they were of little or no significance when compared with the efforts exerted by the women themselves.

This leads us to need to consider: where, conceptually, do these women's efforts fit in relation to prevention? How can we bring these two, obviously connected, elements together? We need, first of all, some way to express the women's coping efforts where preventive services were not really a relevant dimension. This really requires a new concept, or even stage, in relation to the preventive continuum. We choose to call this *proto-prevention*. Proto-prevention refers to the actions of the woman herself, designed to deal with the problems presented by parenting and child care without engaging, specifically for the purpose of managing these problems, formal preventive services.

This is significant, because this adds a fifth dimension to the preventive continuum of primary, secondary, tertiary and quaternary prevention. It is also significant because it is not simply a matter of stages (which now number five). It draws attention to the processes by which the women, children and their families pass from one stage to the next. We are looking here at the filters, or individual or group actions which lead to them passing from one stage to the next. What factors, for example, lead these women to make decisions to pass from one stage to the next? What acts as inhibitors to those decisions? (An obvious example here might be stigma.)

However, it also draws attention to the actions taken by the women themselves alongside preventive services. What do they actually do themselves to deal with the situation when formal preventive services are involved? How do they seek to integrate the work of preventive services with their own coping efforts? What happens if formal services do not respond in the ways they expect? What are the consequences of this for their coping actions, and how do they evaluate the services they receive? This last factor is liable to impact both on their current coping actions and on future decisions about what to do when seeking to manage difficult parenting and child care situations.

Alongside the notion of proto-prevention, therefore, we require a concept which helps us understand the relation between the actions of the women and the formal preventive services alongside which they are engaged. We may call this *parental prevention*, and contrast it with *formal prevention*, which is the preventive effort provided by formal services set up for that purpose. We can have these preventive efforts at each stage; for example, we can have primary parental prevention, secondary parental prevention, and so on. Some of the most important issues involve the relationship between the work of the preventive services, and how these interact with the coping efforts of the mother, or, using our conceptual framework, the interaction between parental prevention and formal prevention at any stage in the preventive process.

However, we have a third dimension, which relates to the help the women engage which is not part of the formal preventive services. This, obviously, involves the use of family, friends and acquaintances to help them cope better with the problems they confront. This draws us into theories and concepts from social support, which, like need, are closely related to the idea of prevention. This third dimension, which again could occur at any stage in the preventive process, may be called *informal prevention*. Here again, we can have primary informal prevention, secondary informal prevention, and so on.

If we were to tabulate this conceptually it would take the following appearance.

Table 1: Dimensions of the prevention process			
Preventive stage	*Parental actions*	*Informal supports*	*Formal preventive services*
Proto prevention	Parental proto prevention	Informal proto prevention	None
Primary prevention	Primary parental prevention	Primary informal prevention	Primary formal prevention
Secondary prevention	Secondary parental prevention	Secondary informal prevention	Secondary formal prevention
Tertiary prevention	Tertiary parental prevention	Tertiary informal prevention	Tertiary formal prevention
Quaternary prevention	Quaternary parental prevention	Quaternary informal prevention	Quaternary formal prevention

Of course, we could, in addition, add the actions of the child as an aspect of this process, which could include, for example, situations where adolescents refer themselves to a young person's advisory service. This, however, has not been the focus for this study, so it is best to concentrate on the conceptual framework we have tabulated. The tabulation also helps us to imagine the processes by which these women and their families pass from stage to stage, how the filters might work through each of these dimensions (parental, informal and formal) either to resolve the problem, or otherwise retain it at one stage, or to result in the families passing from one stage to another.

We can add a further dimension to this when we seek to relate women's coping actions to the purposes of prevention. We can here bring in the distinction between *functional* and *dysfunctional coping strategies*. For this, we need to understand the link between the purposes of prevention and the issue of control, which is at the heart of coping.

Prevention and functional and dysfunctional coping

The central theme of these women's coping efforts was that of control. Women were in a variety of situations, with a range of problems confronting them; each was nevertheless characterised by the ways in which child care was a central feature of it. Women sought to take actions which would enable them to take greater control of those situations. These were most obviously aimed at alleviating the problem. Where teenage children were violent, depressed or defying boundaries (most obviously an issue of teenagers seeking autonomy, as against parents seeking to hold the line with rules or boundaries to behaviour), attempting to control the problem often focused on the child's behaviours. Where women felt they were parenting inadequately, this was the focus for their attention, as it appeared to them that it was associated with child emotional or behavioural problems (particularly with young children).

This search for control – and we need to remind ourselves that in their appraisal of coping the notion of control had various meanings – could lead to an improvement or deterioration in the situation. We can see from case examples, how, for instance, child-controlling actions in relation to child behavioural problems, could lead to a deterioration in the situation. It is not difficult to imagine how communication breakdown and a spiralling cycle of violence, could lead to a journey through the various stages of prevention. Clearly, where such coping actions were occurring, the mother would be carrying out dysfunctional parental coping. This would be the case regardless of the intentions, good or otherwise, of the mother when carrying out these actions. Where the coping actions focused on the problem, we could call this *problem-focused dysfunctional coping*, which would obviously contrast with *problem-focused functional coping*.

Control was as much about the woman's emotions. Where they felt they were parenting their young children inadequately, this could be accompanied by searing feelings of guilt and low self-esteem. Where they confronted violent teenage sons or daughters, the issues of fear and aggression came to the fore. Where boundaries were being transgressed, anger was often the primary emotion, and when bullying occurred, women became frequently anxious and worried. Coping was often as much about coping with themselves and their emotions, as with the problem itself. The issue confronting these women was, however, also one of control: how would they be able to control and direct the emotions they felt? Not all women, it should be emphasised, sought to control their emotions, but many did, and where this was the case, it was clear that they were seeking to engage coping strategies with these emotions.

Again, these actions could be functional or dysfunctional. We would here distinguish between *emotion-focused functional coping*, and *emotion-focused dysfunctional coping*. It is easy to see how some forms of emotion-focused coping, such as denial, might actually be dysfunctional. To deny, for example, that a distressed infant was distressed, because the feelings of guilt would otherwise be overwhelming for the woman's fragile ego, may well mean that the situation deteriorates, with a negative spiral of child distress, guilt feelings, denial (to alleviate the pain of guilt), and further child distress. On the other hand, this could be functional. Where the woman is able to learn from a situation, for example, how to respond more effectively to behavioural difficulties, such as tantrums, of a young child, she may experience not just a growing sense of control, but also personal development, the enhancement of self-esteem, and a greater confidence that she will be able to confront further child care challenges successfully in the future.

We can further formulate the area of parental prevention as follows:

Table 2: Dimensions of parental prevention				
Stage	proto	primary	secondary	tertiary	quaternary
Focus	emotion	problem			
Functionality	functional	dysfunctional			

Thus, given different actions and different stages, we can delineate, for example, *proto-emotion-focused, dysfunctional* parental prevention strategies, or *secondary, problem-focused, functional* parental prevention strategies, on behalf of the parent. These bring together central features of coping with prevention in a productive way, in order to classify actions, and also to create a deeper understanding of the prevention process through the application of ideas and evidence from coping.

These categories clearly arise through a consideration of concepts from prevention and coping as well as the empirical evidence we have presented. However, the focus of the study has been the coping strategies of women in particular circumstances of adversity, and, broadly, in the realm of proto- to secondary prevention. A key element of this is the excavation of meanings attached by the women to their circumstances and actions. What, in the light of this framework, do the findings tell us?

Coping, adversity and control

A central feature of coping is the issue of control, although its meaning to the women is both complex and varied. Control is interesting because of the adversity which was a central feature of these women's lives. Although the adversity was wide-ranging – it could relate to the material circumstances, familial relations, the child, or even the psychological state of the parent – this adversity invariably made the exercise of control difficult. Women made homeless, in bed and breakfast, faced fundamental problems of caring for their children, or even holding the family together, while simultaneously having to deal with their accommodation difficulties. Invariably, such contextual difficulties created new and greater child care threats for the women. The threat presented by their adversity, together with the difficulty in gaining control provided the basis for the crisis situations which were so frequently characteristic for these mothers and their families.

The danger with these situations is that such circumstances can overwhelm, and depression can become a feature. The adversity may make a sense of control of any sort difficult to attain, and feelings of helplessness, considered by many to be at the centre of depression (Abramson, Seligman and Teasdale 1978) will emerge. Depression can be associated with a mixture of emotions, most obviously despair, but also anger, anxiety, low self-esteem and confidence. All these can make coping with the problem more difficult, as women can feel problems are insurmountable at worst, and at the least, extremely difficult. Demoralisation, and difficulties in responding to resolve problems, can emerge. At the same time, coping with these very emotions associated with depression becomes a part of the women's general coping actions and strategy. In this context, women's appraisal of their coping, and in particular their terms of reference – their discourses – when appraising their coping, are important. These discourses provide the frame for reflecting upon themselves, their capacity to control and direct their lives, their self-esteem, and ultimately their perceptions of self. Are they a good mother? Can they manage problems other mothers manage? Can they cope when confronted with severe problems or in adversity? The way these women negotiate these situations can have a major impact on the fundamental ways they view themselves. These are serious issues for the women, of the deepest significance and meaning for them.

The focus: threat meanings

Control was sought in relation to threat, which was engendered by the particular stressors concerning the women. The key to understanding stressors, according to coping theory, is to discover their 'threat meanings'. It is apparent now that this is not simply a matter of some severity rating (although that existed). The stress experiences derived from the 'terms of reference' which women used to appraise those stressors. Threat meanings were complex, but involved interactions in two basic dimensions: those of problem definition and 'site', and of responsibility and blame.

Problem definition

Problem definition contained threat meanings which potentially called upon diverse coping strategies. The *egocentricity* at the heart of the various manifestations of child behaviour problems provided the basis for their threat meanings. This was expressed in terms of an emphasis by the child on their wants, of a refusal to accept boundaries, assertions of rights to do what they wanted, and an absence of concern about the effect of their behaviour on others. The impact was significant, with mothers often describing themselves as living on a knife edge, and with behaviours ranging from routine dismissiveness and social ineptitude to outright violence, generally from teenagers, and at times against the mother herself.

The idea of child *sensitivity* was at the heart of women's construction of child emotional problems. Children were seen as vulnerable, in pain, responsive to negative environmental pressures. The concern of mothers was often protection of the children (conspicuously not an issue with child behavioural problems). Manifestations of emotional problems differed with age, from crying and attention-seeking in young children, or distress expressed in the form of aggression, to depressed mood, sleep difficulties, social withdrawal and low confidence in school-age children. Bullying sometimes provided a context for emotional problems in children.

While egocentricity and sensitivity characterised construction of child problems, the central theme of parenting problems was a *sense of failure*. Women blamed and castigated themselves, often for failing to cope where they really should have, and this was allied at times to a sense of guilt. The interaction with the child was the focus for their attention: women felt they did not spend enough time or give enough attention to the children, that their control and discipline was insufficient or too great, or that they were not sufficiently responsive to the child's emotional needs. Sometimes the problem resided in the partner or ex-partner, eliciting criticism and resentment, but still, at times, a sense of responsibility in the women (they had chosen this partner), feeding their sense of failure.

Responsibility and blame

The ascription of responsibility or blame was another dimension of the threat meanings constructed by the women. This was itself multifaceted. Women distinguished primary responsibility for a problem – the main 'blame' being attached here – from secondary responsibility – which might influence matters. Thus women could recognise that divorce played a formative part in a teenager's attitudes, while nevertheless blaming them for their behaviour. Alternatively, they might 'blame' the behaviour on the divorce. In the first case, divorce would be conceived as an influencing factor, while responsibility remained with the child; in the second, the divorce was causal, and hence 're-sponsible'.

Blaming the mother had significant implications for the women. Women were emotionally involved with their role as mother and performance of their parental role, involving fundamental issues of identity and self-worth. The problem might be the child, but the responsibility lay with the mother. Women could simply blame themselves regarding themselves, as ineffective or poor parents. They could accept responsibility while recognising the influence of environmental factors, such as poverty or single parenthood.

Blaming the environment was another dimension. Material factors, medical problems, relationships, for example, among siblings, peer groups, or even friends or relatives of the mother, could be seen as primary factors responsible for problems. Even so, the women could feel a sense of guilt for failing to manage child care problems, even in the face of environmental difficulties.

Blaming the child very often contained a subtext of the mother as victim. This was practically a universal characteristic of mothers whose children were teenagers. While they could recognise environmental influences, blame was squarely placed on the children. 'It's just the way they are' expressly placed responsibility on the person of the child. Another attribute of some women was the active and expressed exclusion of themselves (the mother) from blame, with women often assuming a self-justificatory tone.

Problem-focused parental preventive actions: proto to secondary

The first course of action in coping by most women involved what they did themselves. These were problem-focused parental prevention strategies. Women generally saw themselves as the major factor in relation to managing the child. This was their responsibility, and where they involved others – informal supports, social services, or other agencies – these were generally to assist (as far as the women were concerned) in their own actions, which were primary. Of course, for some women, the main feature was an unwelcome referral to social services, often involving abuse allegations. Social services were not seen, then, as an assisting agency, but rather as part of the threat the women felt in relation to their children.

A key question for these women was: how could they bring these problems or stressors under control? This was the central and defining feature of their coping strategies. Although this was not always possible – which could at times lead to more emotion-focused coping – problem-focused coping, where it was directed at child care, had a consistent feature in most cases: whether and how the woman would respond *directly* to the threat.

The direct active coping of the women entailed a wide range of actions which could essentially be distilled into two: child-controlling strategies and child-responsive strategies. *Child-controlling strategies* were widely used and were characterised by a focus on the child's behaviour at the level of behaviour, operating directly on that behaviour. Such strategies worked on crude behaviourist principles, in that they worked through consequences for behaviours, positive or negative. *Positive-oriented actions* sought to create a virtuous circle by rewarding behaviours the child was already manifesting which were considered 'good'. Given the nature of the situations, these were generally the exceptions in the child's overall behaviour patterns. By rewarding the positive, mothers were generally hoping to chip away at the overall behaviour patterns, gradually altering the balance between undesirable and desirable behaviour. Two distinctive elements of this involved the mother (a) recognising positive elements within an overall negative behaviour pattern; and (b) being prepared to consider encouragement and rewards as powerful motivators to change behaviour positively.

Much more frequently women adopted *negative-oriented actions*, and a great deal of the confrontational interactions between mother and child revolved around negative-oriented actions. These sought to change the child's behaviour by instigating unpleasant consequences for negative behaviours. These were designed to make the child realise that their behaviour was unacceptable, and that the result of continuing such behaviours was unpleasant consequences. However, rather than getting the child to realise that their behaviours were unacceptable, the tendency to work on the negative with the negative ran the risk of being self-defeating, particularly, as was generally the case, if the women did not adopt positive-oriented actions alongside negative-oriented actions. The relationship could be damaged, and this was more likely, the older the child. The more they were able to subject mothers' actions to critical appraisal, and the greater the impulse towards autonomy, the more the children felt able to defy them. Negative-oriented actions, in short, were liable to break down.

Child-responsive coping focused on the cognitive-affective dimensions of interactions, rather than behavioural. In crises, the women saw the importance of reassurance, clear communication and understanding, and physical care. They sought to use these positively in coping with the situation. *Instrumental-oriented coping* sought to develop and maintain routines of behaviours and expectations, together with the physical safety of the child. Both were designed to contribute to a sense of security and reliability for the child, and involved seeking to avoid placing children in dangerous situations, or extricating them from such situations. Normalising family routines – setting in place routines which would operate, had the crisis not existed – was another of these strategies, based on the idea that instilling routines encouraged a sense of security by giving some sense of certainty and expectation.

Cognitive-affective coping strategies were designed specifically to impact beneficially on the internal, emotional or cognitive state of the child. They were designed to instil a sense of confidence, of being able to direct and control one's life, of being a valued individual, of having the interest of significant others. Amongst the key actions we have identified are proximising, cognitive-affective nurturing, encouragement through firmness. Through *insight-oriented coping* mothers sought to facilitate understanding, either, on the part of the child, of her perspectives and reasoning, or, on her part, of the child's understanding and perspectives of the situation. Such improvement in mutual understanding might reduce tensions between mother and child. Where conflict occurred, matters could deteriorate to the point where neither side was prepared to hear the views of the other. Of course, listening to the child does not necessarily mean taking their views seriously, and could mean expecting the child to respond positively to her views.

Parent-oriented coping occurred where mothers sought to undertake actions or processes which were fundamentally oriented to herself, yet directly affected her interaction with the child. These facilitative actions included reflective consideration, setting boundaries to the self and suppressing competing activities. They were designed to stimulate appropriate actions and prevent destructive actions being taken.

Emotion-focused parental preventive actions: proto to secondary

Coping also involved women acting on themselves, particularly their own emotional state. This clearly forms a part of the preventive process. Preventive practice, particularly when framed in terms of the policy of family support, seeks to avoid family breakdown. This can be threatened by the woman's emotional state, to the extent that this makes managing the problem more difficult. Thus, emotion-focused coping forms another dimension with implications for preventive practice. Women's management of themselves in this respect was, however, a complex matter, with a number of dimensions.

Women were aware that managing their own feelings was a major element of their coping. Some approaches led to women being less likely to act on the problem. Such lack of action was characteristic of *avoidance strategies. Denial and disengagement* was one element of this. While psychoanalytic theory would suggest that, by definition, women would not be aware of denial, a wider definition (often adopted in coping theory) involves some recognition of dissonance between the experience they were having and their recognition of events. Defined in this way, denial was infrequently identified by women. *Mental* disengagement was a strategy where women, deliberately or otherwise, separated themselves from the problem they were confronting. *Behavioural* disengagement involved physically disengaging themselves from the problem.

Adjustment strategies involved adaptation by the woman to the situation, often recognising there was little they could do to change it. *Acceptance* was a response to 'live with it', or could additionally mean they were reconciled to it, perhaps by changing their attitude. However, while women may have accepted that the situation could not be changed, they were rarely reconciled to it. Acceptance was generally a hostile truce. *Positive reinterpretation and personal growth* was another of these strategies. The most positive self-referential coping response involved reframing the situation or self in a more optimistic way. Positive reinterpretation reframed the situation in a more positive light, while personal growth reframed their experience more optimistically, as a contribution to the woman's own development.

Functionality in parental preventive actions: proto to secondary

This is a complex issue, and difficult to excavate where the accounts given were solely from the mother herself. Although often internally coherent, they nevertheless provided only a particular view of the situation. Our exploration of this issue involved examining particular cases to show how the interaction of family history, child behaviour and parental coping style, including their construction of meaning, could play a part in the emergence of the frequently dysfunctional situations leading to referral to social services. They help us understand how, in other words, families pass from managing themselves or with informal supports, to the use of specialist child care services.

Dysfunctional child-controlling strategies

Two case studies involving this kind of dysfunction revolved around the overuse of child-controlling strategies in circumstances where a greater emphasis on child-responsive strategies might have been more constructive. In both cases there is clear evidence of serious emotional needs in the child, which apparently underlay behavioural problems of varying difficulty. In both cases, although there was some awareness of these emotional needs, the mother's understanding of the situation operated at the surface level of the trouble caused by the behavioural problems. The result was the use of child-controlling strategies, where there was a strong case for a greater emphasis on child-responsive strategies. In one case, the daughter's emotional distress, reflected in lack of confidence with peers, social withdrawal, insecurities about making and sustaining relationships with peers, and taking an overdose, took second place, in her mother's mind, to the fear of her getting pregnant, and 'clubbing' until 2.00 a.m. The response was an overemphasis on child-controlling strategy, which arguably, even on the mother's own account, may have been linked to her daughter's overdose, and an under-emphasis on child-responsive strategies. The result was a deterioration of relationships, an incapacity of the mother to gain control, and a degree of bewilderment about what she could next do.

In another case a 15-year-old boy had experienced divorce, rejection from his father, and multiple home environments. He had moved back in with his mother, where he had to cope with a whole stepfamily. He was an aggressive, violent young man, whose aggression was often directed at his stepfamily. He became self-centred and violent if he did not get his own way. While the mother recognised that he was angry, her response was again child-controlling strategies, which were confrontational and undermining, rather than responsive. She struggled to understand the pain of this young man. While it would be naïve to assume that simple nurturing activities would have resolved the problem, there was little doubt that the emphasis on behaviour and child-controlling strategies contributed to a deteriorating situation.

Dysfunctional child-responsive or parenting strategies

One example showed a three-year-old child with difficult behaviour, including tantrums, but no more than that. His mother, however, was overanxious and perfectionist in relation to her parenting. She had an exaggerated feeling of concern, blamed herself for his tantrums, and had feelings of guilt and depression. These were related to her use of amphetamines when she was younger, and she blamed herself for ignoring him. She considered herself a 'selfish bitch', and felt strongly, despite professional advice to the contrary, that her son was angry with her. She seemed unable to understand that his behaviour was not particularly inappropriate to his age, and her guilt and self-criticism had led to depression, which, she was aware, hampered her ability to care for the child. Overanxious, her anxiety led to perceptions and actions which did not help the situation, and was liable to make it worse.

Problem- and emotion-focused informal preventive strategies

Another dimension involved decisions about the use, and meaning, of informal supports in relation to the stress or threat. One of the key elements of bringing coping closer together with prevention is its firm emphasis on the individual as an active being who makes appraisals and acts on them: individuals are not simply 'in need' of something to be provided (and decided?) by others, or people who are processed at a particular stage of prevention. They make decisions themselves, act on them, and by so doing seek to cope with their situation; they can seek to obtain outside help, maybe through informal support from friends, acquaintances or neighbours, and they can initiate and respond to actions by formal support sources, such as social services agencies. What occurs when they do engage themselves with these agencies is as much about their own actions as the provision of help by the agencies themselves. From the point of view of the mothers, they seek and use social support as part of their coping strategy, or they have to cope with the provision of support, especially when unsolicited. This is what happens when child abuse referrals are made, but they may even have to negotiate and cope with this when they have solicited the help themselves. Much the same can be said about informal support.

So seeking informal support can be seen as an element of coping actions when linked with the overall prevention process. Many women talked of seeking social support in terms of 'active coping', a category which firmly identifies social support as something they made decisions about, and they used, much in the way child-controlling or child-responsive strategies were actions with the children. The women are here seeking to prevent matters worsening (or, indeed, to improve them) by enlisting the support of others. Many women talked of seeking social support in terms of how they do this, and the meanings they attach to these actions. This can be seen as an aspect of the prevention process.

Women, however, were in profoundly differing positions. The use of informal support depends upon its availability in the first place. Two key factors impacted on whether or not it was sought or used. First, use depended on availability, whether and what was perceived to be available. Women with no friends or family would have no one to turn to. Secondly, it depended on women's attitude to supports, or confidence in herself. If she had supports, but refused to use them for various reasons – and these could include feelings of not being worthy of support, in those with low self-esteem – then she had to rely on herself.

Problem- and emotion-focused support

Those with *no or little support* included those who were at a loss to describe anyone to whom they could turn for help. This was profoundly demoralising for such mothers, and carried a distinct (negative) psychological 'edge'. Women could feel especially isolated or lonely if they had suffered losses, and some with partners nevertheless felt they 'had to do it all', and without support. Other key factors were where women felt the absence of particular substantive areas of support, without being entirely bereft of it, and conflict, which had the double edge of leading to loss of support while being stressful itself. Where women's attitudes were the chief factor, women generally felt, for whatever reasons, that they did not want to burden others.

In diametrically opposite positions were women who experienced themselves as having *routine support and integration*. For some women, the meaning of 'routine support' was no support at all. There was nothing special about that, and support was identified as something that only occurred in a crisis. Mostly, however, women saw routine help as the very stuff of social support. Their social lives were integrated with their role as parents: their friends were also parents, and the children were often friends with each other. Hence support for each other was a routine and highly valued aspect of their lives. Routine support was something which gave them psychological robustness in the face of everyday challenges, as well as crisis situations. It conferred a sense of 'togetherness' of 'people being there for me'. When women were religious, praying together could be a powerful source of integration.

Reciprocal support was an aspect of the more closely integrated networks. This could be particularly important because here women gained a sense of worth from its being two-way rather than one-way. Women could gain esteem from knowing that they, too, were contributing support to others, rather than just relying on them. They could feel useful to others, rather than just failures themselves because the help was all one-way. The sense of integration occurred where everyone was seen as pulling together for each other.

EMOTION-FOCUSED SUPPORT

There were key elements of support, when it was available: *acceptance and encouragement* were fundamental. Feeling accepted enabled women to feel more confident about using support more widely – it was a prerequisite for seeking and using support. It gave them a sense of validation in relation to their peers, of not being a 'bad person' or 'bad mother', despite the child care problems they were experiencing. Women sought the kinds of friends who would 'stand by you' in a crisis.

Encouragement was of a 'keep going, you're doing the right thing' sort, and could be as basic as that form of reassurance. Some women were only able to accept support where it involved a basic agreement about their behaviour (as parent), interpretation of the situation, or coping strategy (i.e. that they were in the right, or at least not the subject of criticism). Women sought relationships which were non-critical, and involved agreement in fundamentals. The opportunity to express feelings was a key element of feelings of validation: 'listening and not disagreeing' (even if not overtly expressing agreement, or not saying anything) was the bottom line. Useful advice was generally advice which drew out a new possible action, while lying within the broad domain of agreeing (or not disagreeing) with fundamental views of the mother.

PROBLEM-FOCUSED SUPPORT

Practical child care support provided the other major dimension of support – hardly surprising, in view of the nature of the problems. It could comprise part of the routine support – babysitting, taking the kids to school, looking after them, and so on. It could involve crisis respite, where women, stressed out, needed a break from arguments, misbehaviour, tantrums and violence. Others 'talking to' the child could occur if it was seen as supporting the women's position, or otherwise facilitating coping.

Problem- and emotion-focused, formal, secondary preventive action

Women's appraisal of psychosocial resources, and the meaning they attribute to them, inform their use of, and judgements about, formal support apparatus (particularly social services). When women referred themselves, this indicated that they saw social services as part of (or potentially part of) the psychosocial resources available to them. Again, understanding the meaning that they ascribed to these resources helps us to understand their coping strategies.

PROBLEM-FOCUSED ELICITING

Where women sought to bring social services to bear on the problem, this was very frequently characterised by *vague requests for help*: a statement of the problem without an indication of what was being expected, just the hope that social service would 'do something'. This is an indication both of the degree of desperation some women felt, and also of the limited understanding they had of social services remit. As a resource appraisal, therefore, it was, at best, for some women, the idea that social services dealt in some way with child care problems that spurred the referral. Others sought a range of types of help either directly or indirectly aimed to help exert control. These included *backing them up through threat or boundary-setting* – a 'policing the family' role – *advice on parenting and child care* (giving ideas about what to do) and *counselling* (distinctively involving some catharsis or insight), together with assistance with accommodation.

Where unsolicited referrals occurred, they were generally because of outside concerns about child care. Some were considered malicious, for example, an estranged partner made allegations which were clearly not true, of abuse or neglect of the children. Women's agenda here was not to get help, but to *gain control of the definition of the situation*. The main feature was the primary appraisal of threat from the referrer and social services, while their main drive was to convince social services that their care was adequate, and to be redefined as a 'good mother'.

EMOTION-FOCUSED ELICITING

There were also more subtle, emotion-focused purposes to soliciting social services help. Some, like the previously mentioned 'policing the family' (on behalf of the mother) role, involved the same dynamics (from the mother's point of view), characterised by informal support, particularly the expectation that social services should see (and act upon) things from the mothers' point of view. *Seeking and expecting validation* fell into this category, where women expected social services' actions and perspectives to reflect (and hence validate) their own. *Stress relief* focused on the emotional costs of the problems they suffered, while *seeking security and support* involved trying to feel less isolated, its importance lying not so much in relief from the responsibilities of care as in the psychological effects of no longer feeling solely responsible. *Insight-oriented coping* was generally sought in relation to the children: helping them (rather than their mother) to understand better their feelings and actions.

Filters: (a) proto to secondary formal preventive actions

An important feature of this process is whether women experienced themselves as having a *service*, a *block* or a *filter*. A service or block can be defined as circumstances where women were not referred on. The meanings they attached to these experiences were significant dimensions of an ongoing process, whereby they sought to cope with the situation.

The distinctive feature of all these women's situations was the limited involvement they had with social services. One key element here is that, in involving social services, they lost some control of the direction of coping, since decision making about the help they might, or might not, receive was in the hands of others: their (prevention) pathway to formal support relied on the knowledge of social services in referring them on (or not, in some cases). The terms of reference for the woman, around the issue of *control*, merged here into the agency's concern with the issue of *need*.

Most frequently the women were looking for some direct service from social services, yet none of them were taken on to caseload.

A service

Of women not referred on, some were quite happy because they had received a service, which they felt was as much as they could reasonably expect.

A block

More frequently, women were not happy with this: the lack of a referral to an agency they considered appropriate (or an unacceptable delay) could prevent them from getting the input they felt they needed. They did not gain a greater capacity to control the situation as a result of this, and additionally could feel undervalued and unimportant.

A filter

Of women referred on, some were positive, and generally felt that there had been a response appropriate to their own need, even when social services had not directly done what they wanted. The key to satisfaction was the combination of three factors: *appropriateness* (of referral), *timeliness* and *helpfulness*. More frequently, women were negative about referral on. Wherever one of the three criteria was absent, women generally regarded referral on in a negative light. As with the absence of referral, this did not lead to an increase in their control of the situation. Women's attitude to referral on, therefore, was considerably, but not entirely, influenced by the extent to which this led to a greater sense of control, or the view that as much as possible was being done to help them gain control.

Filters: (b) appraising coping and services

Another feature of filters, besides evaluation of actions, was appraisal of coping and services. An appraisal of coping is going to inform the decisions that a woman makes as to how she might, as an ongoing process, develop strategies to deal with the situation. If she felt that her coping was about as good as could reasonably be expected, she was not liable to change her strategy. Where there were weaknesses, she might (where able to) consider altering her strategies, and this could affect the ways in which she engaged and integrated informal and formal preventive resources with parental prevention. Our examination of women's appraisal of services has provided some insight into their reasons for referring to social services, as well as into how they viewed the service provided – which could again influence future strategies. Both could influence the filter processes from proto to secondary prevention and beyond.

Coping appraisal

This again leads us to the central issue of control, since coping theory would suggest that women would appraise their, and others', efforts in terms of the extent to which these enabled them to exert control over the situation. In fact, judgements on coping were practically entirely made with reference to the actions of the woman herself, rather than those of others. However, the discourses women used to consider these matters varied: we find *outcome-oriented judgements*, focusing on the results of their coping efforts, and *process-oriented judgements*, in which continuity – the expectation of needing to negotiate the problem for the foreseeable future – was the central feature. *Performance- and character-oriented judgements* were made with reference to the women's judgements of themselves as individuals, e.g. the 'character' they had shown in managing in adversity. *Personal growth through coping judgements* reflected women's evaluation of their coping in terms of what they had learned in the process. Sometimes this reflected a degree of self-congratulatory and self-righteous appraisal of their own performance. Judgements of *coping as the capacity to use support* were again self-focused, even though they involved others. Here, the way in which social support was integrated into the overall coping strategy was the means by which coping was judged.

Service appraisal

Control was likewise generally at the heart of service appraisal. Much of this was around the circumstances under which women might legitimately turn to services for support. The *right to service discourse* involved notions that in their kinds of circumstances, they ought to be given access to required services. Where it was based on the notion of desert, women felt they had somehow earned the right to service. This was a justice-based idea. Where it was based on *need* – also a justice-based idea – women felt they had a right to service because their problems were such that they fell below a particular standard which should be maintained. The *response of service discourse* focused on what was actually done. Judgements could be *contextualised* in terms of previous experiences of social services, or of some other service such as housing. They could be *abstracted* judgements, which were made without reference to context. The *problem control discourse* was made in relation to the extent to which involvement of services enabled women to gain control of their problems. The *convergence/divergence discourse* occurred where there was a high degree of investment in competing definitions of the situation. This could occur where women were referred for some sort of abuse, and where they sought to gain a dominant definition of themselves as a good mother, when the 'problem' to be controlled was the assessment of themselves as mother.

Concluding comments

We have shown, I hope, that the concept of coping has productively been allied with that of prevention, to enrich our understanding of prevention. It also brings the mother more centre stage, because of the emphasis on her as active agent, making decisions, engaging in the development of meanings, and acting on these. We have been able, at the practical level, to develop an understanding of how women do seek to cope in adversity, and where formal extended social service support is not made available. This is important at the empirical level.

Beyond this we have been able, through a combination of coping theory, and the concepts in prevention and research findings, to develop and enlarge our understanding of prevention considerably. Indeed, we have developed a range of lower-level concepts which apply to these specific circumstances (where women were moving between proto and secondary prevention levels). However, we have not (of course) covered matters at all levels of prevention, or from all angles, and there remains considerable potential for further developments through research. We hope that our framework helps point the way in this respect.

References

Abella, R. and Helsin, R. (1984) 'Health locus of control, values and the behaviour of families and friends: an integrated approach to understanding preventive health behaviour.' *Basic and Applied Social Psychology 5*, 283–93.

Abramson, L., Seligman, M. and Teasdale, J. (1978) 'Learned helplessness in humans: a critique and reformulation.' *Journal of Abnormal Psychology 87*, 49–75.

Ainsworth, M. (1973) 'The development of infant–mother attachment.' In B. Caldwell and H. Riccuiti (eds) *Review of Child Development, Volume 3*, Chicago: University of Chicago Press.

Ainsworth, M., Blehar, M., Water, C. E. and Wall, S. (1978) *Patterns of Attachment*. New Jersey: Erlbaum.

Aldgate, J. and Tunstill, J. (1995) *Making Sense of Section 17*. London: HMSO.

Amato, P. (1993) 'Children's adjustment to divorce: theories, hypotheses and empirical support.' *Journal of Marriage and the Family 55*, 23–38.

Antonucci, T.C. (1985) 'Social support: theoretical advances, recent findings and pressing issues.' In I. G. Sarason, and B. R. Sarason (eds) *Social Support: Theory, Research and Applications*. Dordrecht, The Netherlands: Martinus Nijhoff.

Arnett, J. (1995) 'Broad and narrow socialization. The family in the context of cultural theory.' *Journal of Marriage and the Family 57*, 617–28.

Audit Commission (1994) *Seen But Not Heard*. London: HMSO.

Batchelor, J., Gould, N. and Wright, J. (1999) 'Family Centres: a focus for the children in need debate.' *Child and Family Social Work 4*, 197–208.

Baum, A. (1990) 'Stress, intrusive imagination and chronic distress.' *Health Psychology 9*, 652–75.

Baumrind, D. (1967) 'Child care practices anteceding three patterns of preschool behaviour.' *Genetic Psychology Monographs 75*, 43–88.

Baumrind, D. (1971) 'Current patterns of parental authority.' *Developmental Psychology Monographs 4*, (1, 2).

Bebbington, A. and Miles, J. (1989) 'The background of children who enter local authority care.' *British Journal of Social Work 19*, 349–69.

Baumrind, D. (1977) 'Socialisation Determinants of Personal Agency.' Paper presented to the Biennial meeting of the Society for Research in Child Development, New Orleans. Quoted in D. Shaffer (1999) *Developmental Psychology*, fifth edition. Brooks Cole, Pacific Cove, USA.

Baumrind, D. (1991) 'Effective parenting during the early adolescent transition.' In P. A. Cowen and M. Hetherington (eds) *Family Transitions*. Hillside, N.J.: Erlbaum.

Bebington, A. and Miles, J. (1989) 'The background of children who enter local authority care.' *British Journal of Social Work 19*, 5, 349–68.

Becker, S. and Selburn, R. (1990) *The New Poor Clients: Social Work, Poverty and the Social Fund.* Wallington: Community Care/Benefits Research Unit.

Beckwith, J. (1993) 'Gender stereotypes and mental health revisited.' *Social Behavior and Personality 21*, 1, 85–8.

Belle, D. (1990) 'Poverty and women's mental health.' *American Psychologist 45*, 385–9.

Belsky, J. (1984) 'The determinants of parenting: a process model.' *Child Development 55*, 83–96.

Berridge, D. and Cleaver, H. (1987) *Foster-home Breakdown.* Oxford: Basil Blackwell.

Bifulco, A. and Moran, P. (1999) *Wednesday's Child.* London: Routledge.

Bowlby, M. (1951) *Maternal Care and Mental Health.* Geneva: World Health Organisation.

Bowlby, J. (1973) *Attachment and Loss, Volume 2: Separation.* New York: Basic Books.

Bowlby, J. (1991) 'Postscript.' In C. Parkes, J. Stevenson-Hinde and P. Marris (eds) *Attachment Across the Life Cycle.* London: Tavistock/Routledge.

Bradshaw, J. (1990) *Child Deprivation and Poverty in the UK.* London: National Children's Bureau.

Broverman, I., Broverman, D., Clarkson, I., Rosenkrantz, P and Vogel, S. (1970) 'Sex role stereotypes in the clinical judgements of mental health.' *Journal of Consulting and Clinical Psychology 34*, 1–7.

Brown, G. W. and Harris, T. O. (1978) *Social Origins of Depression.* London: Tavistock.

Brown, G. W., Andrews, B., Harris, T. O., Adler, Z. and Bridge, L. (1986) 'Social support, self-esteem and depression.' *Psychological Medicine 16*, 813–31.

Brown, G. W., Bifulco, A. and Harris, T. O. (1987) 'Life events, vulnerability and onset of depression: some refinements.' *British Journal of Psychiatry 150*, 30–42.

Buchanan, A. (1996) *Cycles of Child Maltreatment.* Chichester: Wiley.

Carver, S., Weintraub, J. K. and Schieir, M. (1989) 'Assessing coping strategies: a theoretically based approach.' *Journal of Personality and Social Psychology 56*, 2, 267–83.

Caspi, A. and Silva, P. A. (1995) 'Temperamental qualities at age three predict personality traits in young adulthood: longitudinal evidence from a birth cohort.' *Child Development 66*, 486–98.

Cassell, D. and Coleman, R. (1995) 'Parents with psychiatric problems.' In P. Reder and C. Lucey (1995) *Assessment of Parenting: Psychiatric and Psychological Conditions.* London: Routledge.

Chess, S. and Thomas, R. (1984) *Origins and Evolution of Behaviour Disorders.* New York: Brunner/Mazel.

Cleaver, H., Unell, I. and Aldgate, J. (1999) *Children's Needs – Parenting Capacity.* London: Stationery Office.

Cohen, F. (1987) 'Measurement and coping.' In S. Kasl and C. Cooper (eds) *Stress and Health: Issues in Research Methodology.* Chichester: John Wiley.

Cohen, F. and Lazarus, R. (1983) 'Coping and adaptation in health and illness.' In D. Mechanic (ed) *Handbook of Health, Health Care and Health Professionals.* New York: Free Press.

Cohen, F., Rees, L., Kaplan, G. and Riggio, R. (1986) 'Coping with the stress of arthritis.' In R. W. Molkowitz and M. R. Haug (eds) *Arthritis and the Elderly*. New York: Springer.

Colton, M., Drury, C. and Williams, M. (1995) *Children in Need*. Aldershot: Avebury.

Conger, R. D., Ge, X., Elder, G. H., Lorenz, F. O. and Simmonds, R. (1994) 'Economic stress, coercive family processes and developmental problems of adolescents.' *Child Development 65*, 80–97.

Cornwell, J. (1984) *Hard Earned Lives: Accounts of Health and Illness in East London*. London: Tavistock.

Coyne, I. and Holroyd, K. (1982) 'Stress, coping and illness: a transactional perspective.' In T. Millon, C. Green and R. Meacher (eds) *Handbook of Clinical Health Psychology*. New York: Plenum.

Department of Health (1989) *Introduction to the Children Act 1989*. London: HMSO.

Department of Health (1991) *The Children Act 1989 Guidance and Regulations, Volume 2: Family Support, Day Care and Education Provision for Young Children*. London: HMSO.

Department of Health (1995) *Child Protection: Messages From Research*. London: HMSO.

Department of Health (2000) *Framework for the Assessment of Children in Need*. London: HMSO.

Department of Health (Diana Robbins) (2001) *Transforming Children's Services: An Evaluation of Local Responses to the Quality Protects Programme, Year 3*. London: Department of Health.

Department of Health and Social Security (1974) *Report of the Committee of Inquiry into the Care and Supervision Provided in Relation to Maria Colwell*. London: HMSO.

Department of Health and Social Security (1982) *Child Abuse: A Study of Inquiry Reports, 1973–81*. London: HMSO.

Department of Health and Social Security (1985) *Review of Child Care Law. Report and Minutes of an Interdepartmental Working Party*. London: HMSO.

Downey, G. and Coyne, J. (1990) 'Children of depressed parents: an integrative review.' *Psychological Bulletin 108*, 50–76.

Dunst, C., Lee, H. and Trivette, C. (1989) 'Family resources, personal well being and early intervention.' *Journal of Special Education 22*, 108–16.

Eckenrode, J., Laird, M. and Doris, J. (1993) 'School performance and disciplinary problems amongst abused and neglected children.' *Developmental Psychology 29*, 53–62.

Elliott, G. and Eisdorfer, C. (1982) *Stress and Human Health*. New York: Springer.

Fahlberg, V. I. (1991) *A Child's Journey through Placement*. Indianapolis: Perspectives Press.

Ferri, E. (1976) *Growing Up in a One-Parent Family*. Slough: NFER.

Fisman, S., Wolf, L. and Noh, S. (1989) 'Marital intimacy in parents of exceptional children.' *Canadian Journal of Psychiatry 4*, 519–25.

Folkman, S. and Lazarus, R. S. (1985) 'If it changes it must be process: study of emotion and coping during three stages of college exam.' *Journal of Personality and Social Psychology 48*, 150–170.

Fraiberg, S., Adelson, E. and Shapiero, V. (1975) 'Ghosts in the nursery: a psycho-analytic approach to impaired mother–infant relationships.' *Journal of the American Academy of Child Psychiatry 14*, 387–422.

Fuhrman, T. and Holmbeck, G. (1995) 'A contextual moderator analysis of emotional autonolmyand adjustment in adolescence.' *Child Development 66*, 793–811.

Fuller, R. and Stevenson, O. (1985) *Policies, Programmes and Disadvantage: A Review of the Literature*. London: Heineman.

Ge, X., Conger, R. and Elder, G. (1996) 'Coming of age too early: pubertal influences on girls' vulnerability to psychological distress.' *Child Development 67*, 3386–3400.

Gibbons, J. with Thorpe, S. and Wilkinson, P. (1990) *Family Support and Prevention: Studies in Local Areas*. London: HMSO.

Gibbons, J., Conroy, S. and Bell, C. (1995) *Operation of Child Protection Registers*. London: HMSO.

Goldberg, D. and Huxley, P. (1992) *Common Mental Disorders, a Biosocial Approach*. London: Routledge.

Goldstein, J., Freud, A. and Solnit, A. (1979) *Beyond the Best Interests of the Child*. New York: Free Press.

Goldstein, J., Freud, A. and Solnit, A. (1980) *Before the Best Interests of the Child*. London: Burnett Books.

Gottlieb, B. (1985) 'Theory into practice: issues that surface in planning interventions which mobilise support.' In G. Sarason and B. Sarason (eds) *Social Support: Theory, Research and Application*. The Hague: Martinus Nijhoff.

Hall, L., Williams, C. and Greenberg, R. (1985) 'Support stressors and depressive symptoms in low income mothers of young children.' *American Journal of Public Health 75*, 518–22.

Hallett, C. and Stevenson, O. (1980) *Child Abuse: Aspects of Inter-Professional Co-operation*. London: Allen and Unwin.

Hammersley, M. and Atkinson, P. (1983) *Ethnography: Principles in Practice*. London: Routledge.

Hanson, N. (1958) *Patterns of Discovery*. Cambridge: Cambridge University Press.

Hardiker, P., Exton, K. and Barker, M. (1991) *Policies and Practices in Preventive Child Care*. Aldershot: Ashgate.

Hardiker, P., Exton, K. and Barker, M (1996) 'A framework for analysing services.' In National Commission of Inquiry into the Prevention of Child Abuse, *Childhood Matters, Volume 2: Background Papers*. London: Stationery Office.

Henderson, A. S. (1984) 'Interpreting the evidence on social support.' *Social Psychiatry 19*, 49–52.

Henderson, S., Byrne, D. G. and Duncan Jones, P. (1981) *Neuroses and the Social Environment*. Sydney: Academic Press.

Henry, B., Caspi, A., Moffitt, T. and Silva, P. (1996) 'Temperamental and familial predictors of violent and non violent criminal convictions: age 3 to age 18.' *Developmental Psychology 32*, 614–23.

Hetherington, E. (1988) 'Parents, children and siblings six years after divorce.' In R. Stevenson Hinde (ed) *Relationships with Families.* Cambridge: Cambridge University Press.

Hetherington, E., Bridges, M. and Insabella, G. (1998) 'What matters? What does not? Five perspectives on the association between marital transitions and children's adjustment.' *American Psychologist 53*, 167–84.

Hobfell, S. E. (1989) 'Conservation of resources: a new attempt at conceptualising stress.' *American Psychologist 44*, 513–24.

Holman, B. (1980) *Inequality in Child Care.* London: Child Poverty Action Group.

Holman, B. (1988) *Putting Families First: Prevention and Child Care.* London: Macmillan.

Holtzman, E. and Gilbert, L. (1987) 'Social support networks for parenting and psychological well-being among dual earner Mexican American families.' *Journal of Community Psychology 15*, 176–86.

Home Office (1999) *Supporting Families.* London: Home Office.

House of Commons (1984) *Second Report from the Social Services Committee, Session 1983–4.* London: HMSO (Short Report).

Howe, D. (1984) *Social Workers and their Practice in Welfare Bureaucracies.* Aldershot: Gower.

Howe, D. (1995) *Attachment Theory for Social Work Practice.* Basingstoke: Macmillan.

Hynd, G. W. and Hooper, S. R. (1992) *Neurological Basis of Childhood Psychopathology.* Newbury Park, CA: Sage.

Kagan, J. (1984) *The Nature of the Child.* New York: Basic Books.

Kagan, J. (1989) *Unstable Ideas: Temperament, Cognition and the Self.* Cambridge: Cambridge University Press.

Kagan, J. (1992) 'Behaviour, biology and the meaning of temperamental constructs.' *Pediatrics 90*, 510–513.

Kagan, J. and Snidman, N. (1991) 'Temperamental factors in human development.' *American Psychologist 46*, 856–62.

Kerr, M., Lambert, W. and Bem, D. J. (1996) 'Life course sequelae of childhood shyness in Sweden: comparison with the United States.' *Child Development 65*, 138–46.

Kurdek, L. and Fine, M. (1994) 'Family acceptance and family control as predictors of adjustment in young adolescents: linear, curvilinear or interactive effects?' *Child Development 65*, 1137–1146.

Lamborn, S., Mounts, N., Sreinberg, L. and Dornbusch, S. (1991) 'Patterns of competence and adjustment amongst adolescents from authoritative, authoritarian, indulgent and neglectful families.' *Child Development 62*, 1049–1065.

Lamborn, S. and Steinberg, L. (1993) 'Emotional autonmy redux: revising Ryan and Lynch.' *Child Development 64*, 483–99.

Layder, D. (1993) *New Strategies in Social Research.* London: Polity Press.

Lazarus, R. S. (1993) 'Coping theory and research: past, present and future.' *Psychosomatic Medicine 55*, 234–47.

Lazarus, R. S. and Folkman, S. (1984) *Stress, Appraisal and Coping.* New York: Springer.

Lefcourt, H. M. (1991) 'Locus of Control'. In J. P. Robinson, P. R. Shaver and L. S. Wrightsman (eds) *Measures of Personality and Social Psychology Attitudes.* London: Academic Press.

Littlewood, J. (1992) *Aspects of Grief: Bereavement.* London: Routledge.

MacDonald, K. (1992) 'Warmth as a developmental construct: an evolutionary analysis.' *Child Development 63,* 753–73.

MacKinnon-Lewis, C., Starnes, R., Volling, B. and Johnson, S. (1997) 'Perceptions of parenting as predictors of boys' sibling and peer relations.' *Developmental Psychology 30,* 325–33.

McLanahan, S., Wedemeyer, N. and Aldberg, T. (1981) 'Network structure, social support and psychological well-being in the single-parent family.' *Journal of Marriage and the Family 43,* 601–12.

McLanahan, S. and Sandefier, G. (1994) *Growing Up with a Single Parent: What Hurts, What Helps.* Cambridge, Mass: Harvard University Press.

McLoyd, V. (1998) 'Socioeconomic disadvantage and child development.' *American Psychologist 53,* 185–204.

Maccoby, E. E. and Martin, J. A. (1983) 'Socialisation in the context of the family: parent–child interaction.' In M. E. Hetherington (ed) *Handbook of Child Psychology, Vol. 4: Socialisation, Personality and Personal Development.* New York: Wiley.

Main, M. (1991) 'Metacognitive knowledge, metacognitive monitoring and singular (coherent) vs multiple (incoherent) model of attachment.' In C. Parkes, J. Stevenson-Hinde and P. Marris, (eds) *Attachment Across the Life Cycle.* London: Tavistock/Routledge.

Main, M. and Goldwyn, R. (1984) 'Predicting rejection of her own infant from mother's representation of her own experience: implications for the abused–abusing intergenerational cycle.' *Child Abuse and Neglect 8,* 203–17.

Measor, L. (1985) 'Interviewing: a strategy in qualitative research.' In R. L. Burgess (ed) *Strategies of Qualitative Research: Qualitative Methods.* London: Falmer.

Melville, J. (1983) 'Looking for a mother.' *New Society* 8 December, 391–3.

Milham, S., Bullock, R., Hosie, K. and Haak, M. (1986) *Lost in Care: The Problem of Maintaining Links between Children in Care and their Families.* Aldershot: Gower.

Miller, J. and Glassner, B. (1997) 'The "inside" and the "outside": finding realities in interviews.' In D. Silverman (ed) *Qualitative Research: Theory, Method and Practice.* London: Sage.

Miller, N., Cowan, P., Cowan, C., Hetherington, E., and Clingempeel, W. (1993) 'Externalising in pre-schoolers and early adolescents: a cross-study replication of a family model.' *Developmental Psychology 29,* 3–18.

Mirlees Black, C. (1995) 'Estimating the extent of domestic violence: findings from the 1992 British Crime Survey.' *Research Bulletin 37,* 1–9.

Moos, R. H. and Schaffer, J. (1993) 'Coping resources and processes: current concepts and measures.' In L. Goldenberger and S. Breznitz (eds) *Handbook of Stress.* New York: Free Press.

Newman, D., Caspi, A., Moffitt, T. and Silva, P. (1997) 'Antecedents of adult interpersonal functioning: effects of individual differences in age 3 temperament.' *Developmental Psychology 33,* 206–217.

Newton, T. (1989) 'Occupational stress and coping with stress: a critique.' *Human Relations 42,* 441–61.

Norman, P. (1995) 'Health locus of control and health behaviour: an investigation into the role of health value and behaviour specific efficacy beliefs.' *Personality and Individual Differences 18*, 213–18.

Norman, P. and Bennett, P. (1999) 'Health locus of control.' In M. Connor and P. Norman (eds) *Predicting Health Behaviour.* Buckingham: Open University Press.

Packman, J. (1981) *The Child's Generation.* Oxford: Basil Blackwell.

Packman, J. (1986) *Who Needs Care? Social Work Decisions about Children.* Oxford: Blackwell.

Packman, J. (1993) 'From prevention to partnership: child welfare services across three decades.' In G. Pugh (ed) *Thirty Years of Change for Children.* London: National Children's Bureau.

Parker, R. (1980) *Caring for Separated Children.* London: Macmillan.

Parry, G. (1986) 'Paid employment, life events, social support and mental health in working class mothers.' *Journal of Health and Social Behaviour 27*, 193–208.

Parry, G. and Shapiro, D. (1986) 'Social support and life events in working-class women.' *Archives of General Psychiatry 43*, 315–23.

Parton, N. (1985) *The Politics of Child Abuse.* Basingstoke: Macmillan.

Parton, N. (1997) (ed) *Child Protection and Family Support: Tension, Contradictions and Possibilities.* New York: Routledge.

Paterson, R. and Neufield, R. (1987) 'Clear danger situations: determinants of the appraisal of threat.' *Psychological Bulletin 101*, 404–16.

Patterson, G., Raid, J. and Dishion, T. (1994) *Antisocial Boys.* Eugene OR: Castalia.

Payne, S. (1991) *Women, Health and Poverty: An Introduction.* London: Harvester Wheatsheaf.

Peterson, R., Gazmararian, J., Spitz, A., Rowley, D., Goodwin, M., Saltzman, L. and Marks, J. (1997) 'Violence and adverse pregnancy outcomes: a review of the literature and directions for future research.' *American Journal of Preventive Medicine 13*, 5, 366–73.

Pierce, G. R., Sarason, B. R. and Sarason, I. G. (1990) 'Integrating social support perspectives, working models, personal relationships and situational factors.' In S. Duck (ed) *Personal Relationships and Social Support.* London: Sage.

Pithouse, A. and Holland, P. (1999) 'Open-access family centres and their users: positive results, some doubts and new departures.' *Children and Society 13*, 167–78.

Pound, A. and Abel, K. (1996) 'Motherhood and mental illness.' In K. Abel, M. Busszewikz, S. Davidson, S. Johnson and E. Staples (eds) *Planning Community Mental Health Services for Women.* London: Routledge.

Pringle, M. Kelmer (1974) *The Needs of Children.* London: Hutchinson.

Quinton, D. and Rutter, M. (1984a) 'Parents with children in care I: current circumstances and parenting skills.' *Journal of Child Psychology and Psychiatry 25*, 211–29.

Quinton, D. and Rutter, M. (1984b) 'Parents with children in care II: inter-generational continuities.' *Journal of Child Psychology and Psychiatry 25*, 231–50.

Ratner, P. (1998) 'Modelling acts of aggression and dominance as wife abuse and exploring their adverse health effects.' *Journal of Marriage and the Family 60*, 453–65.

Reis, J. (1988a) 'A factoral analysis of compound measures of social support.' *Journal of Clinical Psychology 44*, 876–90.

Reis, J. (1988b) 'Correlates of depression according to maternal age.' *Journal of Genetic Psychology 149*, 535–45.

Rogers, B. and Pryor, J. (1998) *Divorce and Separation: The Outcomes for Children.* York: Joseph Rowntree Foundation.

Rose (1994) 'An overview of the development of services – the relationship between protection and family support and the intention of the Children Act, 1989. Department of Health paper for Sief Conference, 5 September, quoted in N. Parton (1997) (ed) *Child Protection and Family Support.* London: Routledge.

Rotter, J. B. (1966) 'Generalised expectancies for internal versus external control of reinforcement.' *Psychological Monographs: General and Applied 80*, 1–28.

Rotter, J. B. (1975) 'Some problems and misconceptions related to the construct of internal versus external control of reinforcement.' *Journal of Consulting and Clinical Psychology 43*, 56–67.

Rotter, J. B. (1990) 'Internal versus external control of reinforcement: a case history of a variable.' *American Psychologist 45*, 489–93.

Rowe, J. and Lambert, L. (1973) *Children Who Wait.* London: Association of British Adoption and Fostering Agencies.

Rutter, M. (1977) *Maternal Deprivation Reassessed.* Harmondsworth: Penguin.

Rutter, M. and Quinton, D. (1984) 'Parental psychiatric disorder: effects on children.' *Psychological Medicine 14*, 853–80.

Sarafino, E. P. (1998) *Health Psychology.* Chichester: John Wiley.

Schutz, A. (1964) *Collected Papers II: Studies in Social Theory.* The Hague: Martinus Nizhoff.

Sheppard, J. (2000) 'Learning from personal experiences: reflections on social work practice with mothers in child and family care.' *Journal of Social Work Practice 14*, 1, 37–50.

Sheppard, M. (1990) *Mental Health: The Role of the Approved Social Worker.* Sheffield: University of Sheffield Press.

Sheppard, M. (1993) 'The external context for social support: towards a theoretical formulation of social support, child care and maternal depression.' *Social Work and Social Sciences Review 4*, 1, 27–59.

Sheppard, M. (1994a) 'Maternal depression, child care and the social work role.' *British Journal of Social Work 24*, 33–51.

Sheppard, M. (1994b) 'Child care, social support and maternal depression: a review and application of findings.' *British Journal of Social Work 24*, 287–310.

Sheppard, M. (1996) 'Depression in the work of health visitors: clinical facets.' *Social Science and Medicine 43*. 1637–1648.

Sheppard, M. (1997a) 'Social work practice in child and family care: a study of maternal depression.' *British Journal of Social Work 27*, 815–47.

Sheppard, M. (1997b) 'Double jeopardy: the link between child abuse and maternal depression in child and family social work.' *Child and Family Social Work 2*, 91–109.

Sheppard, M. (1998) 'Social profile, maternal depression and welfare concerns in clients of health visitors and social workers: a comparative study.' *Children and Society 12*, 125–35.

Sheppard, M. (2001a) 'The design and development of an instrument for assessing the quality of partnership between mother and social worker in child and family care.' *Child and Family Social Work 6*, 31–47.

Sheppard, M. (2001b) *Social Work Practice with Depressed Mothers in Child and Family Care.* London: Stationery Office.

Sheppard, M. (2002) 'Depressed mothers' experience of partnership in child and family care.' *British Journal of Social Work 32*, 93–112.

Sheppard, M. and Watkins, M. (1998) 'The parent concerns questionnaire: evaluation of a mothers' self-report instrument for the identification of problems and needs in child and family social work.' *Children and Society 14*, 194–206.

Sheppard, M. and Woodcock, J. (1999) 'Need as an operating concept.' *Child and Family Social Work 4*, 1, 67–77.

Smith, T. (1996) *Family Centres and Bringing Up Children.* London: HMSO.

Snidman, J., Kagan, J., Riordan, L. and Shannon, D. (1995) 'Cardiac function and behavioural reactivity.' *Psychophysiology 32*, 199–207.

Srouffe, L. (1985) 'Attachment classification from the perspective of infant–caregiver relationships and infant temperament.' *Child Development 56*, 1–14.

Stark, E. and Flitcraft, A. (1995) 'Killing the beast within: woman battering and female suicidality.' *International Journal of Health Services 25*, 43–4.

Steinberg, L. (1996) *Adolescence* (fourth edition). New York: McGraw Hill.

Steptoe, A., Wardle, J., Vinck, J., Tuomisto, M., Holte, A. and Wickstrom, L. (1994) 'Personality and attitudinal correlates of healthy and unhealthy lifestyles in young adults.' *Psychology and Health 9*, 331–43.

Stewart, G., Stewart, J., Prior, A. and Peelo, M. (1989) *Surviving Poverty: Probation Work and Benefits Policy.* Wakefield: ACOP.

Strauss, A. and Corbin, J. (1998) *Basics of Qualitative Research: Techniques and Procedures for Developing Grounded Theory.* Thousand Oaks, CA: Sage.

Suls, J. (ed) (1983) *Psychological Perspectives on the Self, Vol 1.* Hillsdale, NJ: Erlbaum.

Tetzloff, C. and Barrera, M. (1987) 'Divorcing mothers and social support: testing the specificity of buffering effects.' *American Journal of Community Psychology 15*, 145–59.

Thoits, P. (1982) 'Conceptual, methodological and theoretical problems in studying social support as a buffer against life stress.' *Journal of Health and Social Behaviour 23*, 145–59.

Thoits, P. (1986) 'Social support as coping assistance.' *Journal of Consulting and Clinical Psychology 54*, 4, 416–23.

Thomas, A. and Chess, S. (1986) 'The New York longitudinal study: from infancy to early adult life.' In R. Plomin and J. Dunn (eds) *The Study of Temperament: Changes, Continuities and Challenges.* Hillside, NJ: Erlbaum.

Thompson, M. and Ensminger, E. (1989) 'Psychological well-being among mothers with school-age children: evolving family structures.' *Social Forces 67*, 715–30.

Van Ijzeldoorn, M., Juffer, F. and Duyvesteyn, M. (1995) 'Breaking the inter-generational cycle of insecure attachment: a review of the effects of attachment-based interventions on maternal sensitivity and infant insecurity.' *Journal of Consulting and Clinical Psychology 36*, 225–48.

Van den Boom, D. (1995) 'Do first year intervention efforts endure? Follow up during toddlerhood of a sample of Dutch irritable infants.' *Child Development 66*, 1798–1816.

Van den Boom, D. (1997) 'Sensitivity and attachment: new steps for developmentalists.' *Child Development 68*, 592–94.

Vingerhoets, A. and Marcelissen, F. (1988) 'Stress research: its present status and issues for future developments.' *Social Science and Medicine 26*, 279–91.

Vieil, H.O. (1985) 'Dimensions of social support: a conceptual framework for research.' *Social Psychiatry 20*, 156–62.

Waller, K. and Bates, R. (1992) 'Health locus of control and self-efficacy beliefs in a healthy elderly sample.' *American Journal of Health Promotion 6*, 302–9.

Wallston, K. (1989) 'Assessment of control in health care settings.' In A. Steptoe and A. Appels (eds) *Stress, Personal Control and Health.* London: Wiley.

Weiss, G. and Larson, D. (1990) 'Health value, health locus of control, and the prediction of health protective behaviours.' *Social Behaviour and Personality 18*, 121–36.

Weiss, L. and Schwartz, J. (1996) 'The relationship between parenting types and older adolescents' personality, academic achievement, adjustment and substance use.' *Child Development 67*, 2101–2114.

Weissman, M. M., Paykel, E. and Klerman, G. (1972) 'The depressed women as mother.' *Social Psychiatry 7*, 98–108.

Whipple, E. and Webster Stratton, C. (1991) 'The role of parental stress in physically abused families.' *Child Abuse and Neglect 15*, 76–82.

Williams, J. (1999) 'Social inequalities and mental health.' In C. Newnes, G. Holmes and C. Dunn (eds) *This Is Madness.* Ross on Wye: PCCS Books.

Williams, M. (1997) *Parents, Children and Social Workers.* Aldershot: Avebury.

Wolf, L., Noh, S., Fisman, S. and Speechley, M. (1989) 'Brief report: psychological effects of parenting stress on parents of autistic children.' *Journal of Autism and Developmental Disorders 19*, 157–66.

Woods, N. (1985) 'Employment, family roles, and mental ill-health in young married women.' *Nursing Research 34*, 4–10.

Younniss, J. and Smollar, J. (1985) *Adolescent Relations with Mothers, Fathers and Friends.* Chicago: University of Chicago Press.

Zuvarin, S. (1989) 'Severity of maternal depression and three types of mother to child aggression.' *American Journal of Orthopsychiatry 59*, 377–89.

Subject Index

abandonment 56, 66
abstracted judgements 256-7,
  259-60, 267, 324
abuse
  allegations 245-50, 265,
    313, 318, 321, 325
  blame 122, 124, 134
  mother's past experience
    41, 144, 299
  paternal 122, 124, 134,
    144, 168
  prevention policy 21, 24,
    25, 36
acceptance
  adjustment strategies 14,
    187-9, 193, 194, 316
  informal support 225, 226,
    233, 320
  parenting 57, 199
accommodation see housing
accounts, women's
  denial and dissonance 182,
    194, 316
  internal coherence 87-8,
    91-2, 195, 316
  study context 85, 86, 89,
    90
active agents
  coping theory 37, 39, 53,
    325
  informal support 225, 231
  problem-focused coping 43,
    314, 318
  social support 14, 74, 87,
    219
ADHD see Attention Deficit
  Hyperactivity Disorder
adjustment strategies
  acceptance 187-9, 316
  personal growth 189-92,
    316
  positive reinterpretation
    189-90, 316
  self-focused coping 13-14,
    181, 193, 194
adolescence see teenagers

adoption 25, 26, 27, 240,
  262
advice
  health visitors 178, 201,
    296
  legal 239, 254, 270
  outside agencies 270, 272
  personal growth 295, 296
  social services
    counselling 239-41,
      321
    emotion-focused coping
      243
    parenting and children
      238-9, 249, 263,
      321
  social support 30, 48, 219,
    220, 227-8
affection for child 113, 117,
  123, 167, 170
affective social support 48, 54
age
  child
    behaviour-oriented
      coping 153-4
    behavioural problems
      59, 108, 116, 204,
      205
    blame 130, 134, 195
    interviewer 88
    mother's care status 28
  aggression
    child
      emotional problems
        110, 312
      marital separation 124,
        125
      neglectful parenting 59
      routine disruption 99,
        101, 102
      teenagers 98, 104
    mother
      child's violence 309
      depression 66, 67, 252,
        298
      smacking 157, 158
      snapping 192-3
      social services 252,
        277
    parental 64
  agreement
    convergence-divergence
      discourse 263-6, 267

informal support 226-8,
  232, 233, 320
Ainsworth Strange Situations
  classification 56-7
alcohol use
  by child 59, 103, 132
  by mother 80, 145, 148,
    181, 187, 194
alienation 33, 106, 107, 170,
  210, 215
allegations of abuse 245-50,
  265, 313, 318, 321, 325
anger
  child 33, 64, 206, 207
  mother 87-8, 192-3,
    247-8, 309-10
  parents 33
antidepressants 143, 144,
  183, 203
anxiety
  child 62, 173, 297
  mother 120-3, 143-4,
    271-2, 309, 310
  parents 64, 70
  stress 40
appraisal see also primary
  appraisal; secondary
  appraisal; women
  coping as process 51, 53
  and meaning 40-2
appropriateness of response
  253-4, 274-7, 283-4, 323
Asperger's syndrome 160
assessment, social services 77,
  78, 80-1, 264, 265, 274
'at risk' children 10, 31, 78,
  298
Attachment Classification
  System 56
attachments
  attachment theory 25, 27,
    55
  parenting
    child characteristics 62,
      63-4
    child development 12,
      27, 55-7
    secure/insecure 62, 65,
      67
Attention Deficit Hyperactivity
  Disorder (ADHD)
  behavioural problems 61-2,
    99, 126, 152, 205, 290
  social services 80, 243, 259

Author Index